Adi Kuntsman

Figurations of Violence and Belonging

Queerness, Migranthood and Nationalism in Cyberspace and Beyond

PETER LANG
Oxford · Bern · Berlin · Bruxelles · Frankfurt am Main · New York · Wien

Bibliographic information published by Die Deutsche Bibliothek
Die Deutsche Bibliothek lists this publication in the Deutsche Nationalbibliografie; detailed bibliographic data is available on the Internet at <http://dnb.ddb.de>.

A catalogue record for this book is available from The British Library.

Library of Congress Cataloging-in-Publication Data:

Kuntsman, Adi.
Figurations of violence and belonging : queerness, migranthood and nationalism in cyberspace and beyond / Adi Kuntsman.
p. cm.
Includes bibliographical references and index.
ISBN 978-3-03911-564-8 (alk. paper)
1. Gay and lesbian studies. 2. Violence. 3. Cyberspace. 4. Marginality, Social. I. Title.
HQ76.25.K86 2009
306.76'6089917105694--dc22
2009007544

ISBN 978-3-03911-564-8

Hochfeldstrasse 32, Postfach 746, CH-3000 Bern 9, Switzerland
info@peterlang.com, www.peterlang.com, www.peterlang.net

Printed in Germany

Contents

Preface

> [T]he seemingly not there [...] is a seething presence. Seething, it makes a striking impression; seething, it makes everything we do see just as it is, charged with the occluded and forgotten past.
>
> —Avery Gordon, *Ghostly Matters*, 1997: 195.

This book was written in the seething presence of violent pasts: some extensively commemorated, like Jewish persecution during the Nazi regime; some remembered only selectively, like the Stalinist political terror; some forgotten, like same-sex relations in the Soviet labour camps. At the same time, writing the book was charged with the violent present: daily homophobia and racism, the on-going colonial enterprise; raging military warfare in Israel/Palestine, simultaneously localised as a national issue and globalised as part of the 'war on terror'. Legitimised, glorified or normalised into the mundane, violence often becomes invisible, especially to those untouched by it or to those who benefit from its fruits. Theoretically and politically, this book is committed precisely to the invisible – to the 'occluded and forgotten', as Avery Gordon puts it. I follow Gordon's powerful insight that what is seemingly not there often has a seething presence and demands our attention – be it the seductive embrace of colonial nationalism; the queer sexiness of war; the unnoticed death and destruction just beyond our doorsteps; the shadows of the past; or what Jasbir Puar in her reflection on Gordon's work calls 'the ghosts of the future that we can already sniff' (2007: xx).[1]

1 In her discussion of 'future that is already here [...] yet unknown but for a split second', Puar puts forward the notion of 'antecedent temporality' – 'ghost [...] that we can already sniff'. She elaborates: 'Haunting in this sense defuses a binary between past and present – because indeed the becoming-future in haunting us – while its ontological debt to that which once was cautions against an easy privileging of the fetish of innovation, of what might otherwise be demeaned as an unthinking reach for that which is trendy or cutting edge' (Puar 2007: xx).

The analysis, presented here, is a form of situated knowledge (Castañeda 2002; Haraway 1991, 1997); it comes from the particular, and in a way, also very personal, perspective of someone writing from both within and outside, someone, simultaneously entangled in the existing regime, privileged by it, and committed to challenging it. Like those queer immigrants who are at the centre of this book, I was born and raised in the former Soviet Union. Like them, I left as part of the large wave of late-Soviet and post-Soviet emigration that began in the end of 1980s, following *perestrojka* and democratisation. Like them, I arrived in Israel, together with many other Soviet Jews and their family members, welcomed by the national project of Jewish repatriation. Like them, I was also part of the emerging 'Russian' queer scene that has developed in Israel and in cyberspace since the late 1990s and continues to thrive to this day.

My generation of post-Soviet queers witnesses both the tremendous changes in the acceptance of queer sexualities, and the stubborn persistence of poisonous homophobia. My life, like the lives of other queer immigrants, goes against what is seen as normal and culturally acceptable by many post-Soviet subjects in both Russia and the émigré diaspora; our public visibility causes rage and violence, verbal and physical, within and outside our émigré communities. At the same time, our queerness hardly prevents us from settling in or moving around what Eyal Weizman (2007) poignantly calls the 'hollow land' of Israel/Palestine, whose 'elastic geography'[2] is about a complex and sophisticated system of land grabbing,[3] settlements, borders

2 '[T]he frontiers of the Occupied Territories are not rigid and fixed at all; rather, they are elastic, and in constant transformation. The linear border, a cartographic imaginary inherited from the military and political spatiality of the nation state has splintered into a multitude of temporary, transportable, deployable and removable border-synonyms [...] that shrink and expand the territory at will. These borders are dynamic, constantly shifting, ebbing and flowing; they creep along, stealthily surrounding Palestinian villages and roads. They may even erupt into Palestinian living rooms, bursting in through the house walls. [...] Elastic territories could thus not be understood as benign environments: highly elastic political space is often more dangerous and deadly than a static, rigid one' (Weizman 2007: 6–7).

3 Which, contrary to the popular view, did not stop but rather intensified after the 1993 Oslo agreement.

and checkpoints, all of which constitute the 'colonial present' (Gregory 2004b) of geographical and political control over Palestinian life, while building the national home for Jewish Israelis.

Past experience of racialisation and non-belonging (as Jews), and ongoing instances of ethnic and sexual marginalisation (as newcomers and as queers) can make the promise of national homecoming particularly tempting. The transition from a racial and ethnic minority into a national majority, when migrating from the former Soviet Union to Israel, indeed has many appealing gains: economic, political and emotional. The intensity of longing to belong, and the pleasure of having *where* to belong, should not be underestimated. Like other immigrants, queer and straight alike, I sensed, on so many moving occasions, the seductive powers of the nation's hug that makes one feel at home in one's country. But belonging should come with responsibility. Rather than accepting the privileges of this given nationhood, it is imperative to ask, what are its costs. Who does it leave homeless? On whose continuous losses – of history, of land, of culture and identity – are the national gains based?

Thinking more specifically about Russian-Israeli queers, I want to face their – and my own – complicity in the Israeli colonial nationalism and its violences; an uneasy and painful, but, I believe, necessary, process. Among other things, this process means questioning the comforts of Israeli nationhood, conditionally offered to Russian-speaking queer 'repatriates', as long as they act as 'docile patriots' (Puar and Rai 2002) and as long as they 'loyally repeat the nation', to paraphrase Jin Haritaworn's (2008) eloquent words.[4] This book aims to confront and interrogate the racism and militarism that make up this nationhood's daily reality within and outside the queer scene. In that sense, the book responds to Puar's call to 'underscore contingency and complicity [of queerness] with dominant

4 In his discussion of white gay sexuality and citizenship in Britain, and in particular, the much celebrated gay inclusion into the military, which happened at the time of military invasion in Afghanistan and Iraq, Haritaworn notes, that 'the performance of military masculinity, once a subversive, parodic repetition of a violently heterosexual masculinity from which gay men were excluded, has become a loyal repetition to the nation' (Haritaworn 2008: n.p.).

formations' (Puar 2005: 122) such as those of nationalism and colonialism. But I am also looking for a more nuanced analysis of queerness that emerges at the intersection of marginality and dominance, privilege and exclusion, production *and* reception of violence. This book is a journey into the profound ambivalences of lives and psyches of those who are simultaneously positioned at the centre and margins of the Israeli nation and of post-Soviet diaspora: as Jews, as Eastern European immigrants, and as queers. It looks into the multifarious webs of race, sexuality and nation; into unexpected twists of collective remembering and forgetting; into moments of connection and alienation; and into ambivalences and contradictions of both violence and belonging.

Writing this book away from Israel/Palestine, from what might appear to some as the 'safe heaven' of my current academic position in the UK,[5] I am facing a double difficulty. On one hand, my critique of Israeli nationalism might be dismissed by people there because I currently live abroad as part of the idea that only those residing in the country have the right to criticise it. Of course, when such critique comes from a resident, other grounds for dismissal are quickly found. On the other hand, writing about issues related to Israel/Palestine for the English-speaking audience *outside* of it, I am often facing a simplistic and reductionist understanding of social, political and cultural life there, coming from both activists and some academics. Les Back in his discussion of the relations between injuries of class and the presence of racism in white working class life in south-east London, notes that 'it is the task of sociological listening to render this moral and political complexity without either becoming an apologist for racism or reducing such lives to a caricature of absolute evil and violent thuggery' (Back 2007: 84). So, too, this book aims to render the complexity of addressing the lives of queer immigrants who can be simultaneously embraced by the national home and symbolically erased from it; and who are both privileged and injured by Israeli colonial nationhood. My aim is precisely to move away from the reductionist and caricaturist understanding

5 I thank Claudia Castañeda for pointing out the importance to account for such a possible reading.

of life in Israel, while not being an apologist for its ongoing violence or for the complicity of those who embrace it. Responding to Back's call for attentive sociological listening, I hope to write critically, yet responsibly, about the community and the country of which I am, however ambivalently, a member. I hope to open up, rather than reproduce, the simplistic dichotomies of 'colonised and coloniser', and of victims and perpetrators, and suggest instead a more compound reading of social and psychic life at the intersection of queerness, migranthood and nationalism.

Listening to the occluded and forgotten, looking into the past and the future, this book is first and foremost about the contested, troubled and ambiguous *present*, in Israel/Palestine and beyond.

PROLOGUE

The Journey to this Book

July 2002. The Pride Parade was about to get underway in West Jerusalem. I remember myself in the middle of a colourful crowd that gathered, laughing and chatting, ready to march on the streets. From a balcony a man with a megaphone screamed in Hebrew about sinners and the Judgement Day. A not unfamiliar scene in the city, where the Jewish population is ridden with tensions between the religious and the secular, and where the most vocal opposition to the Parade comes from the Orthodox Jewish community. Not far distant is the Jerusalem Open House, a GLBT centre that organised this first Parade in the 'Holy City'.[1] Their vision of the Parade is to promote respect and tolerance among all the groups in the city.[2] A deracinated and depoliticised recycling of GLBT rights as 'Western modernity', or a powerful and moving humanistic dream? Probably both. Just a mile to the east lies occupied East Jerusalem. Dreams aside, how out of place, I thought, was the Parade's insistence on sexual freedom and the freedom to take the streets in a city that denies movement, settlement and other basic freedoms to its Palestinian residents.

In the middle of the colourful gathering was a group dressed all in black, carrying pink banners with political slogans, such as 'No Pride in Occupation!' This was 'Black Laundry': a group of radical Israeli queers who had begun organising actions of political awareness within the queer com-

1 For over a decade the annual Parades have taken place in Tel Aviv; since the late 1990s they have also been held in other Israeli cities. Since 2002 The Parade has taken place annually in Jerusalem.

2 As part of its activities, The Open House provides support for gays, lesbians, bisexuals, transgenders and other queers from all segments of the city, including Arabs and Orthodox Jews.

munity. Most of their slogans were about the Occupation.[3] I had marched with 'Black Laundry' in the previous year's Parade in Tel Aviv and was glad to see and join them again in Jerusalem.[4] I was even more excited – and surprised – to spot among them a young woman with slogans, written in Russian. Radical left-wing activism in Israel at that time was a predominantly Hebrew and English-speaking affair (and a middle and upper class one, too). The Russian-speaking immigrants were mostly excluded from it by virtue of class and cultural differences, political opinions or simply prejudice and the lack of welcome. Or else they blended in as 'one of the Israelis', embraced by the left as curious exceptions from 'the rest of the Russians', their activism often seen as a sign of their 'successful integration'. They remained, however, a small minority: most of the Russian Israelis, queer and straight alike, positioned themselves somewhere between the centre and the right of the political spectrum.

Intrigued to see another 'Russian' marching with Black Laundry, I approached the woman carrying Russian slogans. This is how I met Rita, and this is how my journey to this book began. At that time, in the third year of the second Palestinian *Intifada* and the growing warfare in and re-occupation of the West Bank and Gaza, we were both left-wing activists. Both immigrants, feminists and queers, Rita and I 'clicked' immediately. We talked about our experience of being torn between our political alliances with the Israeli left, and the constant othering we encountered there as immigrants. We also talked about right-wing politics, racism and homophobia among Russian-speaking immigrants in the country; about the anger and alienation we both felt towards the immigrant community. We discussed ways of queer organising among Russian Israelis. It was then

3 A few, however, broke out of the expected dichotomies of straight/queer and right-wing/left-wing and addressed disability, transphobia, sexual workers, welfare rights and more.

4 Although I was never formally a member of 'Black Laundry', and have some reservations regarding their politics, a discussion of which lies beyond the scope of this book, it was very important for me to march with them during the Parades. For me, marching with 'Black Laundry' in 2001 and 2002 was about 'critique from within': supporting the Parades while challenging their overall celebratory atmosphere and raising awareness of the ongoing warfare and Occupation.

that Rita told me about the new website, 'The Pan-Israeli Portal of Russian-speaking Gays, Lesbians, Bisexuals and Transsexuals' she had recently joined. 'I hope to find a different Russianness', Rita said, 'one that is not based on raging homophobia or racism'.

I approached the website with curiosity and with hopes, very similar to Rita's. Except for the 'Russian' group at the Jerusalem Open House which I had helped to establish a few years earlier and a group of young immigrant lesbians I had interviewed for my previous research (Kuntsman 2003), this was my only time in a Russian-speaking queer space. Shortly after the Parade, when I was still finding my way around the discussion board of the website, a group of participants, including Rita, began organising against homophobic attacks in the immigrant media, following a particularly hateful publication about the Jerusalem Parade. The website became a vibrant political space of action and empowerment, from which queers could confront media violence and speak back to the immigrant community that often either silenced or demonised them. It generated a sense of shared destiny as well as mutual support. At that moment, the website indeed felt as if it were a place of different Russianness, or rather, a place where Russianness could be reclaimed and re-articulated by queers.

I joined the anti-homophobia initiative and later began participating in other on-line discussions that took place on the site. Several months later, I moved to England to pursue my doctoral studies, which I wanted to dedicate to the emerging queer immigrant scene in Israel, on- and off-line. I continued participating in the discussion board, keeping in touch with friends I knew off-line, and making new ones through the website. The physical distance emphasised – and made me more attentive to – the feeling of connectedness, both my own and that of other people who took part in this on-line space. The website was often described, and indeed felt like, a place one comes to in order to find support, understanding, friendship or love. It is this moving sense of connection in the supposedly disembodied and immaterial terrain of cyberspace that led me to focus on the website as the main site of my research. Originally interested in the website only as an instrument that assists in off-line organising, I soon realised that cyberspace is in itself a site of imagining and making one's home.

But the longer I participated on the site, the more I discovered how complicated this 'homely' space was. For example, the discussion board was frequently galvanised by raging fights between the participants, making one question, whose home it is? More importantly, I began to wonder: what kind of queer politics does the site create? And is this really a site of a 'different Russianness'? While opening up some boundaries, such as those of sexuality and ethnicity, the website often passionately reinforced and reassured others, especially those of race and nation. For example, despite a seeming variety of political views and opinions, voiced on the site, it has been almost impossible to raise a radical critique of Israeli nationalism or the state's policy towards the Palestinians without being mocked, verbally attacked by other participants, or silenced. Anti-Palestinian hate speech, expressions of militant Israeli patriotism and scorn towards the left-wing queers such as 'Black Laundry', on the other hand, were commonly accepted and rarely challenged. The intense and frequent racist hate speech and fights I repeatedly encountered on the site were almost physically painful to me. At times, they made my experience both as a participant *and* as an ethnographer unbearable. But they also led me to ask fundamental questions about the relations between violence and belonging, in cyberspace and beyond.

... After being an active and a tireless polemicist in many debates on feminism, racism and Israeli politics, Rita eventually ceased participating on the discussion board. When I spoke to her during my fieldtrip to Israel in 2004 she told me she had not found her 'different Russianness' there. She continued her political activism with the Israeli queer community and with Russian immigrants elsewhere. To some extent, I shared Rita's disappointment. However, unlike her, I stayed, both because of the many personal connections I had made through the website, and because I wanted to continue with the research. I saw my project as both a way of contributing to the queer immigrant presence, within and outside of academia, *and* as a way to make a difference to queer politics in the immigrant community, and more broadly in Israel/Palestine.

But staying also meant being 'in the closet' about my own activism. I never hid my left-wing views, but I did not put them on display, either.

Nor did I initiate discussions about government policy or the Occupation, although I was an otherwise active participant. Even when my immediate impulse was to try and challenge every expression of racism and nationalism on the Forum, I was also acutely aware that such an intervention might not be effective, or could even be counterproductive in that particular context – for example, by generating a flame war and further circuits of racism, instead of a debate – and so I stayed silent. This was not an easy decision; the activist in me kept saying: *if you do not speak up, you contribute to the legitimating of what is said.* This may not have been the best decision, if there is such a thing in ethnography. But I also sensed that there is more to the binary of speech and silence; the researcher in me wanted to hear the silence speak. Now, looking back on my self-silencing, I want to step out of the simplistic opposition of good 'speaking out' and bad 'non-intervention', and think about the unspoken and the unspeakable, about complexities and violences of homely spaces in and beyond cyberspace, about the limitations of dialogue, as well as about other possibilities of making a difference.

This book offers a reading of Israeli nationalism and of queer migranthood that does not necessarily reflect the state of mind of all the participants of the website. Despite writing 'from within', I am not speaking 'for' them; I am well aware that my opinions might be neither popular, nor representative. Nevertheless, I saw writing this book not only as an intellectual endeavour, but also a political responsibility, precisely because I am a queer immigrant myself. In other words, I see it as a necessary intervention, and also hope that it can become a way of 'speaking to': to those, whom I met on the website, to other Russian-speaking queer immigrants, to Israelis, and to other queers. I began working on this project in the belief that academic writing can, too, be a form of the different Russianness – and different queerness – that I, like Rita, was looking for.

The journey to the book has been made possible by many people – colleagues, mentors, and friends. First and foremost, I owe deep gratitude to my PhD supervisors, Anne-Marie Fortier and Gail Lewis at Lancaster University, UK, who have been an invaluable source of inspiration, encouragement and support. I wish to thank both of them for their theoretical insights, ideas and advice; for guiding me through the doctorate and for pushing me to do my best; for being critical and intellectually rigorous yet always respecting my opinions and my work.

I would also like to thank other teachers, colleagues and fellow PhD students in the department of Sociology, Institute for Women's Studies and Institute for Cultural Research at Lancaster University for their inspiration and productive critique: Sara Ahmed, Ranjini Canchi Raghavendra, Claudia Castañeda, Woo-Joo Chang, Jennie German Molz, David Hansen-Miller, Adrian Mackenzie, Maureen McNeal, Nayanika Moohkerjee, Michal Nahman, Lucy Suchman, Sarah Proctor-Thomson, Imogen Tyler, Laura Watts and Yoke-Sum Wong. My gratitude also to the participants of the *Out of Place: Interrogating Silences in Queeerness/Raciality* conference, held in Lancaster, for the precious exchange of ideas, and for the hope in transnational alliances and different queer politics. I am thankful to Laurent Berlant, Ghassan Hage, Donna Haraway and Jasbir Puar, whose visits to Lancaster and comments on my work were a source of great insight. During my years at Lancaster I benefitted greatly from the warm welcome and help of the support staff of the Sociology Department: Joann Bowker, Pennie Drinkall and Claire O'Donnell.

Several people were invaluable in helping transform the doctorate into a book. I would like to thank my examiners, Les Back and Jackie Stacey, for turning what is usually seen as a scary 'defence' into a truly inspiring intellectual exchange, and for encouraging me to make this crucial step forward from the doctorate to the book. I am indebted to Claudia Castañeda and Martin Manalansan for their dedicated reading, generous engagement and the detailed and insightful comments on the earlier draft of the book. I also thank Raghika Gajjala for her comments on some of the chapters.

My deep appreciation also goes to colleagues at Liverpool John Moores University where this book received its final shape: Iqbal Akthar, Simone Krüger, Siân Lincoln, Nickianne Moody and Steve Spittle. I am grateful to Tina Campt whose visit to Liverpool was a great source of inspiration; thank you for your insights and for reminding me that some contradictions are irresolvable and that some complicities cannot be redeemed. I also thank the participants of *Rediscovering the Domestic: Interdisciplinary Reflections on Contemporary Global Cultures* and *Still Out of Place?* conferences, held in Liverpool, for their ideas and thoughtful and critical questions. And lastly, I thank Jin Haritaworn for our ongoing intellectual companionship in thinking about queerness, racism and the 'war on terror'.

I wish to thank United Kingdom Overseas Research Scholarship; Anglo-Israel Association; Peel Studentship of Lancaster University; Hadassah Brandeis Institute on Jewish Women and William Ritchie Travel Fund, Lancaster University for contributing towards fees, fieldwork and other research expenses associated with the project. I am grateful to the Research Capability Fund at Liverpool John Moores University for contributing towards the production costs of the book. I thank Jane Hardy for her thorough copyediting and indexing.

I thank my friends 'in the field' Anna Talisman, Jeny Sotnikov and Guy Frankovich for opening their hearts and homes for me; I am truly grateful for your friendship and for the ongoing conversations about migranthood, queerness and belonging, conversations we are still able to have, despite the geographical distances and the many disagreements between us. My gratitude also goes to all other participants of the website that agreed to take part in this research. I want to thank my family and my friends in Israel and the UK: Anat Caspi Kaivanto, Denise Carlyle, Lauren Erdreich, Fiona Frank, Lydia Ginzburg, Mary Kinane, Smadar Lavie, Julia Lerner, Edna Lomsky-Feder, Diana Martin, Ronit Moshel, Tamar Rapoport, Sveta Roberman, Laura Staetsky, Sandy Staplehurst, and Elly Teeman who supported and encouraged me all the way, and provided an invaluable source of critical thinking and high spirits. I thank Debra Ferreday and Esperanza Miyake, colleagues and dear friends, who helped me stay sane during the years in Lancaster, and who continue to keep me inspired.

And last but not least, I owe this project to my life partner Yehudit Kirstein Keshet. Our debates on the fate and future of Israel/Palestine have always kept me on my toes; our political and intellectual companionship means more to me than I am able to describe. Without Yehudit I would never have mastered the nuances of English style and grammar; she was a tireless editor of endless drafts and versions of this book, and a sharp reader and critic. But more importantly, without her encouragement, patience and help I would not have been able to carry out the project. Her faith in me carried me through the doctorate, the book and beyond; her love carries me through life.

Some of the chapters were published previously in different versions. I thank the publishers for permitting me to reprint these articles: 'The Currency of Victimhood in Uncanny Homes: Russian-speaking Queer Immigrants in Israel Confront Homophobia', *Journal of Ethnic and Migration Studies*, 35 (1), 2009, pp. 133–149. 'The Soldier and the Terrorist: Sexy Nationalism, Queer Violence', *Sexualities*, 11 (1), 2008, pp. 159–187. 'Between Gulags and Pride Parades: Sexuality, Nation and Haunted Speech Acts', *GLQ: Journal of Gay and Lesbian Studies*, 14 (2–3), 2008, pp. 263–287. 'Written in Blood: Contested Borders and the Politics of Passing in Israel/Palestine and in Cyberspace', *Feminist Media Studies*, 8 (3), 2008, pp. 267–283. 'Hospitality in flames: queer immigrants and melancholic be/longing', in Jennie Germann Molz and Sarah Gibson (eds), *Mobilizing Hospitality: The Ethics of Social Relations in a Mobile World*, Aldershot: Ashgate, 2008, pp. 145–158. 'Belonging through violence: Flaming, erasure and performativity in queer migrant community', in Kate O'Riordan and David J. Phillips (eds), *Queers Online: Media technology and sexuality*, New York: Peter Lang, 2007, pp. 101–122.

INTRODUCTION

Violence and Belonging

This book began with questions of belonging – sexual, ethnic and national. It brings together my years of academic engagement with issues of sexuality and migration, and my recent interest in cybersociality and the making of on-line collective spaces. Cyberspace can provide many opportunities for home-making and home-imagining,[1] especially for migrants and diasporic subjects (Gajjala 1996, 2004). As the extensive scholarship on cybercultures in the last fifteen years has shown, cyberspace can bring together physically dispersed people, create a space of communication for socially marginalised groups and serve as a resource for community organising. With this scholarship in mind, I began an ethnography of queer immigrants' organising, which was centred around, but not limited to, 'The Pan-Israeli Portal of Russian-speaking GLBTs', an on-line space created by (and for) Russian-Israeli queers.

My initial questions concerned the ways queer immigrants can belong to the nation given that both nationalism and immigration are usually imagined in heterosexual terms. For example, the Israeli national ethos is based on heteronormative masculinity and femininity: it defines the men's main role as soldiers who have to defend the nation, and the women's role as mothers who have to reproduce it (Berkovitch 1999; Kadish 2001). Within this ethos the immigrants, too, are channelled into these roles. And while Israeli immigration law and policy do not officially distinguish individuals

1 The imagining of homes in cyberspace is in some ways similar to what Benedict Anderson described as 'imagining communities' (Anderson 1991). In his work on 18th–19th century newspapers Anderson addressed the ways people imagine themselves as part of a community, physically seeing each other. Anderson's notion of 'imagined communities' was taken on by many scholars of cybercultures, see, for example, Baym (1995), Rheingold (2000).

on the basis of sexual orientation, they are based on the concept of the heterosexual family bonded by legal marriage,[2] making the queer immigrants invisible at best and discriminated against at worst. So initially I wanted to explore how Russian-speaking queers imagine their place in the country that is officially defined as their national homeland but ignores or marginalises them as queers. I also wanted to know, how their home-making and home-imagining was mediated by cyberspace.

All these questions are still in place. But the more I progressed with my ethnography, the more I was confronted by issues of violence: nationalist, racial and homophobic; symbolic and verbal; imagined and enacted; violence of which queer immigrants were victims, perpetrators or supporters. Violence was one of the main reasons for their first political organising against homophobia; it was part of their daily experience in cyberspace. But violence was also constantly present as the background of my fieldwork that began at the time of the second Palestinian *Intifada*, Israel's reoccupation of the West Bank, the US invasion of Iraq and the 'global war on terror'. So what about belonging? The two are often envisioned in opposition: violence is viewed as an obstacle to belonging or as a background against which belonging – understood as a creation of 'safe spaces' on and off-line – takes place.[3] This book takes a more complex approach to conceptualising the two,[4] by looking at the ways various forms of violence constitute,

2 So while the heterosexual partner of an Israeli citizen can enter and settle in the country based on marriage, a same-sex partner cannot. However, the question of marriage and citizenship is far more complicated, as Israel has been strengthening its discriminatory mechanisms against the non-Jewish (and in particular Palestinian) citizens, preventing family reunification under various legal excuses. The racialisation of marriage and citizenship is a complex topic that is beyond the scope of this book.

3 Such an opposition can be found, for example, in public debates and in policy research regarding education or community cohesion, where violence (usually understood mainly as an interpersonal affair) is seen as an obstacle to be eliminated. The same opposition prevails in many writings about on-line interactions, communities and 'disruptive behaviours' that threaten them – a topic which I discuss in detail in Chapter 6.

4 For an excellent critical intervention into the dichotomised mapping of violence and belonging in the case of gays and lesbians, see *Sexuality and the Politics of Violence and Safety* (Moran and Skeggs 2004). The authors make a similar argument regarding the interrelatedness of safety and violence. The focus of their book is different from mine in

rather than contradict, the sense of sexual, ethnic and national belonging of Russian-speaking, queer immigrants.

My thinking about the complexities of violence and belonging is informed by extensive scholarship on the role of violence in drawing, negotiating and defending collective boundaries through violence towards outsiders or towards 'others within' (see, for example, Boellstorff 2007; Campt 2005; Daiya 2008; Nevels 2007). Violence can be a technology of constituting 'us' versus 'them' that is exercised through acts of torture, rape, enslavement, lynching and warfare, but also works through cultural knowledge, discourses of political and legal subjecthood, notions of humanness and forms of dehumanisation (Kaplan 2004). In that sense, violence is also, in Gail Mason's words, 'a mechanism through which we distinguish and observe other things. In other words, violence is more than a practice that acts upon individual subjects to inflict harm and injury. It is, metaphorically speaking, also a way of looking at these subjects' (Mason 2002: 11).

One of the main – although of course, not the only – concerns of this book is the way nationalist and racial violence becomes a mechanism of belonging to Israeli society, a society, engaged in ongoing colonisation and military conflict. For example, Israel's 'way of looking' at suffering and victimhood is highly racialised: Jewish suffering in both the past and the present is highly valued and extensively commemorated; Palestinian suffering, on the other hand, is continuously disregarded as non-existent or non-important. This particular way of looking at subjects of violence is both a technology of inclusion into the national collective *and* a mechanism of dehumanisation, marking only some lives as valuable and memorable.[5]

Centring my discussion on queer immigrants and on their location in webs of inclusion and exclusion, I add another layer of complexity: the role of sexual and ethnic marginality in these 'violent belongings' (Daiya

---

that firstly it addresses 'safety' rather than 'belonging' and secondly in that it uses space as the main analytical focus, by exploring the role of law and criminalisation, on one hand, and individual strategies of dealing with violence, on the other.

5 Or what Judith Butler (2004) calls the distinction between 'grievable' and 'ungrievable' lives, and what Paul Gilroy (2004) describes as 'raciology of dehumanisation'. I return to discuss these concepts in detail in the conclusion.

2008; Kaplan 2004). Rather than seeing violence only as a means of exclusion, I examine the economy of violence (Moran and Skeggs 2004) and the cultural capital of *entitlement* to belong (Hage 2000), by looking at how access to and performance of violence might become a move away from margins, carry a fantasy or promise of integration into racialised nationhood (Nevels 2007), as well as signal its irresolvable ambivalence (Campt 2005).

And lastly, this book takes as its point of departure the world of cyberspace where, shaped by accelerated speed (Virilio 1995, 1997), information, words and feelings can circulate momentarily and instantaneously, but where they can also turn into virtual fossils, remaining in timeless and frozen on-line archives (Gajjala 2002). Throughout the book I explore the ways this dual nature of cyberspace shapes and transforms various forms of violence and look into the kinds of belonging it allows. My aim here is not to establish the nature of cyberspace itself or to assess whether or not belonging is possible in on-line environments. Rather, this book is an exploration of how violence and belonging co-constitute each other through movement and stillness, rapid transformations and stubborn persistency; and how the mechanisms and the effects of such co-constitution transcend the boundaries of on and off-line worlds.

The main question of this book is therefore twofold. Firstly, I ask: what is the relationship between violence and belonging? In pursuing this question, the book follows the different forms of violence in and out of cyberspace and the ways they map, constitute and are constituted by different desires and practices of belonging. Secondly, I ask: what are the relations between these different forms of violence? My interest here is firstly in various *types* of violence, such as homophobia, discussed in the first part of the book; racism, discussed in the second part; or intra-communal on-line flame wars, discussed in the third. Mapping each of those, I then explore the ways they are connected synchronically, through metonymic closeness in cyberspace, and diachronically, through shared genealogies of otherness and monstrosity. Secondly, I am interested in the relations between different *forms* of violence, such as physical and verbal, social and psychic, material and semiotic. This book is written with a clear awareness of the differences between them; for example, one must certainly distinguish between hate speech and killing, or between on-line flame wars and off-line warfare. And yet, this book insists on their interrelatedness. With the primary ethnographic focus on on-line home-making and home-imagining, my analysis suggests that violence in and out of cyberspace reverberates through spaces, bodies and psyches, and that the on-line and off-line worlds are always intertwined.

Troubled home-making in Israel/Palestine

Over one million immigrants from the former Soviet Union have arrived in Israel since 1989 (Central Bureau of Statistics of Israel 2002),[6] and been received by the Israeli 'Law of Return' that grants immediate citizenship and financial support to all Jews and their family members regardless of age, gender or sexuality. The immigration of Jews is defined by the state of Israel, and indeed perceived by many of the immigrants themselves, as a national 'homecoming' although many of them also define their immigration as flight from the collapsing Soviet Union and as motivated by eco-

6 There were several waves of 'Russian' migration to Israel, before and after the establishment of the state in 1948. The largest in number is the latest wave of the 1990s–2000s, which is extremely diverse in terms of economic and educational background, and yet considered to be one of the most educated groups of newcomers. 'Russian' immigrants are also diverse in terms of ethnicity and religion: this wave has brought a high number of mixed families of Jewish and non-Jewish parentage. The place of the Russian-speaking immigrants in the country keeps changing, from weak economically and marginalised ethnically in the early 1990s, to increasingly empowered politically and culturally in the late 1990s and early 2000s, to what some see as the future economic and ethnic elite. The book thus captures a very particular moment of this changing reality. For an account of changes in Russian immigrants' collective identity – unfortunately, examined through the problematic concept of 'integration' – see Leshem (2008). The changing role of the 'Russians' in racial, ethnic and classed formations in Israel/Palestine, which includes reaffirmation, challenge and refiguring, is yet to be conceptualised. One notable attempt to do so can be found in Lerner (in preparation).

nomic and practical motives rather than by nationalistic ones (Horowitz and Leshem 1998).

The immigration and settlement of Russian-speaking newcomers – queer and straight alike – are inseparable from the colonial visions of the Zionist project: creating a country for 'people without land' in the 'land without people'. The very Law of Return, for example, defines Jewish immigration as 'return from the Diaspora', as repatriation: the Hebrew word, used to describe it, is *Aliya*, literally meaning ascent (to Zion). The Law of Return, and the 'repatriation' policy of the state, aim to provide Jews from all over the world a safe home,[7] to which they are seen as entitled not only because of persecution in the past or present, but because this home is viewed as historically theirs (regardless of its other occupants). For many Jews this return is indeed a fulfilment of diasporic longing, sometimes carried through generations. But at the same time, it erases other lives, histories and homes and makes Israel into an a colonial state, where Palestinian refugees were driven out of the land in 1948 and not allowed to return to their homes; where the traces – material and mnemonic – of their presence are scrupulously overwritten; where Palestinian citizens, remaining in Israel, many of whom were 'internal refugees', displaced from their pre-1948 areas of residence, are accorded citizenship and *de-jure* equal rights, but suffer *de-facto* discrimination, in regard to ownership of land and the distribution of resources but also in regard to national identification;[8] where the expansion of borders after 1967 and the following Occupation and settlement of Palestinian lands of the West Bank and Gaza appear, to many Israelis, as both natural and necessary; and where so much destruction and injustice had been and continues to be done in the name of the 'safe Jewish home'.

In this book, I choose to use the term 'immigrants' rather than 'returnees' or 'repatriates', to describe the Russian-speaking newcomers to Israel.

7 The state of Israel does not simply support Jewish immigration but actively encourages it through various programmes among the diaspora Jews.

8 Palestinian citizens of Israel should not be confused with Palestinians in the Occupied Territories of the West Bank and Gaza who are stateless and subject to military governance. Only a minority of them have Jordanian citizenship.

Remaining ethnographically attentive to the dreams and desires of many of them for a home, and a national home in particular, my political and conceptual intention is to question and challenge, rather than unproblematically accept, the racialised formations of this homecoming. This book, in other words, is grounded in the reading of Israeli nationalism as a colonial project. Such reading is based in part on the concept of 'settler societies' (Yuval-Davis and Abdo 1995) defined as a specific type of nationalism based on settlement in a land occupied by other peoples. Throughout the book I use the term Israel/Palestine, to distinguish between Israel as a state and Israel/Palestine as a geo-political colonial space, constituted through the complex histories of both Israelis and Palestinians.

But I also view the colonial relations in Israel/Palestine as more complicated than the dichotomy of the (Israeli) coloniser/(Palestinian) colonised, or of a homecomer/a homeless. As several scholars have noted, the Zionist project is not simply Jewish, it is also Eurocentric (Lavie 1996; Shalom-Shitrit 1999; Shohat 1997). From the early days of Jewish settlement in Palestine (mainly since the 1900s), and then from the first days of the state of Israel (1948), Jews of non-European origin have been subordinated economically and colonised culturally. The country's elite were and are the *Ashkenazim* – Jews of European descent. The *Mizrachim* – meaning in Hebrew 'the Orientals', from North Africa and Asia – many of whom arrived in Israel in the 1950s, were robbed of their cultural heritage and language and became second-class citizens. Ella Shohat (1997) and Smadar Lavie (1996) therefore suggest addressing colonial relations in Israel/Palestine as those between the West/'First-Worlders', or the white *Ashkenazim*, and the East/'Third-Worlders', the *Mizrachim* and the Palestinians.

The arrival of Jews from the former Soviet Union – and in particular, its large *Ashkenazi* component, those who lived in the European parts of the former Soviet Union (Russia, Ukraine, Belarus, Lita, Latvia and Estonia) – was supposed to strengthen Eurocentric colonial domination. As Jews, the newcomers were expected to contribute to Israel's demographic war over the Palestinians, that is, to ensure the Jewish majority. And yet, their Jewishness was constantly questioned: due to their many mixed marriages with non-Jews on one hand, and cultural assimilation in the Soviet Union on the other, the Russian-speaking newcomers were seen as 'not Jewish enough' and, as such, constructed as racially and culturally impure. As light-skinned Europeans, many of whom had higher education, the 'Russians'[9] as they are often called in Israel, were desirable for the Zionist project of Israeliness as white middle-classness and Europeanness. At the same time the attitude towards the 'Russians' was ambivalent: as immigrants from the Eastern/communist block, they were seen as not the right kind of Europeans (and as not Western enough),[10] and had to be re-educated into proper Westerness and Israeliness (Golden 2003; Shalom-Shitrit 1999).

The 'homecoming' of the Russian-speaking immigrants is therefore a far more complex process than an unproblematic 'return'; it is a troubled project of belonging and colonisation, both in terms of contested socio-political and cultural location and in terms of subjectivity. As regards their location, they occupy the complex position of citizens who are both privileged and marginalised, desired and othered. As such, they further complicate the coloniser/colonised dichotomy both in relation to their Jewishness and their Europeanness. Their subjectivity as 'homecomers' is, too, profoundly ambivalent. Many of the Russian-speaking immigrants

9 The conflation of Russianness with whiteness and Europeanness has its own internal colonisation and erasure: not all immigrants from the Soviet Union were from the European parts of the country, some came from the Caucasus and regions of Central Asia. The many internal differences – ethnic, economic, cultural and religious – were often overlooked or made invisible by the state policy, the immigrant intellectual and media elite, and, importantly, also by researchers who used the category of 'Russians' as a synonym for 'whites' (Bram 2005). While this book looks at immigrants, most of whom are of European origin, I am aware of my own complicity in this conflation.

10 For example, the 'Russian' immigrant community was seen as politically 'immature' due to years of living under communist rule; their patterns of voting resembled those of lower-class *Mizrachim*, rather than the middle-class *Ashkenazim*, to whom the Russians formally belonged, in terms of both ethnicity and class. Similarly, the 'Russian' women were marked as 'reproductively irresponsible' because of their reliance on abortion rather than other contraceptive methods used by middle-class *Ashkenazi* Israeli women. This, too, was explained by the 'backwardness' of life in the Soviet Union. The very constructions of 'political immaturity' or 'reproductive responsibility' are important subjects that lie beyond the scope of this project; what I want to note here is that the Russian-speaking immigrants often did not confirm to Israeli models of class/ethnic distinction and categorisation.

constitute their colonial belonging through a sense of entitlement to the nation and land (as Jews) and of cultural superiority over 'the Oriental' *Mizrachi* Jews and Palestinians (as Europeans).[11] And yet, their experiences are in many aspects minoritarian: they struggle against everyday racism and feelings of inferiority and alienation.[12] Olga Gershenson describes the relations between immigrants and Jewish Israelis as 'mutual colonisation' where both the 'Russians' and the Israelis repeatedly address each other as simultaneously inferior and superior (Gershenson 2005). I take on her emphasis on mutuality and the complexity of colonial relations and subjectivities: Gershenson extends Homi Bhabha's (1994) notion of colonial ambivalence by pointing out that in the relations between Russian-speaking immigrants and Jewish Israelis the role of the coloniser is in itself is unfixed and shifting.

And what about sexuality? In the past twelve years a large body of research has been written on immigrants from the former Soviet Union, including the analysis of the immigrants' perception of Israeli society and its ethnic make-up (Gershenson 2005; Lomsky-Feder and Rapoport 2003; Lomsky-Feder et al. 2005) and the Israeli-Palestinian conflict (Al-Haj 2004; Shumsky 2004). Many studies have also explored gender and sexuality and the ways they condition and shape immigrants' belonging (Amir and Benjamin 1997; Amir, Remennick and Elimelech 1997; Golden 2003; Lemish 2000; Lomsky-Feder and Rapoport 2003). None of these studies, however, deal with non-heterosexual immigrants; their analyses, even when critical of particular forms of heteronormativity, nevertheless contribute to the view of nationhood and gender relations as exclusively heterosexual. In contrast, this book suggests that queer sexuality can play an important role in immigrant belonging. I aim to challenge both the absence of queers in research on Russian-speaking immigration, and the very heterosexual formations of migranthood and nationalism.

11 I return to discuss the orientalism of the Russian-speaking immigrants in Chapters 3 and 4.

12 I return to discuss these in Chapters 5 and 6.

My deployment of the term 'queer' throughout the book has three purposes. Firstly, I use it as an inclusive category that accommodates the variety of non-heterosexual practices, subjectivities and identities, some but not all of which can fit the GLBT – gay-lesbian-bisexual-transgender – labels. For example, when referring to the queer immigrants throughout the book, I deliberately leave the question of self-identification open. While many participants of the website identified themselves as lesbian, gay, bisexual, transgender or transsexual, many others did not take on a particular sexual identity, some defined themselves as 'interested' or 'exploring', others used the term 'queer', and yet others refused naming completely. Secondly, I use 'queer' as an analytical tool to trace and map this variety, following the ways categories of sexuality are figured and refigured through history, movement and geo-political location. In Chapter 1, for instance, I describe how the multiplicity of categories used for same-sex relations in the Soviet Union and Israel is violently collapsed into one monstrous figure of the criminal. And lastly, I use 'queer' to undermine heterosexuality as a regulatory regime (see for example, Gopinath 2005; Manalansan 2000, 2002), in particular when approaching nationalism and immigration. For example, Chapters 5 and 6 address the ways both Soviet and Israeli practices of everyday life are queered as the immigrants negotiate their ambivalent position in the local clubbing scene, while Chapter 3 traces the ways immigrants' love for the nation is queerly sexualised.

With all three uses of the term 'queer', I see this book as an ongoing conversation with the growing body of research on 'queer diaspora.'[13] Scholars in this field bring to the fore the lives and experiences of queer migrants, often ignored by mainstream research (Luibhéid 2008). Most importantly, they question the very assumptions, surrounding both the notions of national and diasporic belonging on one hand, and of white queer politics, on the other. In Jasbir Puar's eloquent words, they 'queer the

13 To name a few, see Gayatri Gopinath's (2005) work on queer subjects in the Indian diaspora; Martin Manalansan's (2003) ethnography of Filipino queers in the Philippines and in the US; or Jennifer Petzen's (2004) ethnography of queer Turkish migrants in Germany. See also edited collections such as *Queer Diasporas* (Patton and Sanchez-Eppler 2000) and *GLQ: Special Issue on Queer/Migration* (Luibhéid 2008).

diaspora' and 'diasporicise the queer' (Puar 1998: 406). At the same time, it is crucial to remain critical of the transgressive potential of 'queer diaspora': as Puar reminds us, 'queer diasporas are not immune from the forms of cultural nationalism; in fact, they may even rely on them' (Puar 1998: 410). In other words, exploring how nations and diasporas can be queered, we must remember that 'queering' does not necessarily mean transgression and subversion of the dominant regimes; nor does 'diasporicising'.

It is with these cautions in mind that I look at the Israeli constructions of queer sexualities, and the way Russian-speaking queers negotiate their way around them. While the Zionist national project is inevitably heterosexual and heteronormative (Glusman 1997; Kadish 2001), queer sexuality can undoubtedly denaturalise the heterosexualised grounds of the nation state (Eng 1997; Patton and Sanchez-Eppler 2000; Warner 1993). However, the national and the queer tropes are not necessarily mutually exclusive. Rather, queer sexualities can both challenge and reinforce the power of the nation (Har'el 2000). For example, many Jewish-Israeli gay men base their claim for citizenship on the basis of participation in the army, and many middle-class Israeli lesbians choose to become mothers following the Israeli model of (Jewish) female citizenship as reproduction and motherhood (Kadish 2001). And while queers are still sometimes depicted as threatening the nation from within,[14] the mainstream Israeli queer community itself is politically loyal and patriotic, *Ashkenazi* and middle-class, Hebrew speaking and Zionist-oriented (Bar-On 1997; Yosef 2004). In other words, while some aspects of queerness can be seen as threatening or subverting the national project, other aspects can best be described as what Puar coins 'homonationalism' (Puar 2007).[15]

How then are Russian-speaking queers similar to and different from Israeli queers in their relations to the nation? How do Russian-speaking

14 As, for example, happened in the recent debates about moving the Pride Week events from their usual location in Tel-Aviv to Jerusalem.

15 The relations between queerness and nationalism are of course complex and changing over time. My aim here is not to describe what they are but only to point to their complexity. I return to discuss the complicity of queerness within nationalism and patriotism in Chapter 3.

queers locate themselves in relation to the Hebrew-speaking queer community, highly affected by the dominant Israeli 'melting pot' policy? How do they relate to other Russian-speaking immigrants? How do they constitute and negotiate their sense of home, in and out of cyberspace?

Queer homes in cyberspace

A queer immigrant myself, I came out in the early 1990s into a complete absence of immigrant GLBT organisations or queer spaces. At the time of my first research on the topic in the mid-late 1990s, Russian-speaking queers were isolated from the Israeli scene and from each other. Back then, Russianness and queerness were repeatedly constructed as incompatible with each other by both the immigrant media, politicians and the queers themselves. For example, in 1995 a 'Russian' member of the Israeli parliament, a recent immigrant herself, declared that gays and lesbians did not exist in the Russian-speaking community. Young immigrant lesbians, whom I interviewed for my project on immigration and coming out[16] in 1999, echoed her delusion by narrating their lives around the opposition between militantly heterosexual – or even explicitly homophobic – Russianness, which they were rejecting, and liberal Israeli queerness, which they were proudly embracing. A few explicitly spoke of 'unbecoming' Russian: the desire to cease speaking Russian and to become one of the Israeli gays and lesbians (Kuntsman 2003). But there were many others who wanted to connect their Russianness and their queerness; slowly they began

16 My previous research (Kuntsman 2003) was based on immigration stories of Russian-speaking lesbians, and explored the intersection of two homecoming narratives: the Zionist narrative of Jewish immigration to Israel as repatriation and the Western narrative of queer 'coming out' as 'coming home'. In particular, I explored the racialisation and ethnicisation of Russian immigrants and discussed the ways immigrant lesbians escape this othering by adopting a lesbian identity which marked them as white middle-class Israelis rather than stigmatised Eastern European newcomers.

networking and organising. Since the late 1990s several immigrant groups have been established. In 1999 the first 'Russian' group[17] got together at the Jerusalem Open House, bringing together gays, lesbians, bisexuals and other Russian-speaking queers. Another group was organised in Haifa. A year later a larger one was established in Tel-Aviv. Around the same time an immigrant woman, Shunya,[18] began organising 'Russian' evenings at the Tel-Aviv Lesbian Feminist Centre; these evenings later became the first 'Russian' queer night club, *At Shunya's*.[19]

In late 2001 a group of several young immigrants established the site, 'The Pan Israeli Portal of Russian speaking GLBTs', which is at the centre of my discussion. The portal contained information, a newsletter, essays, galleries and a vibrant discussion board called 'The Forum'. Many people from the existing social groups participated in the Forum, maintaining close links between on-line and off-line queer spaces. Later, when the Tel-Aviv group ceased its activities, the Forum became the main 'hanging out' site for queer immigrants; more and more new participants from all parts of the country joined the discussions. For some of them, who, like myself, were already involved in the Israeli scene, participating in the Forum was a way back to their Russianness. 'Speaking about these issues [of sexuality] in Russian', wrote one participant in one of the discussions, 'is like getting back in touch with my roots'.[20] For others the Forum was a place of connection to other queer immigrants. 'It is a place, where I can speak openly about my love for a woman, without being misunderstood', wrote

17 Incidentally, the group was initiated by two people whom I interviewed for my previous research, and myself. The very encounter during interviews and the long discussions about the absence of Russian queer spaces in Israel urged us to create such a space ourselves.

18 All names of the participants mentioned in this book have been changed, except when I refer to publicly known figures: such as Shunya (Tanya Shunevich), the club owner; Anna Talisman, the coordinator of the Russian Forum Against Homophobia and Defamation; and Guy Gomel (Frankovich), the journalist and the main author of articles on the queer immigrants' website.

19 I discuss the club in detail in Chapter 5.

20 All of the discussions cited in this book took place on the website, and were later downloaded and saved on my computer (see also my discussion below). In order to protect the participants, I do not provide URLs of discussion threads.

one woman in an email interview[21] in response to my question 'What is the website to you?' '[For me] it is an outlet, a source of air', wrote one man in response to the same question, 'A place to meet interesting people. And considering that my homosexual life is somewhat virtual, it is one of the main places where I can be myself'.

The website created a vibrant, dynamic and constantly changing collective space. At the time when I first joined the Forum in 2002, and throughout my fieldwork in 2003–2004, there were always several dozen active participants who took part in the discussions on a weekly and, more often, a daily basis. Altogether, the site had several hundreds of registered participants. Many of them came and went, but some stayed for several years, and so did the archives of their on-line encounters.[22] Some participants only took part in the on-line discussions, others were meeting off-line as well as on-line, moving between the two words, undermining what some see as a clear-cut separation of 'cyberspace' and 'the real world'.

The design and functions of the site had also changed over the years: new sections added to the non-interactive parts of the site (essays, news, stories, etc.), new options offered to those participating in the Forum discussions (private messages to individual participants, personalised avatars and individual signatures etc.), and the structure of the Forum itself modified.[23] Some of the administrators and contributors also changed, causing tensions and frictions. And yet, for several years the site has been the space Russian-speaking queer immigrants can come to; a space, where so many of them

21 I conducted a series of email interviews with 20 participants at the initial stage of the research, focusing on the reasons for using the website, and actual practices and frequency of use. I return to discuss the process of my ethnography later in the chapter.

22 I return to describe the nature of my material, which includes – but is not limited to – the archives of Forum discussions, later in the chapter; I then return to address these archives in Chapter 6.

23 The Forum originally consisted of several parts. The *General Forum* section was designed as an open space for discussions, and other sections (*Gay, Lesbian, Bi and Trans*) were designated for personal ads. With time, the *General Forum* became male dominated, and many women (lesbian, bisexual and straight) preferred to hold their discussions in the 'Lesbian/personal ads' section. After a while the latter was transformed into *Lesbi-Forum*, although women continued participating on the *General Forum*.

felt they belonged.[24] In some of the on-line discussions that I took part in and/or observed, the Forum was compared to family, community, one's home country or one's home town. A similar view of the website appeared in the *About Us* section where it was described as an 'association of people, who share similar interests and more.' The text described Russian-Israeli queers as linked together through both their sexuality and their ethnicity. 'We', noted the text, 'are linked by a shared fate'.

> We [are] Russian-speaking Israelis with a sexual self-identification that is different from the majority of people around us. We would like our site to become a virtual association of 'other people' in the global Net. We believe that in the vast internet-space there is a place for everyone. We hope that our site will become one of the most interesting places for you to visit and meet others (http://aguda.org/about.php , saved March 2004).[25]

The internet can provide new opportunities for diasporic and migrant subjects and in that sense, the Russian-Israeli queers' website was no exception. 'Cyborg-Diaspora', using Indira Karamcheti's (1992) and Radhika Gajjala's (2002) words, is a space for creating migrant community through

24 One of the reasons was undoubtedly the newness and the exclusive status of the site, as the only one catering for Russian-speaking queers living in Israel. The situation changed significantly when, in 2006, a competing website, *Raduga* (The Rainbow, Rus,) appeared. Organised by a group of immigrant women, active participants on the queer immigrant scene and former members of the Forum, the site was described as a portal of information and entertainment for Russian-speaking GLBTs in Israel. For two years, since its establishment and until the time of writing this book, *Raduga* has published many original articles. It hosts a vibrant discussion space, and is also linked to two off-line contexts: women's nights and a social group, both organised by the same women who run the site. The activities are advertised and discussed on the bulletin board. In that sense, the work of the new site resembles that of 'The Pan-Israeli Portal ... ' – the website discussed in this book – in its first years of existence. Today 'The Pan-Israeli Portal ... ', which had briefly changed its name to 'The International Portal ... ' but then restored the original one, still publishes articles (mostly reprinted from elsewhere, and not in any way limited to the Russian or Israeli context). It still hosts a discussion space, but predominantly operates as a dating service, linked to an international database of 'personals', straight and queer alike.

25 All the texts from the website are used with the permission of its co-administrators. All translations from Russian throughout the book are mine.

technology that can disrupt dominant discourses of nation, ethnicity and culture. It can also be a space where immigrants can resist the hegemony of the language of their host society. Indeed, the website's description challenges the Zionist idea of Israeli identity as embedded in the Hebrew language.[26] Instead, it proposes a different kind of identity: a Russian-speaking Israeli, and by so doing also creates a new home – in language and in cyberspace. And of course, the website by its very existence as well as by its self-description challenges the heterosexuality and heteronormativity of both nationhood and immigration.

But this challenge does not mean moving away from the nation. Disrupting the dominant notions of language and sexuality, the website's setting suggests that its creators – the Russian-speaking *Israelis* – claim national belonging as both immigrants and queers. The connection of the national and the queer is further expressed in the design of the site's homepage (see Figure 1), a gateway to both interactive and non-interactive parts that make this collective on-line space. The main body of the homepage contains quick links to recently published materials and to the most active discussion taking place on the Forum. It also has a full menu with links to the discussion areas of the Forum and to the various materials available on the site: information on meeting places and Israeli GLBT organisations, essays on life in Israel and on immigrants' organising, reports on homophobia in the Russian-Israeli press, news on Israeli queer life, erotic stories and photographs. This mapping of topics can be read as a practice of immigrants' sexualised belonging: orientation[27] in – and attachment to – Israel is mediated by orientation in the queer scene, news on gay rights, and, importantly also, the erotic attraction of Israel.

The heading of the homepage contains a permanent rainbow-coloured heading with several changing images inside each coloured box.[28] The first image is that of a young man waving a rainbow flag, and in the background

26 I return to the questions of language and identity in Chapter 4.

27 For a further discussion of orientation and queer phenomenology, see Ahmed (2006).

28 The images changed every time the page was refreshed; there is a total of 15 images. The snapshot reproduced here presents one of the frequent combinations I observed.

some metropolis, which looks like the developed part of Tel-Aviv,[29] but could in fact be any other global city; the third image is that of the white and blue Israeli flag; and three others are close-ups of different faces. Some of the pictures in this and other snapshots are recognisable stills from famous films; others are photographs of models; and some seem to be a random collection of faces. These combinations of images can be viewed as merely ornamental, and yet many of them provide intertextual references to global(ised) queer culture. The rainbow flag, and the rainbow-coloured heading too, position the website in the context of globalised Western queerness. But the Israeli flag emphasises the local, geographically located and politicised character of the site; as does the title under the rainbow heading. 'The Pan-Israeli Portal of Russian-speaking Gays, Lesbians, Bisexuals and Transsexuals' say the Russian words that follow a little Star of David. The design of the title and the heading both refer to and reproduce Israel's Jewishness by replaying its national symbols – the blue and white *talith* (Jewish prayer shawl) and the Star of David. The website, in that respect, is a textual as well as a visual claim for a place in the nation: as a site for Jewish newcomers and Jewish queers.

The design of the site's homepage speaks to the mobility of symbols and aesthetic practices that circulate globally through borrowing and de- and re-contextualisation. But it also reminds us of the persistence of the national symbolic in what many people see as the de-territorialised, and therefore essentially nationless and borderless, frontier of cyberspace.[30] However, the visual and textual technologies of queering the national and nationalising the queer through the homepage are only one way in which the immigrants assert their place in Israel. As I demonstrate throughout the book, the claims to the nation and the relations between national and queer

29 Tel-Aviv is the biggest city in Israel; it combines old Arab neighbourhoods, inner city slums, bohemian areas and a growing metropolitan centre with tall glass buildings, financial and trade centres.

30 Scholars of cybercultures are largely critical of such a view; many explore the ways national boundaries can be re-imagined on-line, and the ways cyberspace itself can becomes a site onto which national feelings are projected (see, for example, Everard 2000; Khalili 2005; King 2003; Miller and Slater 2000; Mitra 1997).

belonging can operate in more complex and often subtle ways, for instance, by nationalising the fear of – and the injury caused by – homophobia (see Chapter 2); or by (homo)eroticising state violence and brutal killings (see Chapter 3). No doubt, the national and the sexual home-making in and out of cyberspace was not always about violence – more often than not, the website was a place of warmth, intimacy, welcome and joy. In that respect, the focus of this book on violence is *neither a representative description that follows most frequent patterns or events, nor an exhaustive ethnographic 'portrait' of the community*. I focus on what some of the website's participants would probably see as 'insignificant' and 'marginal' (I may even be accused of blowing things out of proportion), because I want to tackle precisely that which is less evident. What interests me are the ways warmth and welcome can co-exist *with* violence or even be constituted *through* it; and how violence can be normalised into the mundane, to the point of becoming invisible. Here is one example of such normalisation. After the death of the Palestinian leader, Yasser Arafat, on the 11th of November 2004, the following promo of the Russian queer club was published on the site:

> 200 000 mad beasts are burying their leader.
> Palestinians mourn for 40 days.
> 7:40 is the name of a popular Jewish dance.[31]
> I invite you for Jewish dancing – this Friday, in our club,
> Dance all night!!

Arafat was demonised and hated by most Jewish Israelis; his imprisonment by the Israeli Army in his own compound in Ramallah between 2002 and 2004, and his subsequent illness and death, caused little but rejoicing. In that respect, the promo of the club, remarkable for its hatred and its dehumanisation of the Palestinians as 'mad beasts', was not unique to queers or to immigrants; rather, it was embedded in Israel's nationalist violence and imagery. And yet, I found the appearance – and the acceptance – of this promo profoundly disturbing. What I thought was striking here was the constitution of the Jewish queers' celebration through the

31 'The Train 7: 40', a well-known Yiddish song, popular among Russian Jews.

Palestinians' mourning and how this was shadowed not only by the pairing of dance/funeral, but by the broader home-making of Israel (queer and straight alike), the destruction of homes, physical and imaged, and the denial of a homeland for the Palestinians.

This complicity of queerness within nationalist violence, manifested here through the intertwining of celebration/mourning and life/death,[32] was atypical for promos of the club. However, it is symptomatic of the broader context of racial hatred and demonisation within and without the queer immigrant scene. During my research and participation in the Forum, I watched some participants engaging in collective fantasies of orientalist sexual encounters with and torture of 'the enemy' – the Palestinians (see Part II of the book); fantasies that have echoed the political reality of today's Middle East. But nationalism and racism were far from the only type of violence through which queer home was constituted. It is important to remember that this home came into being in the shadows of ongoing homophobic hatred and demonisation of same-sex relations, as well as the cultural memories of anti-Semitism and Jewish persecution (see Part I). Ironically and strikingly, the queer's own discursive and verbal violence towards Palestinians was all too similar to the homophobic violence they faced in the immigrant community and media. Victims and perpetrators of hate speech, the participants of the Forum were also often violent to each other: during my ethnography I followed endless on-line fights in which humiliation and insults were the rule rather than the exception (some of these fights are briefly discussed in Part II and addressed in further detail in Part III). The home, it often seemed, was saturated by violence; despite the many instances of happiness and connectivity, it was burning from within and from without.

How can one address these multiple and intersecting types of violence, without loosing the sense of home and belonging? This book is a search for a complex understanding of home-making that can co-exist simultaneously on several levels: psychic and social; individual, communal and national.

32 Such co-presence and the interrelation of life and death can best be characterised as what Puar coins 'queer necropolitics' (2007), a concept I return to at the end of the book.

In that sense, I aim to do what Kamala Visweswaran (1997) coined fieldwork as 'Home Work' – a critical exploration of the very notion of home, belonging and homeland (see also Lavie and Swedenborg 1996). In that respect, this book is grounded in feminist theorising of home as 'an illusion of coherence and safety based on the exclusion of specific histories of oppression and resistance, the repression of difference even within oneself' (Martin and Mohanty 1986: 1996). Rather than following the website's narrative of queer immigrants' shared fate, this book addresses ruptures, exclusions and erasures within their cyberspace. Instead of simply accepting the notion of Russian-Israeli queerness, I ask what kind of histories of oppression and resistance are excluded and silenced? Focusing on the role of violence in constituting belonging, I explore how the illusion of coherence and safety within the nation, the queer community, and cyberspace itself, works alongside and through violence. But instead of dismissing the possibility of belonging in the face of violence, I want to look into the multifaceted, and at times contradictory, co-constitution of the two. I see my HomeWork as both a form of theorising and a form of political intervention: my aim is to address violence in formations of ethnic, national or queer belonging, in and beyond cyberspace, *and* to think about how these formations might be rethought and refigured.

The social, the psychic, the performative and the affective

My reading of the contested home-making in Israel/Palestine and in cyberspace stems from the theoretical assumption that belonging is not ontologically given, and that collective identities – sexual, ethnic and national – are not pre-existent but made. More specifically, I follow Vicky Bell's idea that belonging is performative. Bell follows Judith Butler's idea that speech acts create what they name (Butler 1990, 1993). Employing Butler's theory of performativity as the constitutive reiteration of norms and extending it from the domain of gender, Bell states that 'we need to question how identities continue to be produced, embodied and performed, effectively, passionately and with social and political consequence' (Bell 1999b: 2). With Bell and Butler in mind, I address 'Russian', 'immigrant' and 'queer' as products of performative repetitions and collective negotiations. Here I am specifically informed by the work of Tamar Rapoport and Edna Lomsky-Feder on Russian-speaking immigrants in Israel and the notion of ethno-national homecoming (Rapoport and Lomsky-Feder 2005).

Rapoport and Lomsky-Feder note that most sociological analysis of Jewish immigration/'repatriation' to Israel assumes that the national ethos is located outside the newcomers and is then imposed on them, while they can adopt or reject it. Contrary to such reading, they suggest that

> [H]omecomers are embedded and embodied in the national ethos from the outset of their arrival, and even long beforehand. To use Althusser's (1971) term, the Zionist ethos of homecoming interpellates the homecomers as subjects before and after their arrival. Indeed, our interviews reveal that while the Russian subjects-homecomers are interpellated into the ethos, they are at the same time pre-occupied with producing their homecoming in various arenas of daily life. We contend that each of these arenas is a performative space (Rapoport and Lomsky-Feder 2005: 3).

Rapoport and Lomsky-Feder explore several specific arenas: the use of past and memory, and the relations between the 'Russians' and other ethnic and national groups. In these arenas the immigrants discursively produce themselves and their home. But the national ethos, the scholars emphasise, is not simply reiterated. Rather, the immigrants create their versions of it, 'reframe and revitalise the meaning of homecoming' (Rapoport and Lomsky-Feder 2005: 3).

I approach sexuality as one such arena, where homecoming can be reiterated and reframed and where it is performed, 'passionately and with social consequence' (Bell 1999b: 2). The passion, or more precisely, the affective dimension of belonging, is one of the themes that run through this book. In that respect I follow Elspeth Probyn's reading of belonging as 'longing to belong' (Probyn 1996: 8; see also Fortier 2000), as yearning, as 'the desire for some sort of attachment, be it to other people, places, or modes of being, and the way in which individuals and groups are caught within wanting to belong, wanting to become, a process that is fuelled by yearning rather than the positing of identity as a stable state' (Probyn 1996: 19).

But the affective aspect of belonging is not only about the desire to belong;[33] it is also about the emotional intensity of belonging. Love and hate, suspicion and fear, mourning, disgust and pain, discussed throughout the book, constitute immigrants' attachment to the nation, as well as its specific sites such as the immigrant community, the queer scene or the website. In that respect, I expand Probyn's and Bell's notion of affective belonging by turning to the constitutive power of emotions. Here I am informed by Sara Ahmed's *The Cultural Politics of Emotion* (Ahmed 2004). Emotions, Ahmed demonstrates, constitute subjects and objects of affect, and work to produce boundaries of and between subjects and communities. For example, in Chapter 1, I discuss how homophobic disgust constitutes the community of Russian Israelis who expel the 'disgusting' queers; in Chapter 3, I show how the queers claim their national belonging through love of the nation and hatred of its enemies. These and other emotions are performed in the text-based cyberspace;[34] they form affective regimes and can make on-line interactions incredibly intense, even when – and sometimes precisely because – on-line communication lacks physical base and 'clues'.[35]

My 'archive,' then, consisting predominantly of on-line texts and records of text-based interactions, can be considered what Ann Cvetkovich (2003) coins an 'archive of feelings'. In her *An Archive of Feelings: Trauma, Sexuality, and Lesbian Public Culture*, Cvetkovich argues that cultural texts are 'repositories of feelings and emotions, which are encoded not only in the content of the texts themselves but in the practices that surround their

33 Or what Avtar Brah calls 'homing desires' (Brah 1996), see my discussion in Chapter 5.

34 My take on the performative power of texts does not distinguish between written language and speech. Rather, I follow Gajjala's idea of on-line texts as 'wrything' rather than 'writing' or 'speaking'. See the discussion below.

35 In the absence of facial clues, many people, including the participants of the Forum, use 'emoticons', such as icons of smiling or sad faces. However, as I show throughout the book and discuss in detail in Chapter 6, the meaning and effects of such emoticons are far more complex than it may seem.

production and reception' (2003: 7). Attentive to the ways emotions circulate in cyberspace, I also approach these texts as performative, informed by Ahmed's notion of the 'emotionality of texts'. For Ahmed, the emotions circulate in texts; and texts, in turn, can perform objects of emotions such as disgust or hate. Emotions work in texts through the metonymic sticking of signs – an idea that I address in further detail in Chapter 1 and return to in the conclusion.

Texts, however, do not simply constitute objects and subjects of emotions. The emotionality of texts, as I demonstrate throughout this book, is also deeply felt. In that respect, texts can create violence not only on the level of discourse and narrative (for example, by constituting something or someone as hateful); violence is also a part of the lived experience, of both those who produce and those who consume the texts.[36] Texts and words, in other words, can inflict injury on subjectivity. In their analysis of racist assaults Charles Lawrence III, Richard Delgado and Mari Matsuda point out that hate speech not only represents racism and its effects, but is in itself injurious (Lawrence et al. 1993; see also Delgado 1993).[37] They introduce the concept of 'words that wound' to address the injury of violent language. The idea of wounding words is further developed by Butler in her notion of 'linguistic vulnerability'. Calling names is one of the first forms of linguistic injury, she suggests, but it is 'also one of the conditions by which the subject is constituted in language' (Butler 1997a: 2). More specifically, Butler relates to the constitutive powers of hate speech that 'constitute[s] the subject in a subordinate position' (Butler 1997a: 18); however she also emphasises that the effects of name-calling are complex and unfixed.[38]

36 Cyber texts are particularly interesting in that respect, since they blur the boundary between 'audience/author, producer/consumer and text/human subject' (Gajjala 2002: 184).

37 Lawrence III also notes that racial invective can produce physical symptoms in the victim. See also Toni Morrison's idea that 'oppressive language is violence' (Morrison cited in Butler 1997a: 6).

38 For example, she suggests that there is a need to loosen the link between act and injury to 'open up a possibility for a counter-speech' (Butler 1997a: 15).

But language, and violent language in particular, is not only a constitutive field; it is a field of struggle and contestation. This contestation becomes particularly clear when words that wound travel across time and space, as happens in immigration. In Chapter 1, for example, I open up Butler's notion of the historicity of injurious names, and demonstrate that wounding words are haunted by the past and inflict injuries on today's subjects through ghosts of other times and places. In Chapter 4, I show that the physical and discursive violence of border crossings in and between Israel and Palestine is transformed into the contested terrain of on-line passing through language. In Chapter 6, I show that the wounding words deployed in on-line fights can become a slippery ground between a game and an injury, exposing ambivalence, anxieties and performative failures of immigrants' subjectivities, in cyberspace and beyond.

Violent language, then, is *both* performative in the sense of discursive constitution, and injurious in the sense that its violence is felt and lived. With such an understanding of violence in mind, I turn to the question of what violence does to belonging. Informed by the idea of affective belonging on one hand, and by the notion of wounding words on the other, this book suggests that violence is both destructive and constructive, and that belonging is constituted *through* and not against violence.

Throughout the book I read violence neither as only internal, coming from within the subject, nor merely external and structural. Instead, I show that violence is always both social and psychic, and that the affective is located at the boundary between the interior and the exterior. In that respect this book is influenced by – even if not always directly engaged with – several scholars working at the intersection of the social and the psychic: Franz Fanon's (1963) account of the effects of colonial violence and the liberation war on the mental and psychic states of both the colonised and the colonisers; Bhabha's (1994) conceptualisation of colonial ambivalence; Gordon's (1997) insistence on haunting and the uncanny as inseparable components of social life; and Butler's (1997b) discussion of the psychic life of power. The approach to violence as both social and psychic also guides my deployment of Sigmund Freud's work on the uncanny,[39] melancholia[40] and jokes.[41]

In my analysis of violence and belonging I also rely on the large body of work in the field of the anthropology of violence (Daniel 1996; Das 1990; Das et al. 2000; Malkki 1995; Shepherd-Hughes and Bourgois 2004) that calls for a more complex and nuanced analysis of the multiple effects of violence. One particularly insightful contribution of these scholars is their emphasis on the different forms of violence that undermines the distinction between 'war' and 'peace'. Veena Das and Arthur Kleinman, for example, note the emergence of the 'new political geography' of whole areas marked as 'violence-prone areas' where ongoing violence has 'blurred the boundaries between violence, conflict and peaceful resolution' (Das and Kleinman 2000: 2). Their other contribution is the call to trouble 'the distinction between public and private, visible and invisible, legitimate and illegitimate forms of violence in times that can best be described as neither war nor peacetime in so many parts of the world' (Shepherd-Hughes and Bourgois 2004: 4; see also Kleinman 2000).

Israel/Palestine is indeed a violence-prone area; its nationalism and colonialism influence and are manifested in all spheres of social and psychic life beyond the shooting and bombing and physical destruction. The violence of the Occupation and the war lives in and through the subjectivities of people, or as Jacqueline Rose eloquently puts it, Israelis and Palestinians occupy each other's heads (Rose 1998: 33). But the complex layers of violence discussed here are not limited to Israel/Palestine, neither geographically nor subjectively. As I show throughout the book, Russian-speaking immigrants also carry and are haunted by the Soviet past that interferes with their Israeli present.

Reading violence and belonging, this book maps the multifaceted topographies and histories of violence as they circulate on the queer immigrants' website and beyond. I show that violence is about the formations of

39 See Chapter 2.
40 See Chapter 5.
41 See Chapter 6.

particular subjects and collectives; boundaries of exclusion and inclusion; and forms of humanising and dehumanisation. I examine the reverberations of violence in and outside of cyberspace, and address the complex relations between different forms of violence – physical, discursive and psychic. In order to grasp the material-semiotic-psychic formations of violence and belonging, and examine their complexity while remaining attuned to the particularity of my ethnographic site, I turn to the tool of figurations.

Figurations

The methodological and theoretical use of figures and figurations, deployed in this book, is inspired by the work of Donna Haraway (1997) and Claudia Castañeda (2002) on the relations between knowledge, practice, power and the making of worlds, although my approach is somewhat different from theirs, as I shall outline below. My engagement with figures and figurations has two interconnected aims: firstly, to signal the intertwinedness of on-line and off-line worlds and the material-semiotic nature of cyberethnographic material, and secondly, to map the complex, messy and contradictory relations between violence and belonging and the ways they work through particular figures.

This book is based on the analysis of a wide range of materials gathered since I began participating in the site in 2002, most of them written by Forum participants and published on the website, as either webarticles or discussion posts.[42] During my fieldwork I read all the non-interactive sections that had been published on the website since its establishment, and continued reading them as they appeared. In 2003–2004 I spent ten

42 Even the materials, external to the site – such as the homophobic publications in the Russian-Israeli newspaper, analysed in Chapter 1, and the articles about the queer immigrants' club, which I refer to in Chapter 5 – were published on the site and attracted my attention first and foremost by being there.

months visiting the Forum daily, usually spending a few hours there. I read all the discussions as they emerged every day; took part in some of them and held private one-to-one conversations with some of the participants.[43] I also downloaded and saved all the archives of past discussions available on the site.[44] And lastly, the on-line fieldwork was complemented by two research visits to Israel, interviews with participants and activists, and by my own recollections of some events I took part in prior to formally engaging in the ethnographic research. Nevertheless, my research was located predominantly on-line; as such, it raises inevitable questions regarding the status of the ethnographic material and the ways cyberwords relate to off-line life.

Most internet studies written and published in the past decade project a feeling of innovation in both the conceptual and the methodological understanding of fieldwork in cyberspace (Fernback 1999; Kendall 1999; Stone 2001). Many have suggested new definitions of the 'field': Annette Markham, for example, claims the concept of discursive – rather than geographical – boundaries of the field (Markham 2004), and Christine Hine (2001) describes the idea of 'virtual ethnography'. But what are the

43 Although the Forum discussions can be considered public documents (they are available to all, as long as they are kept in the archive; no registration was required to read the postings), I nevertheless sought permission to use them, and made an effort to have as many participants informed about the research as possible. With the permission of the website administrators I downloaded and saved all the archives of past discussions available on the site. I also posted the information about my research on the Forum twice during the ethnography, and in addition I posted a question asking for objections to the use of the discussion threads, explaining the aims of the research and the anonymity of anyone mentioned (all the names of the participants and organisers mentioned in this book have been changed, except for 'Daughter of Palestine', discussed in Chapter 4, whose nickname was central to my argument). There were no objections from the participants; the answers to my request varied between positive and indifferent. Unfortunately, there was no way to ensure that each and every person cited in this book gave his/her consent, because participants on the site came and went, rarely leaving contact details. For a detailed discussion and a critical analysis of ethics in on-line research see Gajjala (2002).

44 These, however, were never a full account of *all* discussions that took place on the Forum: some postings or threads were deleted for various reasons. I return to discuss deletions in Chapter 6.

relations between the virtual and the material? The excitement about the new field of/in cyberspace tends to address on-line sociality as a separate domain, essentially different – and separated – from off-line life. Indeed, as this book will demonstrate, wounding words and linguistic vulnerability have their particular manifestations and circulation when performed on-line. At the same time, importantly, I do not read them as independent from – or having no effect on – off-line life. This book comes from an assumption that words in cyberspace may have more weight as they are the main medium of communication; but they are never 'just words'.

Critically approaching the idealised notion of cybersociality as 'virtual' – that is, as disembodied, free of off-line constraints,[45] Radhika Gajjala (2000) puts forward the concept of 'embodied negotiation' of discursive spaces in order to emphasise the connectedness of cybercommunities and off-line materialities. She terms this negotiation 'wrything' (instead of 'writing' or 'speaking'). 'Wrything occurs at the "clashing" point of the material and discursive, where individuals within discursive spaces are confronted with the materiality of their discourses' (Gajjala 2000: 2).

The complexity of the relations between discourse and materiality is what informs my analysis of violence and belonging in cyberspace. Working with words, and more specifically with words that wound, this book follows the reverberating connections between cyberspeech and off-line (material, embodied) violence. But rather than looking at the *confrontation* of discourses and materiality (Gajjala 2002) which assumes separation, I use figures to signal their connection. For example, in Part I, I use two figures – the Shadow by the Latrine and the Jewish Victim – to capture the ways past violence of imprisonment, state terror and genocide lives through contemporary debates about sexuality in print media and on-line; how shadows of the past become injurious words, and how communities come into being through performance of feeling and acts of memory. In

45 Cyberstudies of the 1990s were particularly fascinated by what many saw as the ultimate post-modern experience: life on the screen where you can be anyone you want (see, for example, Turkle 1995). This fascination was much criticised by feminist and critical race scholars of cybercultures (see, for example, Gajjalla 2001; Nakamura 2002; Tal 1996; Tal and Lyman 2000).

Part II, I follow the figures of the Soldier, the Terrorist and Daughter of Palestine to explore how war and conflict structure sexual desires and how these desires circulate in cyberspace; how national borders materialise through cyberfantasies of pain and torture; and how on-line identities are sometimes written in blood, literally and figuratively. In Part III, I use the figures of the Club and the Flamer to trace how everyday materialities – sound, sight, smell, taste and touch – shape and are shaped by the immigrants' longing to belong; how melancholic torments travel in and out of cyberspace; and how raving on-line fights conjure up material and psychic realities of queer migranthood.

The seven figures, presented in this book, are a result of my observations and analysis; all of them emerged out of the ethnographic materials. However, my figures are not what Gajjala would describe as 'embodied digital subjects' (Gajjala 2000: 2); these are not representations of particular people or objects. What unites all the figures is their tropic character. In that respect, I follow Haraway who insists that figures are not representational and mimetic, they 'have to be tropic; that is, they cannot be literal and self-identical' (Haraway 1997: 11). For Haraway, figures emphasise 'the tropic quality of all material-semiotic processes' (ibid.). Taking her insights into the world of cyberspace, I explore the ways material-semiotic practices constitute and are constituted by cyberwords, and add another aspect to Haraway's framework – the figures' affective dimension. Figures, as this book will demonstrate, are always material, semiotic *and* psychic.

But my use of figures goes beyond the account of the material, the semiotic and the psychic in and beyond cyberspace. I adopt the notion of figuration as a *conceptual tool* that allows me to map complex and contradictory relations between violence and belonging. Haraway, for example, describes figurations as 'condensed maps of contestable worlds' (1997: 11). Taking Haraway's work on the making of worlds in technoscience as a point of departure, Claudia Castañeda further develops the concept of figuration as a form of ontology as well as an epistemological practice:

> The concept of figuration makes it possible to describe in detail the process by which a concept or entity is given particular form – how it is figured – in ways that speak to the making of worlds. To use figurations as a descriptive tool is to unpack the

> domains of practice and significance that are built into each figure. A figure, from this point of view, is the simultaneously material and semiotic effect of specific practices. Understood as figures, furthermore, particular categories of existence can also be considered in terms of their uses – what they 'body forth' in turn. Figuration is thus understood here to incorporate a double force: constitutive effect and generative circulation (Castañeda 2002: 3).

In her *Figurations: Child, Bodies, Worlds*, Castañeda uses one single figure – the child – which she follows across geo-political sites and across domains of knowledge and practice. Haraway, similarly, follows some figures, such as the gene or the fetus, across materialised worlds and situated knowledges of technoculture. But Haraway also links together several figures, such as the Modest Witness, FemaleMan and OncoMouse, in order to explain their relations of 'family romance' and address the way they, together, 'take shape within a common, materialised narrative field' (Haraway 1997: 22). My own use of figures is positioned somewhere in between: I follow each figure in detail to explore a particular topic, such as homophobia, nationalism or on-line fights; but I also look at the figures together, in relation to each other. Paying close attention to the relations *between* figures allows me to see how violence and belonging take shape not only through each figure, but also through substitution and transformation of different figures into each other; or through the figures' metonymic closeness or shared genealogies.

And while Castañeda's focus, like Haraway's, is first and foremost on the world of material practices, I find their work extremely useful to my analysis of wounding words and their circulation across material, semiotic and psychic domains in and out of cyberspace. Using figurations to understand 'categories of existence' and to 'unpack domains of practice and significance' is central to my deployment of figures here. In particular, I take on Haraway's idea of figures as 'condensed maps' and Castañeda's notion of the double force of figurations as a way to describe how an entity is constituted, and how it circulates. Examining each figure I will ask how violence and belonging are given particular forms when they operate through particular figures; and how these figures circulate across temporal and spatial terrains. I am also informed by Castañeda's distinction between 'the child's figuration when the child is itself *being figured in a particular way*' and 'the child-figure when the child is used as the *embodied ground of a particular claim*' (2002: 52, emphasis mine). Throughout the book I will examine how the Shadow by the Latrine, the Jewish Victim, the Soldier, the Terrorist, Daughter of Palestine, the Club and the Flamer are figured in particular ways, and how they become grounds for particular claims – of national belonging and racial superiority, of rejection, inclusion or embrace, of adoration, mockery, fear or erasure.

The insistence on particularity is crucial here: figurations, as Castañeda emphasises throughout her book, 'are always particular, even – especially – when they are used to make general claims' (Castañeda 2002: 45). The analytical power of figuration as a tool of mapping the particular and the specific, as well as the tropic, lies in their ability to 'bring disparate elements together' (Castañeda 2008: n.p.). As the following chapters will demonstrate, relations of violence and belonging never work through simple models. It is only through the tool of figuration – the attention to the connection of disparate elements in each figure and to the affective regimes they produce – that we can map what otherwise appear as confusing, contradictory and messy processes, sometimes reduced to simplistic notions of identification versus alienation, inclusion versus exclusion, 'us' versus 'them' and of victims versus perpetrators.

The book

The book consists of three parts, each focusing on a particular group of figures and a particular form of relations between belonging and violence: haunting figures, border figures and flaming figures. Haunting figures – The Shadow by the Latrine (Chapter 1) and the Jewish Victim (Chapter 2) – map the relations between sexuality, immigration and nationhood by examining homophobic attacks within the Russian-speaking community of immigrants, and the queers' response to them. In these two chapters I approach the haunting presence of a violent past in the ways in which immigrants negotiate the national belonging in the present and imagine the national future. Border figures – The Soldier and the Terrorist (Chapter 3) and Daughter of Palestine (Chapter 4) – examine the ways contested borders and borderzones of Israel/Palestine are figured through queer sexuality. In these two chapters, I address the way queerness serves as a form of belonging and attachment to the nation, and examine how Israeli colonialism and militarism are imagined as queerly sexy. Flaming figures – The Club (Chapter 5) and The Flamer (Chapter 6) – follow the ambivalent meanings and effects of on-line fights about belonging to the queer immigrants' collective spaces, on- and off-line. In these two chapters, I address the role of violence from within as a form of being together. In the conclusion I reflect on haunting, 'bordering' and flaming as 'practices of figuration' (Haraway 1997: 9), and argue that violence of a particular type never stands alone. By looking at the figures in relation to each other, I show that violence operates not only through particular figures but through multifaceted relations *between* them, relations that work synchronically, diachronically and affectively. I conclude my discussion by asking how the relations between violence and belonging might be refigured, and what kind of hope such refiguration might bring to queer immigrant politics and to Israel/Palestine.

PART I

Haunting Figures

I begin my discussion of violence and belonging by looking at how the boundaries of nationhood, ethnicity and class respectability are constituted through the injuries of homophobia *and* the response to it. Departing from the debates on sexuality, migration and nation, the next two chapters examine how shadows of violent past are conjured up by Russian-speaking immigrants – queer and straight alike – to imagine a future and constitute belonging in the present.

George Mosse, in his book *Nationalism and Sexuality* (Mosse 1985), points out that morality and respectability are central to understanding modern nationalism. His idea of respectability rests on Elias' notion of modernity and the 'civilising process' (Elias 1982). Extending Elias' analysis, Mosse suggests that the civilised and the respectable, as well as the unruly and the scandalous, are always sexualised. What's more, the very concepts of manners, aesthetics, sexual practices, racial, gender and class hierarchies are constituted by particular kinds of sexual bodies. Immigration is sexualised, too, by both those who move and those who stay put. Migrant and diasporic belonging is often constructed as heteronormative, and queers among them become 'impossible subjects' (Gopinath 2003). Gayatri Gopinath, for example, shows how the images of India, Indianness and Indian diaspora are imagined through familial and domestic metaphors, which are associated with and represented by heteronormative women's bodies. Gopinath employs Alexander's (1997) idea that 'sexual purity is imagined within a geography (and a home) that only heterosexuals inhabit' (Alexander in Gopinath 2003: 264). In the diasporic imagination of Indianness, Indian lesbians occupy a place of impossibility, for Indian space is marked by heterosexuality and women *inside* homes, whereas lesbians are seen as Western and located *outside* of homes and of Indianness. Gopinath's reading of Indian lesbians as impossible subjects resonates with the work of other scholars in the field of queer diaspora who describe the construction of diasporic ethnicity and queerness as opposed to each other: ethnicity in this construction is seen as inherently and inevitably heterosexual, while queerness is located outside ethnic and migrant belonging (Eng 1997; Takagi 1996). But does queerness necessarily mean exclusion? Unlike the image of queer immigrants as excluded from their ethnic and national homes, this research follows Gopinath's insight that 'those who occupy one "perverse" subject position [...] [can] reimagine and reconstitute their particular, fraught relationship to multiple national sites' (Gopinath 2003: 264).

The following two chapters explore one such site – the debates around homophobia – where the Russian-speaking immigrant community and the queers among them negotiate the boundaries of nationhood; they shame and exclude each other, and struggle for acceptance. I look at what happens when queer immigrants claim their place in the nation precisely *as queer subjects*. My discussion will focus on one ethnographic moment: the anti-queer publications that appeared in summer-autumn 2002 in the Russian-language immigrant media in Israel and the response of 'The Russian Forum against Homophobia and Defamation' (RFAHD) – a group of queer immigrants who got together around that time to combat those publications and other forms of hate speech within the Russian-speaking community. The group was created by several participants of the Forum. I became involved in the organising of the RFAHD shortly after joining the website in 2002. At the time of my fieldwork in 2003–2004 I returned to the topic of RFAHD, this time following the records of its establishment and activities.[1] I examined all the debates on homophobia that took place on the Forum; I also looked at the archives of RFAHD from the time of its creation. Following the events and debates of that period brought me to enquire about the relations between the violence of homophobic hate speech and immigrants' belonging to the nation. What were the injuries of homophobic publications that called for response? How did speaking against homophobia constitute the collective 'we' of the queers? And what is the role of the past in negotiating the national present and future?

Chapter 1 begins by staging the debate around homophobia in the immigrant media and follows a ghostly figure of the Shadow by the Latrine that emerged in the homophobic attacks. Throughout the chapter I follow this figure to various sites of the Soviet past, a past that is neither remembered nor commemorated, but lives through haunting. Chapter 2 tracks

1 Anna Talisman, the RFAHD coordinator, has kindly provided me with the hard copies of all the documentation (letters, reports etc.); other activists of RFAHD gave me electronic copies of letters, petitions and records of e-mail correspondence between the organisers. All the materials are used with the permission of the RFAHD.

in detail the responses of the queer immigrants. I show how they turn away from the Shadow by the Latrine, and refigure the injury, inflicted by homophobia, by substituting this shadow with another haunting figure, that of the Jewish victim. This chapter follows the affective and political dimension of such refiguration in queer immigrants' claims for belonging as Jews, Israelis and queers.

My argument here is twofold. Following Butler's theory of performativity (1990, 1993, 1997), I suggest that homophobic hate speech and the response to it are performative acts that constitute (rather than simply express or devastate) individual and collective subjectivities of 'queers', 'intelligentsia', 'Russian immigrants', 'Jews', and 'Israelis'. Yet I also wish to complicate the performative take by introducing the concept of haunting. I approach haunting as both a 'practice of figuration' (Haraway 1997: 9) and a reference to 'the sociality of living with ghosts, a sociality tangible and tactile as well as ephemeral and imaginary' (Gordon 1997: 65). Throughout my discussion I show that injurious speech acts do not simply have a history; they are haunted by traces of the past and practices of cultural memory. My use of the two figures – the Shadow by the Latrine and the Jewish Victim – aims to map the multiple layers of remembering and forgetting, of emotions such as disgust or fear, and of the ways material violence of the past shapes psychic injuries of the present. By following the two haunting figures and their circulation in and out of cyberspace, I try to map the irresolvable complexities and ambivalences of belonging – ethnic, sexual, classed and national – of both the Russian-speaking immigrant community (as it was constituted in the media attacks) and the immigrant queers. Understanding haunting and its effects, as I will show, is essential when reading immigrants' acts of claiming the nation.

CHAPTER 1

The Shadow by the Latrine

A place by the latrine

> As the immortal Schwartz said, 'Shadow, know thy place!'
> And your place was, and is, *u parashi* [by the latrine, Russian].

These words, written by the Russian-Israeli journalist and poet Boris Kamyanov and addressed to queer immigrants, conclude the exchange that took place between *Vesti*, the leading Russian newspaper in Israel, and the RFAHD. 'A place *u parashi*' – by the latrine – is a Russian idiom describing someone's subordinate position. Its origins lie in the criminal jargon: a *parasha* was the vessel used in old prison cells for excrement. Spatially distanced from the bunk beds, it also marked the place of social subordination: the person who occupied the lowest part of the criminal hierarchy had to sleep by the latrine. In men's cells the place by the latrine was reserved for *pidory* – the inmates who were seduced or forced into a passive homosexual role. These men were often called *opuschennye*, literally meaning those who were 'put down', sexually and hierarchically. Once 'put down', they were to remain subordinate, serving as slaves and as targets for beating and sexual abuse. 'Putting down' was often accomplished through an act of rape (sometimes real and sometimes symbolic), and accompanied by the performative speech act: 'your place is now by the latrine!'[1]

1 Tellingly, *parasha* itself served as a symbolic marker of filth in criminal culture; for example, Guberman (2003) describes how cell rules prohibited eating while someone was using the latrine. Passive homosexuals (those doing the penetration were not considered homosexuals – for more discussion see Healey 2001; Kon 1998) and the latrine were metonymically interchangeable (Guberman 2003; Kon 1998; Samojlov 1989).

'Your place is by the latrine!', exclaimed Kamyanov, re-evoking the speech act of prison violence and by doing so, his words *become* violence. In the introduction to her *Excitable Speech*, Butler notes that 'injurious names have a history, one that is invoked and reconsolidated at the moment of utterance, but not explicitly told. [...] [This] historicity [...] has come to constitute the contemporary meaning of a name' (Butler 1997a: 36). But what kind of history is it? Kamyanov's use of the criminal speech act – an act that constitutes the prisoner in a position of total subordination – evokes the long history of physical and sexual abuse in Soviet prisons and camps. His words also refer to the history of the criminalisation of male sodomy in the former Soviet Union, where Article 121 of the Criminal Code was enacted by Stalin in 1934.[2] Between the 1930s and 1980s, about a thousand men were imprisoned every year under its terms (Kon 1998); entering the camps as 'sodomites', they were almost always destined for rape and abuse by other inmates.

The injury, produced by Kamyanov's repetition of criminal language in relation to today's queers, is deeply felt. And yet, the historicity of his words can not be fully known, and not only because, to use Butler's terms, the histories of state control and prison violence are 'invoked [...] but not explicitly told' (Butler 1997a: 36). As this chapter will demonstrate, the conjunction of same-sex relations, criminality and abuse takes us into a past that is both tangible and ungraspable, a past that is about much more than just the criminalisation of male homosexuality under Soviet law. This is a past that includes many layers of violence – political, physical, sexual, affective and discursive. This is a past that is rarely documented or commemorated, a past that refuses words but also refuses to disappear from

2 The Article, commonly known as the Anti-sodomy Law, refers to same-sex acts between men, punishable by 5–8 years imprisonment. Female homosexuality was not criminalised in the Soviet Union, but was defined as a medical pathology and subjected lesbians to compulsory treatment. For more details on the history of de- and re-criminalisation and pathologisation of same-sex relations in tsarist and Soviet Russia see Healey (2001).

affective and political horizons[3] of post-Soviet sociality.[4] Kamyanov calls the queers shadows whose place is by the latrine. But who are these shadows? Who haunts Kamyanov the poet and what haunts his attack?

Gordon in her *Ghostly Matters* (1997) argues that some extremely violent historical events (slavery, displacement, political terror) can be comprehended only through haunting. They are often manifested in what seems to be a form of absence, such as disappearance, erasure, or lack of words, but in fact their 'absent' presence has high significance. Impossible memories and unwritten histories constitute contemporary sociality in the form of what Gordon, following Raymond Williams (1977), calls the 'structure of feeling' – a concept that captures the lived and felt experience of social life, the experience that is neither solely structural and external to the subject, nor solely psychic and subjective, but is always both.

Having described haunting as a structure of feeling, Gordon positions the ghost as a social figure that is not only the marker of haunting but also an epistemological tool for comprehending the past and the present:

> If haunting describes how that which appears to be not there is often a seething presence, acting on and often meddling with taken-for-granted realities, the ghost is just the sign, or the empirical evidence if you like, that tells you a haunting is taking place. The ghost is not simply a dead or a missing person, but a social figure, and investigating it can lead to that dense site where history and subjectivity make social life (Gordon 1997: 8).

3 My use of the term 'horizons' is inspired by Anne-Marie Fortier's work on 'multicultural horizons' – 'the desires, anxieties, fears, and dreams that invest the national structure of feeling' (2008: 12).

4 My analysis here is limited to the particular ethnographic moment and to the particular context of post-Soviet immigration in Israel. In the context of this book, I am committed to the specificity of the debate between Kamyanov and the queer immigrants that took place in Israel in the 2000s. However, since completing this ethnography I have continued to engage with questions of sexuality and homophobia, extending the focus to post-Soviet, Russian-language Internet more broadly. My ongoing observations suggest that the ghostly presence of the Gulag past, as it is unpacked in this chapter, extends beyond the case of Russian-speaking immigrants in Israel.

Departing from this notion of shadows as a form of 'empirical evidence [...] that tells [...] that a haunting is taking place', this chapter follows the figure of the Shadow by the Latrine, and the ways it functions in homophobic publications. I will look at how its presence 'meddles with the realities' of today's Pride Parade, and how the opposition to the Parade becomes a struggle over the national home as Jewish, Zionist, respectable and heterosexual. In order to do so I will have to trace the ghosts of Kamyanov's attack back to the sites where 'history and subjectivity make social life', and then follow the routes of haunting across time and space, back to today's Israel.

Pidory, *kobly* and *kovyrjalki*

It all started with a poem, written by Kamyanov, and published by *Vesti* in June 2002 shortly after the Pride Parade in Jerusalem.

'"The March of Love" in Jerusalem'

Today is Independence day. Independence from God.
From all over Israel, they've come up
Marching along the Jaffa Road,
to the Jaffa Gate they go.

First the swaggering *pidory* with proudly waving butts
Sweet blue balloons float cheerfully above,
Then come the *kobly* and the *kovyrjalki*
in a hot embrace
Pink clouds of balloons in their wake.

The Pilgrims march on Zion with the rights we've let them take:
The right to mock the Torah's truth;
The right to public fornication, the right to profane the holy vessels
The right to copulate upon the Temple's altar.

Our country's elite is here for all to see:
Parliamentarians, writers, musicians, actors and dancers
Gnessin diploma holders – refugees from Russia
Local transvestites, all join the gambolling throng

Oh Jewish democracy, you can be proud today
We too have joined the global pederation[5]
You have succeeded where your enemies failed:
The state of Israel is now a brothel during the plague.

... Evening falls in Independence Park.
Around the fires the demons dance.
They drink the potion of love until oblivion.
Only a half-hour drive from the celebrating vermin
Our ultimate war goes on.[6]
(Boris Kamyanov, *Vesti*, 20 June 2002)

5 In the original text – an invented word that combines 'Association', 'Nation' and pederasty.

6 Translation of the poem is mine. I thank Boris Kamyanov for his approval of the English translation and for his permission to use the poem. When acquiring the permission, I was asked to make several corrections to the translation to ensure that the author's intentions are communicated correctly. For example, Kamyanov insisted on the use of 'half-hour drive' instead of the originally proposed 'short drive'; he stressed that he was referring to the neighbourhood of Gilo which was located a 30 minutes drive from the Parade's route and whose Jewish residents were repeatedly fired at by Palestinian militants around the time of the Parade. Gilo, one of Jerusalem's Jewish neighbourhoods that stretches beyond the green line deep into the Palestinian territory, borders the Palestinian town of Bethlehem and the village of Beit-Jalla.

Another important correction on which Kamyanov's permission was conditioned was the use of the word 'vermin', which I originally translated as 'scum'. The Russian word *gad* means both scum and vermin; in the context of the overall attack on the marchers I assumed this was yet another name-calling. Kamyanov, however, explained that he referred to vermin to signal the animal nature of the marchers and his disgust towards them (he used the word *gadlivost'* – one of the Russian synonyms for disgust). In that respect his correction further strengthens the overall context of queerness as disgusting and bestial. It is important to emphasise, however, that many readers of the poem might have misread his use of the word *gad* in the way I originally did.

The poem had an unmistakable tone of religious rage, condemning the blasphemy of the parade. The first lines bring up the context of the Independence Day – one of the central Israeli holidays, which is celebrated annually by parades and street carnivals. Kamyanov's repetitive insistence on independence is not accidental: the parade, which goes through the main street of West Jerusalem, ends with a happening in the 'Independence Park' – the locus of gay night time sexual encounters. The pictures of the happening that illustrate the poem (see Figure 2), also correspond with the notion of Independence Day, by showing a colourful crowd, and, importantly, the tandem of the rainbow and the national flag. Yet the image of Independence Day (or any other nation-wide celebration) is juxtaposed in the poem to the holiness of Jerusalem and is described here as 'independence from God'. The accusatory tone intensifies through the poem, where the marchers are mockingly called 'pilgrims' and accused of blasphemy and profanation. The poem also attacks Israeli democracy itself, by blaming it for the devastation of Israel, and by mocking its political and cultural elite, who are called a 'gambolling throng'. The marchers who are presented here as both perverts and sinners are in the same breath made the nation's enemies: it is their presence and their rights that destroy Israel more successfully than its external enemies.

The Pride Parade that took place in summer 2002 was the first event of its kind in Jerusalem. Since the early 1990s, annual pride events have been taking place in Tel-Aviv. Additional, small-scale events were also organised in a few other cities. The decision of Jerusalem GLBT organisations to hold a parade in Jerusalem was motivated by the desire to be 'just like any other city in the country' on the one hand, and to establish a public queer presence in the state's capital, on the other. The parade in Jerusalem was a controversial event at the time, and still is to this day.[7] Many have

7 Given the contested status of Jerusalem as a divided city, having a parade there *because* it is the capital is in itself an act of performing Israeli ownership. The debates around the Parade were concentrated around the notion of liberal gay rights on one hand, and religious opposition on the other. Interestingly, the other – much more central and urgent – controversy of Jerusalem itself, as a divided city and as a politically contested space, was barely mentioned in the debates (but undoubtedly haunted them). The Jerusalem

objected to the Jerusalem Parade, and the most vocal among them were the representatives of the Orthodox Jewish community.[8] For many secular Jewish Israelis, queer and straight alike, the Parade came to symbolise one of the core conflicts in Israeli society: that of relations between religion and the state.

Unlike the mainstream secular Israeli media, generally tolerant of queer issues and supportive of the Parades,[9] the Russian-language newspapers were anything but positive. In earlier years such Pride Parades and related events were either ignored or described with mockery (Gomel 2002). *Vesti* and other Russian-language newspapers occasionally published anti-gay essays or intolerably distorted reports on queer issues (Gomel 2002; Lee 2002). Yet Kamyanov's poem, as the news report on the Russian queers' website described it, was seen as unprecedented in the extent of its violence, and in the name-calling and accusations it made. Its publication caused a vibrant debate on the Forum, where many participants expressed their anger and pain. But it seems that what made the poem so successfully offensive was not just the volume but the particular content of the violence.

Despite the easily recognisable religious rage, it was not the accusations of blasphemy that disturbed the participants of the website. In fact, several weeks prior to the appearance of Kamyanov's poem, another *Vesti* publication had been discussed on the Forum. Authored by Arie Baratz who, like

---

Open House which organised the Parade and was struggling for municipal recognition and funding, repeatedly noted that the Parade emphasised their struggle for peace and diversity in the 'city of three religions'. However, the organising of the events did not take into consideration the Christian and Muslim populations of the city; the Parade took place in the Western (Jewish, Israeli) part of Jerusalem; and the debate itself was figured as a confrontation between secular/liberal/modern/queer and Orthodox/conservative/traditional *Israelis*. Figuring gay rights as Western modernity, the debate performed Israel's Westernness (rather than Jerusalem's geo-political embeddedness in the Middle East) and its ownership of Jerusalem.

8 In the third Jerusalem Parade in 2005 many Orthodox demonstrators protested the Parade, and one man broke through police lines and stabbed three marchers. In 2006 the Parade was postponed from summer to November due to the Lebanon war. In November 2006, at the very time of writing this note, the Orthodox parties are sending threats to bomb the Parade and kill its participants should it take place.

9 Which of course does not mean that Israeli society is free from homophobia.

Kamyanov, identifies as an Orthodox Jew, the publication described the sickness and sin of homosexuality, appealing to Biblical sources. Although hurtful and appalling, it was dismissed by the participants because the author was 'just another religious cuckoo'. In the case of Kamyanov's poem, it was the words used to describe the marchers that were seen as most violent, not his accusations of 'mocking the Torah's[10] truth'. Kamyanov did not use 'gays', 'lesbians', 'homosexuals' or 'sexual minorities' – words that have their own limitations and politics, but are generally seen as neutral. Instead, he chose the words *pidory*, *kobly* and *kovyrjalki* – all originating from Russian criminal jargon. *Pidor* (also, pederast) was used in men's prisons for passive homosexuals, usually describing those who were forced into this role by rape and abuse. It was also used outside prisons as a popular insult among men. *Kobel* (*kobly* in plural) and *kovyrjalka* (*kovyrjalki* in plural) designate the 'masculine' and the 'feminine' roles in lesbian relations in prison that were based on gender differentiation and strict division of roles (Zhuk 1998). While less known than *pidor*, these terms, too, have a strong negative connotation of ugliness and violence.

The response to Kamyanov's publication on the Forum constituted the poem as a meaningful event in the life of Russian-speaking queers; later it was constituted as *the* event that was not to be tolerated.[11] Several days later I was among a group of about a dozen immigrants that gathered in Tel-Aviv's building of the Israeli Association of GLBTs. They established the RFAHD – a group that would monitor homophobic publications and respond to them, and also engage in wider educational work. As a first step it was decided to seek media coverage in Hebrew; several people noted that the Israeli audience was unaware of what was going on in the Russian media. Two of the RFAHD activists contacted Vered Lee, a journalist from *Haaretz*, the leading liberal Israeli newspaper, asking her to write about homophobia in the Russian media. Several of the group members (myself included) met with Lee, telling her about their experiences as queer

10 The Five Books of Moses in the Hebrew Bible, which set out Jewish canon law.

11 I will return to a detailed reading of some of the responses in the next chapter.

immigrants. Some specifically noted the hurtful impact of homophobic publications on them or their families.

Soon Lee published a long piece, describing many examples of anti-gay publications. She added personal stories of the immigrants as well as some commentary from academics in the field of media and social studies. 'It is never easy to be a gay or a lesbian', starts the article, 'but for Russian immigrants this is particularly hard. The Russian media, like most of its readers, is infected by homophobia; it attacks gays and lesbians in a wild manner' (Lee 2002). After the publication came out, Dov Kontorer, a political commentator with *Vesti*, called the publication 'an act of public disciplining' (*Vesti*, 20 August 2002). He stated that *Haaretz* was ruled by the gay elite that was manifesting its perverse life style through parades offensive to good taste. 'This ruling elite', wrote Kontorer in his piece, entitled 'Gay Censorship', 'was trying to limit Russian immigrants' freedom of speech'.

Making the Israeli (read: the Hebrew-speaking, *Ashkenazi*, liberal middle-class audience of *Haaretz*) 'aware' of the anti-gay hatred of the immigrants' journalists can indeed be seen as calling for surveillance and intervention in immigrants' cultural life. The immigrants' marginal location in Israeli society and their status as newcomers 'to be acculturated' make them available for the disciplining gaze of the establishment.[12] Defending the queers against their own ethnic community resembles many other cases where gay rights are associated with Westernness and progress, while ethnic minorities and immigrants are seen as yet to be educated into this freedom (see for example Haritaworn et al. 2008; Ritchie forthcoming). However, limiting the reading of this debate to the relations between the

12 As well as for that of the local queer community. It was interesting to see the immediate willingness of the Israeli queer community to condemn *Vesti*: an Israeli gay portal has published a short piece describing immigrant homophobia, and the Lesbian Feminist Community offered their legal support in filing an official complaint against the newspaper (see also footnote 2 in the next chapter). However, as Chapter 5 shows, the Israeli queer scene is not always welcoming to the all Russian-speaking immigrants, and is not devoid of stereotypes and prejudices. So the case of the support here might have had to do with the opportunity to 'name and shame' some of the immigrants and to channel the image of the 'Russians' into the 'bad' heterosexual and 'good' queer ones, where the latter is figured as 'good' as long as they follow the liberal Western model of queer politics.

dominant majority and the immigrant minority would be inaccurate. The queer immigrants' approach to the Israeli media was mainly motivated by a sense of despair and powerlessness vis-à-vis the unrestricted textual violence of Russian journalists, whose anti-queer writings were often wrapped in a veneer of intellectualism and debate on aesthetics and taste. The desire to be located among Israelis who will understand, as opposed to Russians who do not and will not, indeed constitutes Israeliness as a site of liberation. Russianness as a site of identification, however, is not rejected (as in some other cases of migrant or diasporic queers, see for example Takagi 1996), but becomes a space of pain and struggle. In addition to contacts with the Israeli media, the RFAHD decided to write a statement in Russian, presenting the group and its aims – monitoring homophobic hate speech in the media and engaging in wider educational work – to *Vesti*'s readers.

A community of disgust

The statement issued by the RFAHD was indeed published in *Vesti* (in addition, its Hebrew version was sent to all the Israeli GLBT organisations). Kamyanov immediately wrote a response which this time was rejected by *Vesti* (to the great excitement of the RFAHD) but published in another Russian-speaking newspaper. There it was located as a commentary on a short and extremely unsympathetic report by another journalist on the activities of Russian-speaking GLBTs in Tel-Aviv's community centre. Kamyanov wrote:

> 'Shadows demand rights'
> 'The Russian Forum Against Homophobia' is the title of the letter published in *Vesti* on 26–08–02. As the author of the poem 'March of love in Jerusalem', I was the first one who threw the stone into the swamp of Israeli pederasty. Today I feel obliged to express myself again, this time in the genre of journalism. [...] I, like most people, feel disgusted by sodomy. Similarly, all normal people [are disgusted by] pedophilia, necrophilia, zoophilia and other immoral deviations [...] Supported by Israeli liberals [...] they [the Russian gays and lesbians] demand total acceptance, because living

> with one's filth is not comfortable, and only public opinion can make filth [a source of] pride. But the public opinion of Russian-speaking Israelis will not indulge you, at least not today. What will happen in the future, I am not sure. Our children and grandchildren are growing, and in a de-ideologised, post-zionist society the notion that 'everything is permitted' could be too tempting for them. In your letter you boldly declare that you plan to widen your activities to educational and explanatory work. This we cannot allow you.
> As the immortal Schwartz said, 'Shadow, know thy place!'
> And your place was, and is, by the latrine.
> (Boris Kamyanov, *The Russian Israeli*, 18 September 2002)

Kamyanov's response demonstrates the multiplicity of categories used for non-normative sexualities, and the violent collapse of some of them into each other. Gays, lesbians and bisexuals become pederasts and sodomites, while the latter are merged with pedophiles, necrophiles and zoophiles. Male homosexuality is framed as sinful and deviant and at the same time as criminal, while lesbians, scornfully described in the poem in criminal terms, disappear entirely. All queers are merged into one single figure – a shadow by the latrine.

But Kamyanov's text not only names the RFAHD members (and by association, all other queers) as shadows. He also constitutes the community of Russian Israelis as a community of feelings, more specifically, of disgust. 'I feel disgusted by the filth of sodomy', writes Kamyanov in his essay. His text produces the Russian Israelis as 'normal people' who are disgusted, and positions the queers as those who seek indulgence from them. The queers are presented in alliance with 'Israeli liberals', and at the same time are depicted as part of the Russian-Israeli community. The filth of homosexuality threatens the existence of the Russian-Israeli as well as the whole Zionist national collective. Kamyanov seems to be particularly outraged about the very demand of indulgence: the queers' speaking out makes claims not only from the Israeli nation but also specifically from the Russian immigrants. By doing so they create an unbearable proximity to all other Russian Israelis, and therefore become the abject, the filth, that has to be expelled to protect the morality – and the heterosexuality – of the community.

Disgust as fear of proximity has been extensively discussed by several feminist scholars (Ahmed 2004; Kristeva 1982; Probyn 2000) who suggest that disgust works to produce a collectivity by drawing boundaries between (some) bodies. Elspeth Probyn, for example, notes that

> when we designate something or someone as disgusting, we seek reassurance that we are not alone in our relation to the disgusting object. Through public statements, we want to distance ourselves from the uncomfortable proximity. In uttering the phrase, we call upon others to witness our pulling away. Indeed the phrase 'that's disgusting' sounds more often than not like a plea to establish a common ground that would comfort in the recognition that what offends me also offends you: to assuage doubts that we have not been contaminated, that we are not disgusting or shameful (Probyn 2000: 131).

Probyn examines disgust as a boundary between different bodies, at the same time desiring and fearing proximity. The reassurance of not having come in touch with the disgusting, she notes, is achieved through calling witnesses, that is, through the common ground of recognition and imagined collectivity of feeling. This idea is developed further by Debra Ferreday in her work on pro-anorexic (known as 'pro-ana') websites and the response to them from a wider public (Ferreday 2003). Ferreday shows that the readers of the websites express disgust, an impulse to gag, when encountering the pro-ana websites and the images of anorexic bodies displayed there. Through the repetitive notion of gagging they create a community of disgust, which is a community of 'healthy' bodies trying to expel the abject of the anorexics.[13]

The link between calling witnesses of disgust and constituting a community of feeling, observed by Probyn and Ferreday, is evident in Kamyanov's text. He calls for witnesses by positioning himself as the voice of the Russian Israelis, on whose behalf he attacks the 'swamp of Israeli pederasty'.

13 The move to sustain the boundary between the anorexic and the non-anorexic subject, however, is always doomed to failure: Ferreday shows that the sickening effect of pro-ana websites on the non-anorexic viewer cause the latter to want to vomit, bringing about 'a final ironic assault on the boundary between anorexic and healthy subjects in which the onlooker is forced into a parodic repetition of anorexic praxis' (Ferreday 2003: 291).

The sense of collective belonging produced by this move is complicated: it is the national dream of the Jewish state, based on Zionist ideology; but also the ethnic dream of Israel as the place for the Russian-Jewish intelligentsia.[14] The queer's public presence and later their demands for respect and recognition, signify the betrayal of this double dream: the queers for Kamyanov threaten his vision of the classed, ethnic and national future. Instead, they bring with them the horrors of criminality, terror and violence: Israel is in danger of becoming a filthy prison cell.

The link between feelings, boundaries and collectivity is further developed by Ahmed (Ahmed 2004). She is particularly interested in the performative aspect of disgust. Ahmed ties Probyn's argument on the 'community of witnesses' generated through disgust to Butler's idea of performative speech: speech acts that generate that which is named. Here, Ahmed suggests, speaking of one's disgust constitutes the object that is disgusting *and* the community of those disgusted. Her analysis positions text at the centre of the work of disgust. The community is performed by text, and bodies and signs 'stick' to each other through speech acts, so that one becomes associated with the other. Ahmed's discussion of disgust works around the concept of otherness. Her extensive discussion of the responses to September 11, for example, shows how the bodies of others are constructed as hateful and sickening, as 'non-human, beneath and below the bodies of the disgusted' (Ahmed 2004: 97). The disgust towards these bodies works through what Ahmed calls 'sticking together signs'. 'The naming of disgust metonymically sticks these signs together ["Middle Eastern" and "terrorists"], such that the terror and fear become associated with bodies that are already recognised as "Middle-Eastern"' (Ahmed 2004: 97).

The work of metonymic sticking is particularly clear in Kamyanov's figuration of the queers as disgusting. Just as in the case of the community of disgust, described by Ferreday, Kamyanov and his imagined audience are transferring their feelings onto others. Those disgusted by pro-anorexic websites constituted the latter as disgusting; Kamyanov's feelings of

14 This dream is of course Kamyanov's vision as constituted in his texts. It is in no way representative of all Russian-speaking Israelis, or even of all readers of *Vesti*.

disgust are similarly transferred onto the queers. He sticks *his* disgust to *their* bodies; haunted by the Gulag shadows, he turns the queers of today into ghosts of the horrifying past. The injury of his words is precisely in this transferral that sticks the haunting horrors to those he attacks. This transferral is performative, too: Kamyanov's 'Shadow, know thy place!' aims to push the disgusting out and beneath to keep the intelligentsia as necessarily heterosexual. But who are the 'non-human' shadows, located 'below and beneath' the heterosexual intelligentsia?

The intelligentsia's shadow

'Shadow, know thy place' is a quote from a well-known play, *The Shadow*, by a Soviet playwright Evgenij Schwartz. It is a story about a Learned Man whose shadow got a life of its own, became a tyrant and nearly executed the Learned Man. *The Shadow* was seen by many as an allegory about power and tyranny; some suggested that the shadow represented Stalin. In the play the Learned Man is saved by the powers of an ancient magical spell, when he exclaims: 'shadow, know thy place!'

Written in 1940, *The Shadow* was censored soon after, together with other of Schwartz's plays, to return only during Khrushchev's democratisation of the 1960s, and then again in the late 1980s. For the educated Soviet intelligentsia, Schwartz's plays became a symbol of freedom and of fragile moments of resistance under Soviet rule. Re-evoked by Kamyanov, 'the immortal Schwartz' here performs a double task: it figures Kamyanov's imagined audience of Russian Israelis as heterosexual and free from the 'filth' of homosexuality. But at the same time this act of citation constitutes them as an imagined community of Russian-speaking intelligentsia: they are assumed to share both the literary memory and the very practice of speaking through literature, a distinctive practice of the (post)-Soviet educated class and intellectuals. According to cultural historian Svetlana Boym, since the 19th century – a time when the concept and status of the 'intelligentsia' was established – belonging to the intelligentsia is defined 'not by blood or by class but by their allegiance to Russian literature. [...] Russians are an imagined community of readers (Boym 1995: 139).[15] Peter Kriksonov, a Russian-Israeli translator, strengthens Boym's argument when he notes the common practice of quoting literary texts, with or without quotation marks, while speaking (Kriksonov 2001). The quoting, he says, is an act of belonging to the mythic community of readers.

Kamyanov's citing, then, merges the boundaries of sexuality and class. At first glance there seems to be a clear separation between the intelligentsia and the gays and lesbians/homosexuals/sodomites/shadows by the latrine. The former are brought together by memories and feelings, the later are expelled and sent back to non-existence, just like the shadow in Schwartz's play. And yet, the shadow never really disappears. The notion of the 'shadow', of one's voiceless and ghostly double, suggests that the relationship between the intelligentsia and its (queer) shadow is far more complicated, historically and culturally, than it may first appear. In order to understand this complexity we must 'unpack the domains of practice and significance' (Castañeda 2002: 3) built into the Shadow by the Latrine and follow the intertextual hauntings of Kamyanov's language into other realms of literary and cultural memory where the criminal haunts the intelligentsia and where 'history and subjectivity make social life' (Gordon 1997: 8).

'This is the problem of the Russian language', said Sergej Podrazhanskij, the editor of *Vesti*, when Vered Lee asked him why he chose to publish Kamyanov's offensive poem. 'Half the country spoke in the prison slang. [...] It was an abnormal country with an abnormal lexicon' (Lee 2002). Indeed, as millions of Soviet citizens – political dissidents, religious practitioners, former prisoners of war and simply 'family members of the enemies of the people' – were forced to spend some part of their lives in Gulag during the Repression, 'Gulag-speak' became part of the everyday language. Prisons and camps in the Soviet Union were much more influential than in other countries. Russian sociologist Anton Olejnik, for example, notes

15 For an interesting historical analysis of 19th century practices of intelligentsia's emotional selfhood through literature see Zorin (2008).

that criminal subculture played – and still plays – an important role in both Soviet and post-Soviet society and culture in the spheres of economy, interpersonal relations and everyday language (Olejnik 2001, 2004, 2005). In regards to language he specifically notes that 'the fact of dissolution of prison slang in everyday Russian is evidence not of the opposition of prison and society but of their special "affinity"' (Olejnik 2004: n.p.).

But this special affinity of the two worlds has its historical specificity as well as particular literary figurations. The conjuncture of sexuality, criminality and class distinction leads us to Gulag memoirs, as *the* site where the intelligentsia meet the ghostly shadow of the homosexual. Many of the survivors of the Soviet labour camps wrote about their experiences, forming what is known today as the 'Gulag literary corpus' (Toker 2000).[16] Memoirs of the 'Repression', the purges and decades of imprisonment vary in tone and style, and in the periods described: for example, memoirs of the Stalinist 1930s–1950s differ from the memoirs of the 1970s–1980s.[17] Yet what unites almost all of them is the lack of sympathy for – and often an active disgust and scorn towards – same sex relations in the camps (Zhuk 1998). Importantly, the Gulag memoirs are written exclusively by the educated classes and intellectuals who were imprisoned as 'politicals', accused of anti-Soviet actions. The distinction between the 'politicals' and the 'criminals' is central in all the memoirs and recollections of former prisoners.[18] It is a classed distinction, too: for many of the 'repressed' it was their first close encounter with the mass of the 'lower classes'. Not surprisingly, their take on homosexuality is classed, and often merges the fear of blurring class distinction with the fear of being touched by the filth

16 Leona Toker's (2000) groundbreaking *Return from the Archipelago: Narratives of Gulag Survivors* provides a detailed analysis of the survivors' literary narratives and also addresses the complex status of the memoirs as both an historical testimony and artistic work.

17 Many dissident authors explicitly distinguish between these two generations of Gulag experiences and writing. Guberman, for example, juxtaposes his imprisonment as relatively bearable (and therefore, easy to discuss) with the unbearable suffering of those imprisoned under Stalin (Guberman 2003).

18 In reality, the distinction between 'political' and 'criminal' prisoners was far more blurred and not at all as clear-cut as many memoirs describe it.

of homosexuality.[19] For example, when the Russian historian Olga Zhuk interviewed educated women survivors of the Gulag, they were very keen to distinguish themselves from the 'low brow' criminal prisoners. When asked whether they [the interviewees] had any lesbian ties, some of them answered 'never!' or 'I was blessed not to be touched by *this*' (Zhuk 1998: 99, 103). Others recalled some stories of lesbian relations among the political prisoners, but noted that unlike the 'criminals' these were always discreet and never manifested publicly.

The older generation of today's Russian immigrants were raised during the Soviet regime, when the memoirs such as those by Alexandr Solzhenitzyn, Evgenija Ginzburg and Varlam Shalamov[20] were secretly read and distributed, and received as *the* truth about the Soviet regime. Today's immigrants who are in their thirties or older also remember the 'discovery' of these authors in the late 1980s, when these memoirs were officially published and widely read in the Soviet Union for the first time. The status of these memoirs as true testimony and as the 'real history' metonymically granted them the unquestioned authority about other issues, described by the survivors.[21] Among them was homosexuality, which for the memoirs' authors – and later for their readers – was forever linked to criminality, violence and monstrosity.

Sexuality in the Gulag memoirs often functions as a sign of class distinction. Love, partnership and marriage among the 'political' prisoners are never described in explicitly sexual terms; narrations of public manifestations of attraction or desire are extremely rare. One explanation of such absence is Boym's suggestion that 'the representation of sexuality in Russian culture is at particular risk of being not only immoral but also distasteful'

19 It is important to emphases that Gulag historiography almost completely ignore the topic of same-sex relations; so does the scholarship on the memoirs themselves. My detailed analysis of the memoirs' affective politics of sexuality and class (Kuntsman 2009) – a topic which lies beyond the scope of this book – is the first intervention into the subject.

20 The most famous authors of Gulag memoirs of the Stalinist period.

21 The memoirs received their status of truth and unquestionable moral authority not only because they were censored by the Soviet regime, but also because of the suffering that their authors had undergone.

(Boym 1993: 158). The juxtaposition of sexuality to moral aesthetics is reflected in an untranslatable Russia world, *poshlost'*, that refers to 'artistic triviality, banality, lack of spirituality and sexual indecency' (Nabokov cited in Boym 1993: 157). Further to Boym, I suggest that the fear of the tastelessness, or of the anti-aesthetic, is not merely an artistic anxiety but has to do with class distinction, or rather the fear of blurring it.

The criminals, on the other hand, are presented as explicitly and disgustingly sexual. Shalamov, one of the most famous Gulag authors, himself imprisoned during the Stalinist repression, writes:

> *Blatari* [gangsters, criminals] are all pederasts. Each of them in the camp is surrounded by young people with swollen and muddy eyes – 'Zojkas', 'Man'kas', 'Verkas', whom the *blatar'* is feeding and with whom he sleeps.
> In one of the camps where there was no hunger, *blatari* had tamed and corrupted a female dog. They fed and patted her, and then slept with her, like a woman, openly, in front of everyone in the barrack.
> One does not want to believe these cases, because of their monstrousness. But this is [everyday] life.
> It is hard to imagine that a human being can think of something like this, but *blatari* have nothing human (Shalamov 2003: 564).

The *blatari*, who, according to Shalamov, are all pederasts, embody the monstrous: they are cruel and abusive; in the absence of women in camps they have sex with young men and dogs. Shalamov's description of *blatari*'s relations with the dogs emphasises their monstrosity, but it also equates male-on-male sex with bestiality.[22] Shalamov also describes the *blatari*'s violence towards the doctors: *blatari* do not want to work and force the doctors to give them false sick leaves. Those who refuse are threatened and even killed. But while narrating in detail the fearful existence of the 'politicals' alongside the *blatari*, Shalamov shows no compassion for their victims among the 'criminals' – women or men, who act as effeminate pas-

22 For an interesting discussion of animal metaphors in relations to sex between men in Soviet camps, and the ways these metaphors are played out in post-Soviet popular fiction, see Borenstein (2008).

sive homosexuals. On the contrary, the latter – 'Zojkas' and 'Verkas' – are depicted with disgust or scorn.

Zoja, Manya and Vera are common Russian female names. Their shortened forms (i.e. Verka instead of Vera), normative when used for little girls, come to signify familiarity or disrespect when applied to adult women. In the latter case they are also associated with low-class language. Passive homosexuals in prisons were also often given shortened female names to signify their subordinate status (Healey 2001). Shalamov's text is one example of such use, but the names used here do not refer to specific people. Rather, their use in the plural and with quotation marks, constructs the passive homosexuals as a nameless crowd of disgusting deviants. Their eyes are muddy and swollen – is this a result of their 'deviant' sex? – and they surround their man, behaving like tamed animals. Their shortened, 'gender-bending' names and bestial appearance express the author's revulsion that is communicated to the readers.

Shalamov's account is remarkably similar to a description of same-sex relations in the female camp written by Ginzburg, another famous author and survivor of the Stalinist terror. Ginzburg, like Shalamov, dehumanises all criminal inmates through the conjunction of morality – or rather, the lack of mores – and bestiality. 'Criminals', she writes, 'are beyond the borders of human. I do not want to describe their orgies, although I suffered enough, having been a captive witness' (Ginzburg 1979: 42). It is within the non-human world of criminality and monstrosity that Ginzburg locates her description of sexual relations between women:

> And here is a disgusting little goggle-eyed toad, Zojka the lesbian. With her there are three so called *kobly*.[23] Hermaphrodite-like creatures with short hair, hoarse voices and male names – Edik, Sashok and some other. These humanoids live a fantastic life, where the boundaries between day and night are blurred. [...] Almost none of them sleep at night. They drink some kind of alcohol [...], smoke something.

23 In English the term *kobly* is usually translated as 'studs' or 'dogs' (see, for example, Healey 2001: 237). The masculine women – *kobly* – were sometimes also referred to as 'its' (*ono*). In many memoirs the masculine women are depicted as particularly ugly, fearsome and violent, and their feminine counterparts – the *kovyrjalki* – appear as subservient, docile and pathetic (Zhuk 1998).

> Where they take this potion from is not clear. A huge metal 'stove' is red hot. In it these infernal creatures always cook something, dancing around it, nearly naked (Ginzburg 1979: 113).

Ginzburg, like Shalamov, figures same-sex relations as disgusting. The masculine women – the *kobly* – in her description are, like Shalamov's *blatari*, marked with low-class and gender-bending names ('Sashok' and 'Edik' are male names, short forms of Sasha (Alexander) or Eduard); they are symbolically placed outside of the human world by using words such as 'humanoids' or 'infernal creatures'. Zojka-the-lesbian – here Ginzburg users the term lesbian only in relation to the woman, playing the 'feminine' role in same-sex relations[24] – is also positioned in the animal world, which in the Russian language carries a strong negative connotation and is clearly opposed to humanness.

In Shalamov and Ginzburg's texts, same-sex relations are not simply disgusting. Those engaging in them are described as non-human, whereas the imprisoned intellectuals become victims, 'captive witnesses' to their savage presence. And while direct sexual abuse towards the political prisoners is not mentioned here, it has a haunting presence. It lurks through literary substitutions, such as an account of the ruthless theft by a 'criminal' inmate of precious personal belongings, narrated by Ginzburg; or the story of a political prisoner who was put into a barrack with the 'criminals', described in Shalamov's writings. On his arrival, the 'political', a former cinema scriptwriter, was beaten and ordered to sleep by the latrine; then he was told to rub the feet of the barrack's leader – a 'job' usually done by a young male inmate with a female name (i.e. a passive homosexual). Then one of the inmates asked the leader, referring to the 'political': 'The new [guy] ... would you like to try [him]?' But instead of rape as one might anticipate, the *blatar* 'tries' the storytelling abilities of the newcomer. The latter survives and avoids a 'place by the latrine' because he can recite novels to entertain the inmates – a common practice in prisons and camps where the illiterate *blatari* used storytellers as books.

24 These women were usually called *kovyrjalki*, see also the previous note.

Thrown into the mob of criminals, it was the educated 'politicals' who were forced to become 'captive witnesses' and who were often destined to be 'by the latrine', humiliated and abused physically and/or sexually. This is why *pidory*, *kobly* and *kovyrjalki* haunt Kamyanov the poet; this is why the Russian-Israeli intelligentsia is supposedly so threatened by the queers among them.

But the fearful effect of the queers' presence, importantly, lies not in the queers themselves; rather, it is generated by the emotionality of Kamyanov's own figurations, operating through the movement of memories, meaning and words. Terrifying bestial shadows travel to the streets of Jerusalem, when Kamyanov names the marchers as *pidory*, *kobly* and *kovyrjalki*. The horrors of history meddle with the realities of today through striking intertextual resemblances. Note for example, how Kamyanov's account of the Parade reproduces Ginzburg's description of the humanoids' 'fantastic life', cited earlier, almost in its entirety:

> Where they take this potion from is not clear. A huge metal 'stove' is red hot. In it these infernal creatures always cook something, dancing around it, nearly naked.

Now Kamyanov:

> Around the fires the demons dance.
> They drink the potion of love until oblivion.

It is the circulation of Gulag imagery and the use of Gulag language that makes the Soviet past part of the Israeli present. This resonance of texts, times, and spaces has the effect of uncanny horror:[25] the familiar turns into the monstrous, the streets of Jerusalem become the Gulag, the national home turns into Russian immigrants' worst fear of being made 'captive witnesses' one more time.

The intertextual links to Gulag imagery also work to tie the classed fear and disgust with the religious rage and national anxiety: the criminal monsters are marching on Zion; 'Independence Park' becomes the site

25 I return to engage with Freud's notion of the uncanny in the next chapter.

of a demonic feast. The horror of being thrown into the criminal mob becomes the angst of the Jewish nation, fighting its last battle, while the 'vermin' celebrate their sins. Zion, Holy Jerusalem, the Jewish democracy and the state-at-war come together in this haunting figuration, informing Kamyanov's homophobic violence, shaping and justifying it. The Israeli nation of Kamyanov's texts is a complex entity of several, often contradictory, discourses. The pain and concern about the national future interweaves with the condemnation of 'Jewish democracy' (GLBT rights seem to have synecdochic relations with it for Kamyanov), creating an opposition between the (Jewish) democratic state and the Jewish people. Ethnic and class anxiety about (secular) Israeli norms taking over the children of the Russian Israelis ('our children are growing up in a de-ideologised post-Zionist society') merge with the mourning for Zionism and with Biblical anxiety about profanation and war.

Kamyanov's own self-presentation as the first one speaking out against the sinful 'swamp of Israeli pederasty', and in particular his reference to the loss of ideology, morals and the coming loss in the ultimate war, is a stance of moral authority. It links him to the authors of the Gulag memoirs, many of whom, following the traditions of Russian literature, presented their stories not as private autobiographies and individual narratives, but as documents of transcendental historical significance. They positioned themselves as the voice of, and for, their generation, erased and tortured by Soviet terror. But Kamyanov's moral stance also positions him as what is known as a 'prophet of rage'. The image of a righteous prophet is embedded in Jewish tradition and is familiar not only to religious, but also to secular Jewish Israelis. Moreover, the speaker's position as the 'prophet of rage' who warns against loss and destruction is a common trope in Israeli political rhetoric. But Kamyanov's position, extensively supported by Biblical imagery, exceeds the context of Judaism and the discourse of homosexuality as sin, associated in Israel predominantly with the Orthodox Jewish community and political parties. It relates to the wider imagery of horror, more familiar to Russian Israelis who grew up in the Christian literary tradition. His 'demons', 'drinking potions' and 'dancing around fire' recall descriptions of pagans and witches and their deeds, in both the European Christian and the missionary context. The notion of 'demons' also nods to Dostoevski's famous *Demons*, a dystopian social analysis, heavily influenced by Orthodox Christian philosophy. Together with Ginzburg's 'infernal creatures' Kamyanov's imagery also brings to mind images of Hell, notably the comparison of the Gulag with Hell, and more specifically, with Dante's Inferno or Orpheus' Hades, both widely known among educated Russian-speakers and appearing very often in relation to Gulag memoirs. Disgusting perverts become beastly creatures from Hades – the Kingdom of Shadows.

The violence of ghosts

This chapter took us on a journey into 'dense site[s] where history and subjectivity make social life' (Gordon 1997: 8) in order to understand how material and semiotic violence of the past transforms into a psychic injury of the present. Following the figurations of the Shadow by the Latrine in Kamyanov's homophobic attacks and in the memoirs of former political prisoners of the Gulag, this chapter illuminates the ways in which the history of Soviet political terror is formative to Soviet and post-Soviet views of same-sex relations as disgusting and dangerous; and as particularly fearful for those who see themselves as belonging to the intelligentsia.

Using haunting as a 'practice of figuration' (Haraway 1997: 9), I showed that the absent presence of the camps – their haunting – in national horizons (Fortier 2008) of Russian Israelis is mediated by language, and more specifically by intertextual reverberations and hateful name-callings. It is precisely this haunting presence that brings up constant slippages between various definitions of sexuality. And while there are significant historical differences between the queers of today and criminalised Soviet homosexuals, or between male and female sexualities in and outside of the Gulag, the evocation of same-sex relations in various post-Soviet contexts, such as the one described here, seems to often lead back to the criminal *pidory*, *kobly* and *kovyrjalki*, collapsing everything into the Shadow by the Latrine. This figure signals both the persistent and distorted hypervisibility of male homosexuality as distasteful and perverse, and the frequent disappearance of queer women as sexual subjects while they remain objects of mockery and scorn.

Attention to these refigurations and their effects brings a more complex conceptualisation of the relations between violence and belonging than the one usually deployed in discussions of homophobic violence. As I suggest throughout the chapter, layers of material, semiotic and psychic violence shape claims for belonging by creating a particular form of affective sociality – the sociality of living with and speaking through ghosts. The understanding of belonging as haunted and the attention to particular ghostly figures, such as the Shadow by the Latrine, is particularly important in analysing immigrants' claims for and attachment to the nation. Multicultural nations, notes Sneja Gunew (2004), are haunted by their multiple histories (including colonialism and genocide). So too Israel as a nation, and the Russian-Israeli community of immigrants, are constituted through layers of past violence which can not be fully known but whose presence never disappears. Instead, it can resurface through ghosts that emerge at the moments of national, sexual or class anxieties. The ghostly figures can then become 'grounds of a particular claim', to use Castañeda's words (2002: 52). In the case of Kamyanov, this is a claim of respectability, humanness and national subjecthood, or rather, a violent defence of its purity against the 'filth' of public queer presence, such as Pride Parades.

But what about the ghosts' circulation? In her *Haunted Nations* Gunew asks: 'Can ghosts emigrate?' (Gunew 2004: 107) I want to reformulate her question by asking: What happens to ghosts when they migrate? What happens when they are called on by haunted speech acts? In other words, how is the figure of the ghost refigured in immigration?

The Shadow by the Latrine does not simply move from the Soviet past to present day Israel when it is evoked by Kamyanov. It undergoes transformation in a cross-cultural transition. The Shadow is refigured on Israeli soil in the struggle among Russian speaking immigrants over who deserves to be a proper Israeli, a respectable citizen, a legitimate subject. Haunted by the Gulag demons, Kamyanov and the immigrant community he imagines become 'paranoid nationalists' (Hage 2003), whose belonging is constituted through worrying about the nation's future. Here the worrying works not only to exclude queers from the Russian-Israeli community; it also positions this community as the *real* national subjects who care about the nation's morals and soul. The (heterosexual) Russian-Israeli intelligentsia claims the high moral ground over Israeli liberals who supposedly endanger the nation by 'turning filth into pride', to paraphrase Kamyanov's words.

Kamyanov and the community of the Russian-speaking intelligentsia are haunted not simply by the collective trauma of political terror, but by the intelligentsia's own position in the Gulag as powerless victims in the hands of those whom they hardly consider as human beings. Lev Klein (writing under pseudonym of Lev Samojlov), a Soviet ethnologist and a former Gulag prisoner, called his book on the criminal subculture *A Journey to the Upside-down World* (Samojlov 1989). Indeed, everything in the Gulag was about reversals. Former criminals were the rulers and the executioners; the country's former elite were 'the enemy of the people', consigned to the Hades of the camps. In the Gulag the social hierarchy, both formal and informal, was often reversed: in many camps, especially during the Stalinist period, the 'common criminals' were positioned at the top, and were even explicitly incited against the political prisoners by the prison authorities; the 'politicals' were at the bottom, given the hardest work and the smallest food ration.[26] An upside-down world – this is how the Gulag figures in the collective memory shaped by the intelligentsia's memoirs.

But these memoirs have their own reversals: narrating the political prisoners' struggle to survive, physically, emotionally and morally,[27] they make all the criminal inmates – and by association, all those engaged in same-sex relations – into beastly monsters. 'Captive witnesses' and victims of abuse in the past, they gain both the epistemological power and the moral authority of defining and guarding the boundaries of the human,

26 This was not true for all camps, and happened more frequently during the Stalinist period of the 1930s–1950s. In the later period of the 'Stagnation', political prisoners were often positioned above the 'common criminals', enjoyed special privileges (such as access to books) and were respected by the 'criminals'.

27 For a detailed analysis of the relations between physical and moral survival as it is narrated in the memoirs, see Toker (2000).

thus turning the world upside down one more time. It is these reversals that shape and feed today's homophobic figurations. Kamyanov, for example, employs historical, literary and emotional manipulation to shame and eject the queers from the Russian-Israeli intelligentsia and from the whole Jewish nation. He calls on the ghost of the past through haunted speech acts that become wounding words. In his and other journalists' description, the violence of homophobia is refigured, too: their writings present the Russian-Israeli intelligentsia as the victim of (Israeli) gay rule. Pride Parades become an offence against good taste; and anti-homophobic actions are presented as censorship. As in many other cases of verbal assaults based on ethnicity, gender or sexuality, the notion of free speech, employed by Kontorer against *Haaretz*, becomes yet another violent way of silencing a marginal group. It also evokes the Soviet past once again, by referring to the fear of state-induced censorship and the reign of those who are in fact only shadows.

Kamyanov's use of the Shadow by the Latrine as a ground for his claims of nationhood and heteronormativity is a double-bind: in the same move he positions himself as the speaker for the (Israeli) future while pushing the queers to the (Soviet) past; he reduces the queers to disgusting monstrousness while constructing the heterosexual Russian-Israeli intelligentsia as the victim of the queers. His haunted violence demonstrates that the signs stick not only through emotions performed in the present but also through the ghostly figures of the past. It is not simply the naming of queers as demons or as disgusting filth that is at stake here. And it is not just the performativity of disgust in the present. Rather, it is the *sticking through time* and *performing with ghosts* that gives Kamyanov's words their wounding power.

The constant and complex refigurations, outlined in this chapter, suggest that the Shadow by the Latrine is both persistent *and* mutable. As such, it can allow various claims of belonging, but can simultaneously mute others. For example, the conjunction of sexuality and class in memoirs of imprisonment made it difficult, if not impossible, to remember and commemorate queer victims of the Gulag. While in itself epistemologically questionable and problematic, such a move can be empowering and is indeed common in contemporary queer politics, where the past is (re) claimed and histories are (re)written. 'No one ever counted the number of victims of criminal persecution of homosexuals in the Soviet Union', wrote bitterly the Russian poet and journalist Gennadij Trifonov in an essay, published on the leading Russian gay website, www.gay.ru. 'Even the Soviet human rights activists of the "Stagnation" period never did and never tried to do it' (Trifonov 1991). A similar remark was made by Michael Foucault regarding the silence of dissident intellectuals about the repression of homosexuals and about sexuality more generally, as Jan Plamper notes in his 'Foucault's Gulag' (Plamper 2002). But it is not only the (heterosexual) dissidents who are reluctant to acknowledge queer victimhood and humanise same-sex relations in the camps. As the next chapter demonstrates, the queer immigrants, too, turns away from the ghost of the Gulag in their own claims of respectability and national belonging.

CHAPTER 2

The Jewish Victim

(Not) admitting the ghost

> What kind of case is the case of a ghost? It is a case of haunting, a story about what happens when we admit the ghost – that special instance of the merging of the visible and the invisible, the dead and the living, the past and the present – into the making of worldly relations and into the making of our accounts of the world.
>
> — Avery Gordon, *Ghostly Matters*, 1997: 24–25.

The previous chapter showed how homophobic texts work through multiple reversals, and in their attempts to push away the shadows of the past, inflict violence on queers of the present. For Kamyanov and other Russian-speaking journalists homosexuality was forever linked with monstrousness and criminality; they saw Pride Parades as the Gulag past leaking into the Israeli present, turning their national home into a place of uncanny horror. But what about the queer immigrants themselves? Was *their* home turned uncanny? What were *their* relations to the Shadow by the Latrine? How did they 'reimagine and reconstitute their particular, fraught relationship to multiple national sites' (Gopinath 2003: 264)? Did they constitute their resistance through the marginal, the excluded and the banished? Did they 'admit the ghost'?

In order to answer these questions, this chapter takes a close look at the organising of the RFAHD, which was established following the publication of Kamyanov's offensive poem. Subsequently its struggle was supported by Israeli GLBT organisations. During the short period of its intensive activity (mainly in the months following the publication of the poem, in 2002)[1] the RFAHD worked on two fronts: establishing alliances and seeking the support of Israeli organisations, and engaging in discussion within the Russian-speaking sphere. The first front brought up immediate support and enthusiasm: for example, the Lesbian Feminist Community offered help in filing an official complaint against the paper.[2] The meaning of such support is a complicated matter that lies beyond the scope of my discussion here. As I briefly noted in the previous chapter, it should not be simplistically addressed as playing into Israeli hegemonic notions of acculturation and the surveillance of immigrants 'behaving badly'. But more importantly, alliances with Israeli organisations constituted only a part of the queer immigrants' struggle, while the rest took place on the Russian-speaking frontier. This chapter specifically addresses the latter, looking at the ways the queers aimed to reclaim their respectability and nationhood in a dialogue with other immigrants. In particular, this chapter follows the responses to homophobia published on the website, in articles written for the Russian-speaking media; and in the polemic with *Vesti*'s journalists and editors.

The responses triggered by Kamyanov's violence, ranged in form and style. Some opposed Kamyanov's rhetoric by trying to reclaim homosexuality as not only normal, but also as *cultural*. In an essay, prepared by the RFAHD for publication in *Vesti*, Michail Laskov (a pseudonym, used by one of the activists), wrote:

> Homophobes like to position homosexuality in line with sexual perversions. They deliberately ignore the spiritual aspect of the relations between two individuals. How could the relationships between Marina Tsvetaeva and Sofia Parnok, Paul Verlaine and Arthur Rimbaud, whose love gave the world the most moving poems, be positioned alongside sexual perversions? (Michail Laskov, *Vesti*, 5 September 2002).

1 The RFAHD continues its formal existence until this day, although it is not very active as a group. Some of the activists who took part in its establishment in 2002 now contribute to the Russian queer scene in one way or another.

2 Letter dated 8 October 2002, from Ira Eden, the Community's solicitor, to the Israeli Attorney General.

Laskov's act of naming the authors positions him within the cultural practice of the intelligentsia. In a move, similar to Kamyanov's claim of cultural knowledge and class authority, Laskov establishes *his* authority through mentioning Russian and foreign poets, well known and admired by many educated Russian speakers. These poets were also known for their same-sex relationships, as well as for the poetry and prose these relationships produced. Laskov's reference to the 19th century French and early 20th century Russian authors does not argue with the homophobic criminalisation of queer bodies in camps. Instead, he presents queer sexuality as inherent in the spirituality and cultural capital that are central to the identity of the intelligentsia. Later in the article Laskov emphasises that homosexuality exists across class, racial, ethnic and age groups. Yet it is its existence among well known poets that is evoked to defend the respectability of queerness: the queer here is figured first and foremost as a person of high culture, while high culture, in turn, holds the ability to distinguish between 'homosexual love' and 'sexual perversions'.

Laskov's 'name dropping' is strategic: his text indeed talks to the class and aesthetic anxieties of Russian Israelis regarding same-sex relations as not cultured. He, however, does not mention those known artists and intellectuals who were imprisoned in the Gulag *because* of their sexuality. Among the convicts sent to the camps since the beginning of the Stalinist terror were also those imprisoned according to the Anti-sodomy 'Article 121'. Among them were the famous singer Vadim Kosin (convicted in the 1940s and again in 1959); cinema director Sergej Paradjanov (convicted in the 1970s); and the ethnologist Lev Samojlov (Klein), the author of several ethnographic studies of the criminal world that were based on his own experience of Soviet camps. The fact of their imprisonment is widely known but the law under which they were charged is rarely mentioned, even today. The figuration of the Shadow by the Latrine, it seems, cannot include the 'queers of high culture'; evoked by Kamyanov as the monstrous ghost of criminality and bestiality, it makes people like Kosin, Paradjanov or Samojlov invisible. Laskov's appeal to high culture, in that respect, does not refigure Kamyanov's mapping; paradoxically, it further emphasises the split between dehumanised 'perversions' and the literary spirituality of the intelligentsia. By doing so, it makes a claim for queer respectability, which can only include some queers, and not others.

Other responses to Kamyanov did refer to the Gulag, but only in the discussions on the Forum, and only in a very particular way that in fact reproduced the link between Gulag imagery and the undesirable abjects. Some participants tried to throw the offence of Kamyanov's name-calling back at him. For example, Kamyanov's 'Shadows demand rights', discussed in the previous chapter, was reprinted on the website under the title 'Kamyanov leaves a vacancy by the latrine'.[3] This title was a paraphrase of the exclamation 'your place is by the latrine', used by Kamyanov. The title reverses Kamyanov's attack by placing *him* in the criminal context, at the bottom of the prison hierarchy he reserved for the queers. The publication on the site was illustrated by a computer-modified image of Kamyanov behind bars, with a label 'phobia' attached to it (see Figure 3). The image and the word 'phobia' on it can be read as a suggestion that homophobia and hate speech should be put away. But it can also be interpreted as a reversal of the homophobic imagery within 'Gulag-speak', by attempting to stick the haunting horror of the Gulag to homophobes, rather than to queers. Forum discussions around the same time also threw the criminal imagery back at Kamyanov. One participant wrote a parody in which Kamyanov was shown humiliated in prison, raped by proletarians and turning into a 'swaggering homosexual' ('swaggering' was the word used in Kamyanov's poem to describe participants in the Pride Parade, see previous chapter). This parody, in itself unmistakably violent, presented the act of being 'put down' as embedded in the sexual as well as class hierarchy – a witty, even if disturbing, response to Kamyanov's own class anxieties and to Gulag memoirs' demonisation of low-class criminals.

Another participant noted that Kamyanov's homophobia is typical of the older generation that 'grew by the latrine', and therefore was impervious to change. 'It is to the younger generation that we need to turn', he concluded. This response is particularly interesting, for it suggests that ghosts of the past do not move across generations. The struggle to refigure

3 *Gay News* section of the site, entry published on the 12th of September 2002.

queerness as acceptable and normal becomes a generational rupture, resembling Kamyanov's own fears of the 'de-ideologised' society of the future. The queers' struggle is at the same time hopeless ('they' will never change) and hopeful ('we' are different). Strikingly, it is all too reminiscent of the 'acculturation' and assimilation policy practiced by the Israeli authorities towards the immigrants: you are here, not in Russia, things are (will be?) different now. But just like the parodies of Kamyanov, or Laskov's reference to poets, this refiguration, too, turns away from the Gulag ghost itself. The queer immigrants of today were not – refused to be – figured through it, hoping to leave the shadows behind, in the past. The existence of same-sex relations in the Gulag remained 'exclud[ed] and banish[ed]' (Gordon 1997: 25). The person by the latrine – this time, the homophobe – still had to be humiliated, incarcerated or expelled. The link between criminality, deviation and dehumanisation was not disturbed; rather, it continued to live exactly the way it was figured by the intelligentsia survivors and by Kamyanov himself.

To paraphrase Gordon, cited at the opening of the chapter, what happens when the ghost is *not* admitted? How is the haunted injury communicated *then*? And how – if at all – can we *then* merge 'the visible and the invisible, the dead and the living, the past and the present – into the making of worldly relations and into the making of our accounts of the world' (Gordon 1997: 24–25)? As the rest of this chapter demonstrates, queer immigrants' injury inflicted by homophobia and their claims for victimhood, respect, political rights or a place in the nation were made through a different haunting figure, that of the Jewish victim of anti-Semitism and the Holocaust. So what was it about this figure that made their pain of homophobic injury communicable and their claims possible? What kind of 'accounts of the world' did it constitute? And how does this figuration of queer victimhood as Jewish, map the relations between violence and belonging?

Another haunting

> For a person of different sexual orientation discussing the topic of same-sex love in a 'Russian' newspaper in Israel is as difficult and pointless as for a Jewish publicist to enter a debate about the possibility of his very existence in an anti-Semitic publication, where the negative answer to this question is predetermined as an ideological axiom. What kind of discussion can take place when one has to argue not about one's political or aesthetic views, but about one's human dignity and one's right to love (Michail Laskov, *Vesti*, 5 September 2002).

When several outraged people approached *Vesti*'s editor, Sergej Podrazhanskij, protesting about the publication of Kamyanov's poem as well as earlier hostile publications, Podrazhanskij argued that the only reason the paper published anti-gay material was because it had not received materials expressing different points of view. In response, several members of the RFAHD prepared a long article for *Vesti*. The extract cited above opens the article. It is a direct response to Podrazhanskij's claims: there were no supportive publications about same-sex relations, notes the author, because these were simply not possible in *Vesti*. Laskov compares queers with Jews in order to communicate the pain and despair of many queer immigrants vis-à-vis the hateful publications they encountered in the Russian-speaking media. But his rhetorical move also creates an eerie feeling of a ghostly presence: the one who speaks is the one who is not – cannot be – there. The article is written by a person whose very existence is deemed impossible by the paper: a queer in a 'Russian' newspaper in Israel, or a Jew in an anti-Semitic journal. Of course, this is more than just a textual impossibility. Laskov's reference to a Jew who cannot argue for his existence is haunted by the history of physical annihilation that followed this impossible textual presence. The rhetorical twist of comparing queers to Jews brings to the fore the ghost of the Jewish victim of anti-Semitism, a figure that conjures up both the dead and the living and is evoked here as a reminder that hateful words are more than just words, and violent publications in newspapers can lead to physical extermination.

Laskov's comparison between homophobia and anti-Semitism 'replays' the relationship between queer immigrants and *Vesti*'s journalists as the relationship between Jews and Judeophobes. This move resembles Kamyanov's metonymic transformations, when times and places shift and one figure becomes the other, producing an image both strange and familiar. In order to better understand Laskov's refiguration of homophobia as anti-Semitism, I turn to Freud's notion of the uncanny as the familiar turning eerie or monstrous (Freud 1919/1934). What particularly interests me here is the relationship between the uncanny and the figure of a double. In his discussion of the double as uncanny Freud notes:

> [Thus] we have characters who are to be considered identical because they look alike. This relation is accentuated by mental processes leaping from one of these characters to another – by what we should call telepathy – so that the one possesses knowledge, feelings and experiences in common with the other, identifies himself with another person, so that his self becomes confounded, or the foreign self is substituted for his own – in other words, by doubling, dividing and interchanging the self. And finally, there is the constant recurrence of similar situations, a same face, or character-trait, or twist of fortune, or a same crime, or even a same name recurring through several generations (Freud 1919/1934: 386–387).

Kamyanov's attacks and Laskov's public response both share the element of uncanny doubleness. In Kamyanov's texts it was the shadow of the imprisoned homosexual, Kamyanov's own historical shadow, that he so passionately tried to repress. In Laskov's article somewhat different relations are at stake: the attacked queer turns out to be a Jew, producing – again – the sense of the uncanny, but this time not for Kamyanov and the heterosexual intelligentsia, but for the queer immigrants themselves. In the remainder of this chapter I will take a close look at the move that constitutes the relations between the queer and the Jewish victim as doubleness, as a form of connectedness and substitution that produces links between figures across histories and generations. What does it mean, I will ask, that the two are 'considered identical', and that one – a queer of today – is figured as 'possesses[ing] knowledge, feelings and experience in common with the other', a Jew from Russia, Europe, the Soviet Union or Nazi Germany?

In all the material I collected about the anti-homophobic organising in 2002 the most frequently repeated argument against homophobia was its comparison to anti-Semitism and the Holocaust. Kamyanov's and others' texts were repeatedly called 'fascist': in an article called 'Do no harm!' written for a Russian-language newspaper and reproduced on the website, the author notes that the immigrant media is either completely silent about same-sex relations or uses the insulting criminal jargon, sometimes adding 'tit-bits of pseudo-scientific argument that could with ease have been signed by Dr. Goebbels himself' (Plotkin 2002). One Forum participant wrote in her open letter to *Vesti*'s editor, that their anti-gay publications 'are not suitable for a paper that tries to be a cross-road of opinions; their place is in a course on "An Introduction to Modern Fascism"' (RFAHD archives). On the website Kamyanov's poem was presented as a purportedly fascist text. Immediately after its publication in *Vesti*, the poem was reprinted on the website, in the *Community* section. It was accompanied by a short comment written by Guy Gomel, the website's journalist. The Russian-speaking media, he wrote, has never been particularly friendly to the issues of same-sex relations and GLBT rights, either avoiding the topic completely or writing about it in an aggressive or sarcastic tone.

> But this time *Vesti* outdid itself. Kamyanov's openly fascist text is full of criminal homophobic terms; gays and lesbians are demonised in a manner that would do credit to the Nazi's *Der Sturmer*. Accompanied by photographs of the Jerusalem parade, this 'poetic masterpiece' occupies half a page in a *Vesti-2* supplement, a space generously offered by the editor, Sergeij Podrazhanskij. Here is the text of this new 'blood libel' (http://aguda.org/n.php?mode=lenta&news=109, saved March 2004).

Butler reminds us that injurious names have history. She points out that the force of a name works 'through an encoded memory of trauma, one that lives in language and is carried in language' (Butler 1997a: 36). Kamyanov's violent language, as I demonstrated in the previous chapter, is haunted by the Soviet intelligentsia's collective memory of the Stalinist terror, of imprisonment, of the camps and of sexual abuse. But for Guy, Kamyanov's (and other journalists') haunted words resonate with – and are transformed into – another collective trauma, that of anti-Semitism and the Holocaust. Kamyanov's language is the language of the Nazis, writes Guy, sticking the two together.

In his figuration of homophobia-as-anti-Semitism, Guy deploys two specific signposts, well known and almost paradigmatic in the history of Jewish victimhood: *Der Sturmer* and the 'blood libel'. *Der Sturmer* was a Nazi newspaper, published from 1923 to 1945 by Julius Streicher, one of Hitler's earliest followers. It was known for its anti-Semitic caricatures and its calls for the extermination of the Jews. During the German occupation of parts of the Soviet Union during World War II, many newspapers there reprinted articles from *Der Sturmer*, inciting anti-Semitic hatred among the occupied peoples, many of whom eventually collaborated with the Nazis. The term 'blood libel' refers to a long history of anti-Jewish violence, predominantly in Western and later also Eastern Europe. It found expression both in theology and popular belief and often led to the physical violence against the Jews. The libel accused Jews of the ritual killing of non-Jews (mainly Christians) and of using the blood of non-Jewish infants in order to make *Matzot.*[4] A common form of anti-Semitism in Europe in the Middle Ages, blood-libel reached Russia in the early nineteenth century, leading to violent pogroms. The accusations kept appearing across the Tsarist empire and later also in the Soviet Union; the image of Jews drinking the blood of Christian infants figured in common fear as well as in theological and scientific books (Reznik 1999). One of the most notorious blood libels in Russia was the 'Beilis Case' – the trial of Mendel Beilis, a Jewish man accused in 1913 of the ritual murder of a Christian boy. Another, more recent example, is the so-called 'Doctors' Trial' of 1953: an accusation of conspiracy against Jewish physicians that led to the extermination of many members of the Soviet Jewish intelligentsia. Stalin's plan at the time included a 'final solution' for the rest of the Soviet Jewry which was foiled only by his death in 1953.

The two signposts – the Nazi *Der Sturmer* and the 'blood libel' – as they are deployed by Guy, tie the history of Jewish persecution together with the experience of homophobic hatred. Evoked by Guy in his stand against homophobia, they bring up the horrors, known to all Russian-speaking Jews, whether directly through their own experiences or those of their

4 Special bread used during the celebration of Passover.

families, or indirectly by exposure to collective memories of Jewish persecution. But what does it mean when these images are evoked by a Jewish newcomer to Israel, a newcomer whose very immigration is narrated by the national ethos as 'return' to the safety of the Jewish homeland? Framing homophobic violence through the haunting history of anti-Semitism and the Holocaust can be read as queers' own experience of their home turning into uncanny horror. Having arrived in the country that welcomes them as Jews they suddenly find themselves helpless against homophobic violence. The injury inflicted by homophobia is refigured as the pain of other suffering, experienced directly or indirectly, through family, community or collective memory.

But the comparison of the two forms of victimhood also inevitably reads as part of Israel's manipulation of the Holocaust. In the Israeli national ethos the persecution of the European Jews is narrated as validating the foundation of the state, and the persecution of Jews in the diaspora figures as the main reason and justification for their immigration to Israel. What's more, as Juliana Ochs notes in her discussion of victimhood discourse in Israel, 'references to Holocaust victims turned into a discursive instrument of political legitimacy, used specifically to justify military operations and to argue for Israel's right to "security" on its own terms' (Ochs 2006: 359).[5]

I suggest that the figure of the Jewish victim here does double work. Firstly, when the injury of homophobia is figured through it, it gives weight to the queers' self-positioning as victims because the trope of Jewish victimhood in the Holocaust is something not to be questioned. And secondly, this figure becomes a powerful ground from which the response to homophobia is channelled into the national ethos. In the two following sections I explore two different moves, involving the figuration of the Jewish victim. The first one shows how the comparison between homophobia

5 The discourse of Jewish victimhood as the core of the national narrative is also used to determine *Ashkenazi* domination and to constitute the Jewishness of the state as European (see, for example, Shohat 1997). It is important to emphasise here, however, that referring to anti-Semitism or the Holocaust as a 'discursive instrument of political legitimacy' may or may not mean the speaker's alliance with Israeli nationalism; rather, it reflects the enormous symbolic weight of this discourse in the Israeli collective.

and anti-Semitism aims to make readers relive the horrors of the past – as Jews – and to recognise the anti-queer violence of the present. The second describes the use of victimhood and in particular, of fear, to lay claim to the national home.

Speech acts of memory

Shortly after the publication of Lee's article in *Haaretz*,[6] *Vesti*'s political commentator Dov Kontorer attacked Lee for her 'public disciplining' of the leading Russian-language newspaper (*Vesti*, 20 August 2002). Kontorer presented homosexuality as a private illness that has to be treated individually and not encouraged as a life style. He was particularly aggressive towards the Pride Parades, which he called a ridiculous ceremony that put perversion on display, a ceremony offensive to good taste. Following his attack, activists of the RFAHD decided to send letters of protest to the paper. 'Unwillingness to accept people's freedom of choice', wrote Dana, the author of one of the letters, 'is one of the characteristics of a totalitarian regime'. Evoking the experience of living in a totalitarian state, she continued:

> Let us remember what it meant to be a Jew during Soviet rule [...] Declaring one's Jewishness openly was [...] considered a subversive activity. It is very similar – being a Soviet Jew and being a homosexual, don't you think? Being a Jew is a biological fact. [...] Yet being culturally Jewish, with everything that is linked to it (passport registration, going to synagogue, celebrating Jewish holidays etc), was a matter of choice, to some extent. Many people did not make this choice, despite the biological facts, isn't it true? Many people were persecuted, and it did not matter whether they 'put their Jewishness on display' by participating in 'ridiculous ceremonies', or stubbornly followed 'old and ridiculous principles', even if they tried to hide their Jewishness (RFAHD archives).

6 See previous chapter.

In the introduction to *Acts of Memory* Mieke Bal emphasises that cultural memory is not just something one bears, but something one has to actually perform (Bal 1999). Such a performance is never individual: moving away from the conceptualisation of memory as (merely) an individual psychological process, Bal and other contributors to the book focus on the context in which acts of memory take place, as well as their audience, real or imagined.[7] Memories can be acts of power, resistance, projections of desire or erasure. Following Bal, I read Dana's 'let us remember' as a performance of memories about anti-Semitism. Describing the life of Jews in the Soviet Union, Dana makes her imagined audience – the *Vesti* collective and their readers – take a 'memory tour' into the Soviet past as Dana presents it. She narrates the life of a Jewish person in the Soviet Union along the themes discussed by Kontorer in his essay: sexual orientation that the person is born with and a way of life that one can choose.

Of course, the idea of sexuality as a biological and/or a social fact is a contested subject in itself. But what interests me here is not so much Dana's perception of sexuality, as the parallel she creates between being a homosexual and being a Jew. She depicts them as a similar combination of biology and choice, pointing out that Jewishness, like homosexuality, is not only and not so much a matter of biology but also of choices and social identity. Being culturally Jewish, she emphasises, was made up of many elements, all of which were intertwined with persecution and prohibition. For example, going to synagogue and openly celebrating Jewish holidays was seen as an anti-Soviet activity for which one could be imprisoned. Nevertheless, many people still engaged in it secretly, and some openly protested the discrimination. Among the latter were the *refusniks*, those Soviet Jews, predominantly from the big cities, who were denied permission to leave the country. Since the late 1980s most of them have reached Israel. Many are part of the Russian-Israeli cultural and political elite, including the editorial collective of *Vesti*. The figure of the *refusnik*, as well as all those others whose Jewish life was denied them or caused their persecution, haunt Dana's reference to Jewishness as social identity.

7 For more specific discussion, see Spitzer (1999) and Bardenstein (1999).

There are other ghosts in her text, too: those who chose not to live a Jewish life. In today's Israel many of the post-Soviet immigrants celebrate their return to the Jewish identity that they could not have in the Soviet Union. *Vesti* in particular dedicates much of its efforts to this revival, as well as welcoming those journalists who turned to religion after their arrival in Israel, or were finally able to practice their beliefs in an open way. Among those is Kamyanov as well as another Orthodox author, Arie Baratz, who has frequently spoken out against homosexuality.

Some Jews lived a Jewish life and others did not, writes Dana, but they were persecuted nevertheless. Her reference to persecution appears next to the words that mimic anti-Semitic language but in fact are paraphrases of Kontorer's description of gays and lesbians. This textual proximity of homophobia and anti-Semitism in Dana's letter does not simply emphasise the parallels between two victimised groups; it also links hateful language with discrimination and physical persecution. It demands remembrance of the past in order to recognise the violence of the present.

But importantly, it is not just any past – it is a past Dana and her imagined audience share. Reading Dana's letter as a performance of memory, I turn again to Butler's notion of the performative. Unlike Bal, who emphasises the existing audience or the witness to one's acts of memory (Bal 1999), I suggest that such acts in themselves have constitutional power. 'Let us remember' is a speech act that brings into being the 'us' that remembers. Dana's letter constitutes the collective of those who have a shared past to remember, and by doing so, it becomes a counter-move to Kamyanov's exclusion of queers-as-abject. Dana's speech act of memory sticks the Russian-speaking immigrants, straight and queer, (back) together: as Jews, as victims of persecution, and as those who had – or still have – to make complex choices regarding identity, visibility and lifestyle.

A somewhat similar move can be found in Guy's article 'Hating in Russian' written for the *Community* section of the website in August 2001, and reappearing in the *Homophobia* section[8] that was established on the

8 I return to discuss the *Homophobia* section in more detail later in this chapter.

website in summer 2002, following Kamyanov's attacks. In the article,[9] Guy presents the series of homophobic publications that appeared in *Vesti* and other newspapers over the years. Like Dana, he compares anti-Semitism to homophobia. He does not simply call on readers to remember experiences of anti-Semitism but animates this memory by transforming an anti-gay attack into an anti-Jewish text. This is how he cited one of the publications, a report about a Pride Parade in Haifa, published in *Vesti* in 1998:

> 'Transvestites and transsexuals, homosexuals and lesbians gathered in the city square under the boiling sun. *The raw smell of flesh* was in the air. *Swaggering* chaps, dressed in evening dresses, waved their hips and ogled passers by; *grinning gays* flaunted their butts, restraining their Rottweilers; *giddy lesbians* merged in a juicy kiss every time the march stopped.'
>
> Let us imagine a similar 'report', lets say, about a demonstration of Orthodox Jews:
>
> '*Bearded zhids* in old-fashioned kapotes walked, shaking their side locks, swaggering Abrahams and Sarahs waggled their fat Jewish butts. *The raw smell of blood* was in the air' (http://aguda.org/community/rus/php, saved April 2004, emphases in the original).

The description of the marchers as disgusting abjects by the journalist reminds us of elements of Kamyanov's poem, discussed in the previous chapter. But what I want to concentrate on now is not the description itself but the way Guy comments on it. 'Let us imagine', he suggests, what would happen if the Jews were described in a similar way. 'Let us imagine', he invites, and by doing so, he makes his audience to listen and to (re)experience the violence of homophobia through the violence of anti-Semitism. He then rewrites the homophobic text, substituting Orthodox Jews for queers, and deploying similar tactics as were used for the latter: derogatory name-calling, expressions of disgust and passionate demonisation.

This tactic effectively deconstructs, demonstrates and animates the injury of homophobia, instead of simply shaming it as fascist. Jews are

9 The article, written a year before Kamyanov's poem, demonstrates that the poem may have been the most notable attack on queers in the immigrant media, but was in no way the first or the only one.

called 'zhids' (kikes), an offensive and derogatory Russian term,[10] frequently used in assaultive language, hate speech and racist jokes. They are described with disgust, using the same technology of documentation-and-distortion applied to queers. For example, Orthodox Jews indeed have side locks, and some wear clothes that maintain the dress mode of 18th century Eastern Europe; but this description is mixed with derogatory and caricature images – 'shaking their side locks', 'waggled their fat Jewish butts'.

The violently anti-Semitic text, fabricated by Guy, evokes tropes that are immediately recognisable by people who grew up in the Soviet Union. 'Sarah' and 'Abraham', for example, were often used as nouns that represented Jews in many jokes. Here they are used in the plural, to stereotypically describe all Jews. The caricaturist depiction of Jews resembles anti-Semitic cartoons of 19th and 20th century Europe. And last but not least, the 'smell of blood' recalls the 'blood libels', evoking once again the long and continuous history of persecution.

By substituting Jews for queers, Guy also figures his imagined audience – the 'us' who should imagine an anti-Semitic attack. This audience is simultaneously victim and perpetrator: they are a collective brought together by the traumatic recognition of anti-Semitism, but they are also a collective who accepts (and maybe even supports) the violence of homophobia. When Butler discusses the injury of names as an effect of their historicity, she notes that '[t]he force of a name depends not only on its iterability, but on a form of repetition that is linked to trauma, on what is, strictly speaking, not remembered, but relived, and relived in and through the linguistic substitution for the traumatic event' (Butler 1997a: 36). Here, it seems, the injurious names used for Jews are doing even more complex work. 'Zhid', 'Jewish butts' and the 'raw smell of blood' indeed are linguistic substitutions through which the trauma of anti-Semitism can be relived again and again. Their traumatic effect may be suspended since they are declaimed by a Jewish person, declaring that this is *only* a demonstration, pretence, an act of imagination. And yet, they still carry the haunting history of centuries of violence against Jews.

10 It originates in the Yiddish word Yid (a Jew).

But most importantly, these words are enacted not to inflict injury upon Jews but to figure – and thus make communicable – another pain, to bring to the surface a different ghostly violence through the substitution of one victim for another. This refiguration through substitution is emotional as well as political.[11] On the emotional level, it communicates the violence of homophobia back to the imagined community of heterosexual immigrants: figured as *Jewish* pain, the pain of the queers is expected to become intelligible, meaningful, worthy of empathy and understanding. But at the same time the refiguration of homophobia as anti-Semitism is embedded in the Israeli national ethos that regards Jewish persecution as the greatest, most intolerable, evil: as *that which must not happen again*. Calling up the ghost of the Jewish victim marks homophobia as equally intolerable, and what is also important, equally dangerous. The political effects of this substitution are therefore complex as I will show in the next section, they nationalise the injury of homophobia, claim the nation as a safe home, but also constitute Jewish victimhood as the universal marker of suffering.

Nationalised fears

This is how the RFAHD's statement, mentioned in the previous chapter, begins:

> We are a group of gays and lesbians from the former Soviet Union who got together to combat expressions of homophobia in the Russian-speaking community in Israel. Many of us have to carry a double burden: the difficult adaptation process of new repatriates/immigrants in Israeli society is accompanied by the everyday experience of ignorance and insulting stereotypes that prevail among our former compatriots towards people of different sexual orientation (RFAHD archives).

11 Or rather, it is simultaneously both, since emotions, as shown below following Ahmed (2004), are always political and always involved in the production of politics.

In the opening sentence of the statement the Russian-speaking queers are positioned as double victims: of the hardship of the immigration process and of homophobia of the immigrant community that treats them with ignorance and insulting stereotypes. The former is supposed to be shared with other Russian Israelis, but the latter separates the straight from the queer. Throughout the debates about homophobia on the Forum, as well as in the dialogue with the immigrant media, queers were figured as victims of violence coming first and foremost from their own ethnic community. The idea of homophobia as residing in 'migrant' or 'ethnic' communities is not new: such communities are often perceived as more homophobic (Takagi 1996; Heidenreich 2006) by dominant (white) queers as well as by many queer migrants and diasporic subjects themselves. Scholars working on queer diaspora, migrant organising and anti-racist politics warn against the danger of the ethnicised figuration of homophobia that becomes a new form of racism (Puar 2005; Heidenreich 2006).[12] They also note the difficulty that queer diasporic subjects have in speaking about anti-gay violence in their communities within the racist context of the 'host' society (Dhawan and Castro Varela 2006). The question of context is particularly important here. The case of Russian-speaking queers is similar to and yet different from other queer migrants. Their position in Israel is ambivalent: they are both welcomed as Jews and stigmatised as new-comers.[13] Notions of specifically 'Russian' or post-Soviet homophobia can therefore add to – and intensify – already existing anti-Russian stereotypes where the latter are presented as non-democratic, unable to shake off the legacy of totalitarianism, and politically immature for the 'liberal' Israeli political sphere (Tachtarova 2005). At the same time, however, Russian-speaking queers

12 Recently, the relation between homophobia and racism has been specifically examined in the context of the 'war on terror': Puar (2007), for example, introduces the concept of 'homonationalism' in her discussion of white US queers who become complicit within US nationalism by constructing 'Muslim sexuality' as at the same time deviant and anti-queer. Haritaworn et al. (2008) similarly show how the language of queer rights and freedoms in Germany and the UK is constituted through defining Muslims as both anti-queer *and* as a threat to Western democracy.

13 I return to this ambivalence again in chapters 5 and 6.

can make claims to Israeli home and nationhood as Jewish repatriates and thus nationalise their victimhood. By doing so they can simultaneously escape their marginal position as 'Russian' newcomers in Israel and their status as disgusting monsters in Russian-Israeli imaginary.

But how exactly is their victimhood nationalised? Let us take another look at the RFAHD statement. The statement was jointly written by several people: I volunteered to make a first draft, which then underwent additions and editing through an email exchange between the RFAHD members. The text was drafted in Hebrew, discussed and modified, and then translated into Russian. One of the few points of disagreement was the use of the term 'immigrants' versus 'repatriates'. In my first draft I used 'immigrants', and the term was changed to 'repatriates' by another RFAHD member. This correction generated a lively discussion between us. The term 'repatriates' – *olim* in Hebrew, literally meaning 'those ascending' – is widely used in Israel, to signify the ideological meaning of immigration to Israel as ascending to Zion and returning to the national home. The term 'immigrants', on the other hand, can be seen as neutral because it describes any person who has moved from one country of residence to another. The use of this term for Jewish 'homecomers', however, is often viewed as a politically subversive act, opposing the Zionist ideology.[14] In the email exchange that followed the editing we finally agreed on using both terms, but in the Russian translation the ambivalence disappeared, leaving only the word 'repatriates'.

Of course, claiming gay rights as *repatriates* was not the only way of nationalising the injuries of homophobia; however I see it as a telling moment in the overall turn to the nation which characterised the RFAHD mobilising and the refiguration of homophobia as a *Jewish* injury. Another, very powerful moment was the evocation of fear by emphasising the threat of homophobia, figured through the threat of fascism. For example, when Kamyanov's poem was reprinted on the website, not everyone took it as seriously as the RFAHD organisers. Kamyanov is an old-fashioned Soviet

14 For me the use of 'immigrants' indeed expresses my anti-Zionist position regarding Israeli nationalism and immigration policy.

fool, said some. It's just religious craziness, noted others. One participant, Ricky, suggested that the paper was simply desperate for any material and therefore did not care what it published. 'We live in a democracy, anyone can say whatever they like', he wrote. But he was immediately contradicted by Guy Gomel and Anna Talisman, two participants and activists, who later became the driving forces of the RFAHD. They described homophobic attacks in the immigrant newspapers as unacceptable.

> <Anna>: Hey, it's the 21st century! One has to pay for such actions. All this is reminiscent of the situation in Germany in the 1920s, when anti-Semitism was no longer censored, but Jews kept saying 'Why pay attention to fools??' As we all know, this didn't serve the Jews very well. Not a single Israeli newspaper (unless it's Ultra-Orthodox) would dare to publish something like this. I think today we can provide a proper response.

> <Guy>: Anna, I totally agree with you. This is the last straw [of our patience]. The 'leading' Russian newspapers have to pay for their fascist tricks.

Anna strongly disagrees with those who suggested ignoring Kamyanov's – or any other – offensive posts. She compares the escalating anti-gay publications of the Russian-speaking media to anti-Semitism in Germany of the 1920s. Anna and Guy's call for action, because the offenders have to 'pay for their fascist tricks', also resembles Israeli national militancy in protecting Jewish lives at all costs, militancy narrated through the idea that the Holocaust must not happen again. This call for action is based on exactly this type of warning: homophobic attacks in newspapers, they predict, can lead to mass physical violence, just like in Nazi Germany.

The articles that appeared on the website as well as those that were prepared for publication in immigrant newspapers by the RFAHD, also depicted the homophobia of the Russian-speaking immigrants as dangerous and fearful. They presented it as a phenomenon that distinguishes the immigrant media from the secular Hebrew-language newspapers which were depicted as liberal and tolerant. The Israeli media, we read, treats GLBT issues with seriousness and respect. Open and poisonous attacks on sexual minorities, as well as tabloid-style sensationalist materials are no longer possible there. The Russian-language media, on the other hand, is shamelessly violent towards same-sex relations and other expressions of queerness.

The titles of these articles, too, metonymically stick the 'Russian' and the 'homophobic' together. One of Guy's pieces, published on the website, was 'Hating in Russian' mentioned above; another one prepared for *Vesti* was called 'The Russian Lynch, Deliberate and Merciless'. But importantly homophobia is presented as not only an issue of the (Russian-language) media; rather it is narrated as a problem of the whole Russian-speaking community. For example, shortly after Kamyanov's publication and the establishment of the RFAHD, Guy created a new section on the site, dedicated solely to homophobia. This section had an archive of hateful publications that appeared in various Russian-language newspapers in Israel. It also contained links to other materials, such as the above mentioned articles and other homophobia-related materials.

The main page of the *Homophobia* section opened with the following introductory text:

> It would be easy to blame only the journalists and the editors of the Russian newspapers for the total ignorance and die-hard homophobic stereotypes. But let us be honest. Almost the whole community of immigrants from the former Soviet Union is infected with homophobia. In order to confirm this diagnosis it is enough to raise the issue of same-sex love in an on-line discussion forum of Russian-speaking Israelis or in a conversation with our straight compatriots. Homophobic texts published in the Russian-speaking newspapers are only the tip of the iceberg that came from the cold Russian seas, an iceberg named 'hatred' (http://aguda.org/phobia/index.php, saved March 2004).

This introduction emphasises the totality of homophobic hatred as well as its brutality. Paired with the repeated comparison with anti-Semitism and Nazism it creates the feeling of fear, not so much of what is explicit but of what is unseen or is about to come. The text on the 'Homophobia' page warns that the newspaper publications are not only dangerous in themselves, but conceal the whole 'iceberg' of hatred.

Discussing the affective politics of fear, Ahmed (2004) notes that fear often works through displacement between objects, a displacement that can also link these two objects together. She follows Freud's analysis of fear and in particular his analysis of a little boy's phobia of horses (Freud 1926/1964). Freud reads this phobia as a symptom of another profound fear, the fear of castration as the fear of the father. But contrary to Freud's intra-psychic model, Ahmed reads fear as embedded in collective histories. She suggests that 'the sideways movement between objects, which works to stick objects together as a sign of threat, is shaped by multiple histories. The movement between signs does not have its origin in the psyche, but is a trace of how such histories remain alive in the present' (Ahmed 2004: 66).

Ahmed's analysis provides an insight into why the effects of the Gulag ghosts are repeatedly refigured as anti-Semitic/Nazi attacks and why one ghost substitutes the other through fear. The fear of homophobic attacks is also a fear of the haunting violence against homosexuals in the Gulag that becomes a fear of violence against the Jews in the Nazi concentration camps. Imprisonment, humiliation, annihilation – they are 'shaped by multiple histories' (Ahmed 2004: 66) of Stalinist and Nazi terror. 'Objects of fear become substituted for each other over time', notes Ahmed, 'through the sideways movement of fear' (Ahmed 2004: 67). But why is it that the fear of the Holocaust substitutes for the fear of the Gulag?

Elaborating on Fanon's discussion of the Negro as the object of fear for the white child (Fanon 1986), Ahmed points out that turning away from fear is also a turning *towards* the object of love and safety. The white child turns to the mother, and this turn is a 'protective and safe form of enclosure, or a transformation of the world into home' (Ahmed 2004: 68). Refiguring Kamyanov's move to expel them from the nation, the queer immigrants are *turning* to Israel, as a safe home for Jews fleeing anti-Semitism. In the Israeli national ethos, Jewish immigration is constructed precisely as a move to safety from persecutions in the diaspora (Rapoport and Lomsky-Feder 2005). The sideways movement of fear locates the queers within the collective of victims-coming-to-safety.[15] Claiming Jewish victimhood through

15 It is worth remembering here that among the first actions of the RFAHD was to turn to the Israeli media and to Israeli GLBT organisations for help and support: approaching the Israeli establishment in order to seek protection against other Russian-speaking immigrants, is yet another example of turning towards safety.

the idea of similarity, as well as through merging their personal experiences as Jews and as queers, they write their queer sexuality into the nation.

The currency of victimhood in uncanny homes

This chapter followed the uncanny transformation of the queer victim of homophobic violence into the Jewish victim of anti-Semitism and the Holocaust. The queer immigrants shamed the homophobes by calling them 'fascists' whose anti-gay tactics repeat those of the Nazis against the Jews. The straight immigrants were asked to relive their memories of Soviet anti-Semitism to empathise with gays and lesbians, demonised in the immigrant press. Fellow Forum participants were called upon to act against expressions of hatred because ignoring them could lead to fearful consequences, as had happened in Germany.

In my discussion of these RFAHD activities I tried to understand why the anti-homophobic organising, triggered first and foremost by the haunting violence of the Gulag imagery, did not attempt to refigure the links between imprisonment, criminality and sexual subjecthood. I suggested that it may have been because the Shadow by the Latrine was figured as mute, as not possessing an intelligible language in the world of the educated and the respectable. Indeed, as long as claims for rights and recognition are made from the standpoint of intelligentsia's mores and 'high culture', shadows of the Gulag will continue to remain what Gordon calls 'lost subjects of history' (1997: 195) – those whose existence can never be documented or even acknowledged but whose lives (and deaths) haunt the present. The ghosts of the Gulag, in other words, could only figure some queers and some queerness, and it was not the kind of queerness that the RFAHD members longed for.

The desire to belong to both the Russian-speaking intelligentsia and the Jewish national collective, collectives that were constituted precisely through the exclusion of the haunting Gulag past, made the RFAHD members turn away from the Shadow by the Latrine. But this was not a turn away from victimhood, on both a psychic and political level. On the contrary, the injury of homophobia was embraced and politicised, rechannelled through the figure of the Jewish victim. In this refiguration the injury became nationalised, through what Lauren Berlant defines as techniques of trauma and insecurity as a form of claiming the nation, and what Moran and Skeggs describe as cultural capital of claiming belonging through the need of safety (Berlant 2001 in Moran and Skeggs 2004: 8; see also Berlant 1997). The queer immigrants were positioned as being persecuted and injured like the Jews and therefore, in need of recognition *in* a safe home, like the Jews in Israel. Being subjected to violence, and *being able to claim the injury*, was what gave them their path to national belonging, or, at least, created the illusion of such a path.

In this chapter I traced the affective regimes produced by this refiguration of queer victimhood – despair, worry, fear – which now leads me to raise the following questions: What is the political context in which queer victimhood can be refigured as national and what kind of claims does this refiguration make possible? Who is entitled to evoke the ghost of the Jewish victim, and how does this evocation itself perform the entitlement? And, last but not least, does it work?

It is important to remember that the violence of homophobia, legitimised and normalised within the framework of criminal hierarchy and Gulag memories, was given voice and weight through the figure of the Jewish victim, not only because of the suffering of the Jews, but also because of the special place this suffering occupies in the Israeli ethos. Jewish victims of the past, and in particular the victims of the Holocaust, have what Gordon calls a 'seething presence' (Gordon 1997: 8) in today's Israel. While the collective memory and commemoration of the Holocaust is in itself complex and changing (Ochs 2006), Jewish victimhood very often figures as unique suffering, incomparable to any other.[16] Yet, such comparisons are

16 The extensive commemoration of the Holocaust does not contradict the ghostly status of the Jewish victims themselves. For more discussion of the haunting nature of the Holocaust memory, see Agamben (1999); and Levi (1988).

made repeatedly.[17] In the Israeli context claiming that one is persecuted 'just like the Jews under the Nazis' is an extremely loaded move that may or may not work, but is always burdened with intense emotions. Jewish victims haunt the Israeli nation, but are also constantly mobilised and transformed in politics. Discussing their mobilisation in anti-homophobic organising, it is not enough to explore what the evocation of such victimhood does. We must also be attuned to who is seen as having the right to evoke it. For example, the comparison between Jewish-Israeli victims of recent terrorist attacks and the victims of the Holocaust are very common, although, of course, this comparison is also criticised internally (Ochs 2006). At the same time, the critique or the evocation of Holocaust discourse by *Mizrachi* Israelis or by Palestinians is met with anger and objection, guarding, as it seems, both the uniqueness of Jewish suffering and the hegemony of *Ashkenazi* Jews in their use of this suffering.

For the Russian-speaking queers claiming that their injury 'is just like that of the Jews' was mediated by their personal experiences of anti-Semitism, or rather, by the move to personalise it. 'Lets remember how it was to be a Jew in the Soviet Union', for example, positions the speaker as the one who experienced persecution herself.[18] Another example is when Guy, describing how many homophobic publications positioned themselves as an authority on issues of sexuality, wrote: 'This reminded me of a situa-

17 For example, Israeli settlers did not hesitate to use Holocaust imagery during Israel's withdrawal from Gaza in the summer of 2005. They repeatedly claimed that now, after more than 50 years, Jews are *again* being evicted from their homes. They attached orange stars of David to their clothes, reminiscent of the yellow star that Jews were forced to wear during the Nazi period. Some Israelis protested such historical parallels (although many were supportive).This was not because those 'evicted from their homes' lived on stolen land, or controlled and humiliated an entire population; nor because, unlike the Jews in the Nazi Germany, settlers from Gaza were moved to their own country and heavily compensated by the government. The protest mainly came from those who thought that a comparison was disrespectful and abusive of the memory of the Holocaust. For a detailed analysis of the ways Jewish victimhood is used, see Lentin 2004 and Ochs 2006.

18 Such a move also constitutes the speakers – and by association, all of the queer immigrants on whose behalf they speak – as Jewish, regardless of their actual ethnic background.

tion where I, a Soviet Jewish boy, first learned about Israel from the book 'The Poison of Zionism', published by the *Politiizdat*'.[19]

But they – as immigrants whose very arrival is framed within the national ethos of Jews coming to safety – also felt entitled to mobilise the figure of the Jewish victim and by doing so they have also performed their entitlement. It was only through this entitlement, I suggest, that the queer immigrants could counter the moral authority of someone speaking through the horrors of the Gulag.

Reading the queers' evocation of Jewish victimhood one also has to address the question of its effects, and not necessarily in the sense of how their claims were accepted by different audiences. Examining the audience – for example, how were the essays, such as the *Russian Lynch*, accepted by readers, or how many of the letters to the editor were actually published/responded to – is not my aim here, although it would have been an interesting investigation. What interests me here is the effect on the queers themselves. The speech acts of memory produce a counter move to the exclusion of homosexuality from the nation and from the community of Russian-Israeli intelligentsia; the turn from fear towards the nation is supposed to bring the queers back to safety. But does it? In one of the articles published in the *Community* section of the website and later also submitted to *Vesti*, the author noted:

> One could have expected more tolerance from Jews who, similarly to homosexuals, were persecuted during the Nazi regime, had to wear a distinguishing mark on their clothes and were destined for extermination in death camps (Plotkin 2002).

The homophobia of Russian Israelis, repeatedly constructed as an almost essential quality of the Russian-speaking/post-Soviet intelligentsia, is figured here as something *unexpected*, because of the homophobes' Jewishness. Writing about race and colonialism, Kalpana Seshadri-Crooks notes that the uncanny is an encounter with sameness that was not expected, while in fact this sameness was there all along (Seshadri-Crooks 2000).

19 *Politizdat* was the name of the main Soviet publishing house that printed books on political topics. Its publications had to reflect the communist perspective.

Paraphrasing Seshadri-Crooks, one may say that the unexpected intolerance of Jews turned the Israeli home into an uncanny place for the queers. But the uncanny – *unheimlich* – is also un-homely, which, according to Freud, is inseparably linked to the homely, *heimlich*. Freud connects it with repressed infantile complexes, for example, he notes that neurotic men often see female genitals as uncanny:

> This *unheimlich* place, however, is the entrance to the former *Heim* [home] of all human beings, to the place where each one of us dwelt once upon a time and in the beginning. There is a humorous saying: 'Love is home-sickness'; and whenever a man dreams of a place or a country and says to himself, still in the dream: 'this place is familiar to me, I've been here before', we may interpret the place as being his mother's genitals or her body. In this case too, the *unheimlich* is what was once *heimlich*, home-like, familiar; the prefix '*un*' ['un-'] is the token of repression (Freud 1919/1934: 398–399).

Freud's reading presents the uncanny as a sign of the repression – and the haunting return – of the familiar, the mother's womb, the place of origin. He links the individual *heimlich* to that of a country or a nation. Proposing this relation between the homely and the horrifying is insightful; but Freud's reading can – and should, as Gordon (1997) suggests – be extended from the individual to the social;[20] Freud himself links the uncanny to repressed histories and their recurrence through generations (1919/1934). The debates around homophobia and the national home are inseparable from such repressed – and at times, un-figurable – histories, such as the history of same-sex relations in the Gulag (among criminal as well as political prisoners), or the history of other, non-Jewish victims of the Holocaust (for example, gypsies, queers or the disabled), seldom mention in Israel's claims of victimhood.

Homesickness and longing for the nation are manifested through the uncanny; the national home becomes uncanny, haunted by violence that in fact was there all along. What's more, homesickness can occur when someone is *at* home: the queer immigrants in Israel become homesick *for*

20 For an excellent example of such extension in the context of national fears and desires see Fortier's 'Children of Multicultural Britain' in Fortier (2008).

Israel where they discover the violence they thought they had escaped.[21] The uncanny doubleness, then, is a particular form of figuration, where belonging is *simultaneously a* safe space away from violence, and a place where violence is inevitable, or, in Fortier's words, it 'brings the violence of the world we live in *at the heart of home*' (Fortier 2008: 60, emphasis in the original). The uncanny, in other words, illuminates one of the ways in which belonging can work through violence (I discuss some others in the rest of the book); it does not mean ejection and exclusion: one does not turn away from an uncanny home, but is drawn to it, as well as hurt and terrified by it. The 'particular and fraught relationship' (Gopinath 2003: 264) of queer immigrants to multiple national sites is therefore deeply ambivalent;[22] it simultaneously signals the embeddedness of queer presence within nationalism and the impossibility of ever fully belonging to the nation.

21 I thank Anne-Marie Fortier for bringing this to my attention.

22 I return to discuss this ambivalence in further detail in Part III of the book.

PART II

Border Figures

You need the crossing of bodies for the border to become real; otherwise you just have this discursive construction. There is nothing natural about the border; it's a highly constructed place that gets reproduced through the crossing of people, because without the crossing there is no border, right? It's just an imaginary line, a river or it's just a wall.

—Berta Jottar in Biemann, http://www.geobodies.org/video/performing/performtxte.html, accessed May 2006.

I continue my discussion of violence and belonging by looking at ways in which the nation and its borders are figured by immigrants through adoration of some and violation of other queer bodies. The two chapters in this section follow the circulation of these bodies in and out of cyberspace and map the feelings these bodies generate.[1] At the centre of my discussion are the geographical borders of/in/between Israel and Palestine, the borders of identity categories such as 'Jews' and 'Arabs' and 'us' and 'them', and the affective terrains through which these borders materialise.

Berta Jottar, a Mexican artist, scholar and activist who moves through and works in the US–Mexico borderzone, reminds us that borders are performative: we need crossing bodies to make the border real. But such a crossing does not necessarily mean freedom of movement, despite the metaphor of mobility that it embodies.[2] Nor is it necessarily transgressive (of identity categories or of state sovereign powers) despite the fact that 'borderland theory' has been successfully appropriated as a symbol of subversion in the 'post-modern celebration of fragmentation' (Lavie and Swedenburg 1996: 159). Borders are spaces where 'formations of violence are continuously in the making' (Alarcón 1996: 44). Surveillance, minefields, pain, death, loss and clashes of impositions, discussed by scholars of

1 For an excellent analysis of the ways national borders can be felt through – and by – particular bodies see Fortier's discussion of 'feeling states' in Chapter 5 of her *Multicultural Horizons: Diversity and the Limits of the Civil Nation* (2008).

2 Crossing borders is always about both mobility and immobility. What's more, there are many different types of movement embedded in borders.

borderlands,[3] operate in borders both in the realms of identity and cultural formations and in the physicality of the everyday struggle.

In Israel/Palestine everything is about borders: borders of the state of Israel that were never clearly defined; border settlements of the 1950s where newly arrived immigrants from Morocco, Yemen, Algeria and Iraq were forcibly settled in order to provide a living fence for the recently established state and a protection against *mistanenim*[4] – Palestinians trying to return to the homes from which they were expelled during Israel's War of Independence/the Palestinians' *Naqba*;[5] the expansion of Israel's borders in 1967 to the whole West Bank and to the Gaza strip; Jewish settlements behind electronic fences and watch towers;[6] the 'green line', separating the internationally recognised state of Israel from its occupied and illegally settled territories – a line that does not exist on official Israeli maps; checkpoints and road blocks that monitor movement in, out and across the West Bank and Gaza; the Separation Wall, a fantasy of separating 'us' from 'them' made of concrete, a giant prison under the open sky, like Gaza enclosed in its own Separation Fence. Far from 'just a wall'.

Borders are both material and semiotic, and so are the bodies that cross them. But borders are not only about those who move around them: sometimes the borders move around people – when a new roadblock is erected at the entrance to a village; when a wall is built on the farming land; or when the military invades a home. The following two chapters follow three figures that are specifically associated with the borders of Israel/Palestine, and trace their movements. Chapter 3 is built around

3 For the foundational work on borderlands see Anzaldúa 1987; Alarcón 1996; Fusco 1989; Lavie and Swedenburg 1996; also for the discussion of borders and (im)mobility see Luibhéid 2002; Verstraete 2003.

4 Infiltrators (Hebrew), literally 'those who seep through the cracks'.

5 Disaster (Arabic).

6 In his analysis of settlements post the 1993 Oslo agreement, when, contrary to the popular perception, the process of land grabbing in the West Bank and Gaza did not stop, but simply became more sophisticated, Weizman puts forward the concept of 'frontier architecture' (Weizman 2007) where, he suggests, the politics of borders turn into the politics of frontiers, making the possibility of ever establishing the borders of sovereign Palestine practically impossible.

the Soldier and the Terrorist: two figures that map the relations between sexuality, masculinity, nationalism and war. Their figurations mirror each other like a distorted looking glass, but, as I will show, the two figures are also co-dependent, they complement and co-constitute each other. Tracing their presence in several publications and discussions that appeared on the Forum, I address different forms of (im)mobilities across and around borders and their relation to sexuality and belonging, on the Forum and in Israel/Palestine. Here I approach border crossing as a movement in geographical space as well in the terrains of gay modernity, legal subjecthood and queer sexiness. In Chapter 4 I describe Daughter of Palestine, a mysterious figure who appeared on the Forum causing much ado among the participants. Looking into her performance and the responses her appearance caused, I follow various forms of on-line passing and outing. Here I address border as movement across terrains of sexuality, identity, speakability and humanness.

The two types of movement are of course closely related, and together operate in the figuration of the border and its material, semiotic and psychic effects in and beyond cyberspace. The refusal to let someone pass at a checkpoint, for example, reverberates in the mobilisation to 'out' someone who is passing on-line; adoration of those who protect the national borders by killing the trespassers transforms into the protection of cyberspace from those whose politics disturb the consensus. I address the complex relations between these movements, following reflections, distortions and transformations of the three figures. The border itself, as I will show, always comes into being through violent encounters between those who cross it and those who are assigned – and/or feel entitled – to protect it. In these encounters the nation and its borders become a form of 'spatial-affective aspiration' (Hage 2000: 42):[7] they are figured through affective regimes of love, hate, suspicion, pain and sexual desires. The encounters, described in the two following chapters, indicate the centrality of national and racial

7 In his *White Nation* Hage (2000) explores practices of nation that include the national space; the image of the 'nationalist manager' who not only belongs him/herself, but also feels privileged in relation to the nation and entitled to guard it; and the ethnic/racial other as an object to be managed within this space.

borders in queer immigrants' claims for belonging as Israelis and point to the great deal of violence – both physical and imagined – that goes into securing and maintaining them.

By drawing the attention to the role of violence in the formation of borders, I also raise the question of the *sexiness* of national and military violence and the ways it can appear tempting and promising to the immigrants. I look at the ways queer immigrants *become* Israelis through the embrace of, or fantasies about, torture, pain and violation of those who are constituted as 'the enemy' – the Palestinians. I argue that it is important but not enough to focus on the general complicity of queerness within nationalism and racism (Puar 2005, 2007) – in itself a necessary and urgent task. Rather, I demonstrate that violence can carry a particular promising path of belonging for those who are positioned as 'white but not quite' – as this is the case of Russian-speaking Jewish newcomers who are constituted as almost, but not quite Jewish; almost, but not quite European and Western; almost, but not quite Israelis (yet).[8]

8 In that respect, my argument resonates with Cynthia Nevels' *Lynching to Belong: Claiming Whiteness through Racial Violence* (2007). Nevels looks at three groups of immigrants in the American South, Italians, Irish and Bohemians, and shows how they resolved their position of racial ambiguity – as neither white nor black – through taking advantage of or directly participating in lynching, 'claiming whiteness with a vengeance' (2007: 7). There are of course many fundamental differences between Nevels' and my material, both in terms of political context and in terms of the types of violence discussed. Nevertheless, both our works points to the cultural and political capital of violence precisely for marginalised and racially ambiguous subjects. My analysis, limited here to the queer immigrants, has, I believe, a broader relevance for understanding phenomena such as growing patriotism and right-wing politics of the Russian-speaking immigrants in the last two decades since arrival in Israel.

CHAPTER 3

The Soldier and the Terrorist

An Israeli soldier praised for killing terrorists in their homes, and adored as a gay prince charming; a Palestinian gay man called either a lying terrorist or a cute Arab boy with an almond ass; an Abu-Ghraib prisoner, whose naked body pornographically mediated and distributed by the media, generates a fantasy of the homosexual rape of all Arabs in-the-name-of-Israeli-security. These images appeared on the queer immigrants' website during 2001–2004, the years of the second Palestinian *Intifada* and raging Israeli warfare, severe control over the civilian Palestinian population, checkpoints, segregated roads and the 'Separation Wall', the years in the aftermath of 9–11 and the US 'war on terror'. Some of these images were mentioned in passing, other discussed at length; some were part of the website's permanent publications, others surfaced in the Forum discussions, but all of them were part of the figurations of the Soldier and the Terrorist. These two figures, as this chapter will demonstrate, condense the ways in which sexuality and nationalism are intertwined through violence, where violence itself can function as a practice of queerness, a technology of belonging, a sign of national entitlement *and* a promise of a home.

The figures of the Soldier and the Terrorist that are at the centre of this chapter, both have a synecdochic relationship to the nation. In Israeli ethos IDF – Israeli defence forces – is a people's army, and the soldier stands for the whole nation. In the same ethos the Arab is always the enemy (or rather, the Arab is simultaneously the other of Israeli nationhood, the synecdoche of the Palestinian nation *and* a sign of the Arabic and Muslim threat that 'surrounds' Israel all throughout the Middle East). Since the establishment of Israel and the Palestinian resistance that followed, but more so since the appearance of the Palestinian Liberation Organisation (PLO) in 1964 and in particular in the recent years of the Second *Intifada*, 'the Arab' for most Jewish Israelis equals 'the terrorist'.[1] But the two figures do not simply tie sexuality and the nation. They mirror each other by demonstrating the central role of queer masculinities in the formations of nationalism and war.

Feminist scholarship has long been interested in the ways women's bodies come to represent nations and mark symbolic boundaries of national and ethnic collectives (Anthias and Yuval-Davis 1989; Kandiyoti 1994; Mayer 2000b; Mookherjee 2003; Yuval-Davis 1997). Later works on gender and nation further suggested that nationalisms constitute and are constituted not only by particular femininities but also by particular masculinities (Derné 2000; Mayer 2000a; Mookherjee 2004; Mostov 2000; Sasson-Levy 2003; Žarkov 2001); these femininities and masculinities, however, were mostly conceptualised as heterosexual. Some scholars, in turn, raised the importance of queer sexuality in examining nations and nationalism (Berlant 1997; Puri 2004). 'Queer' in these theories was used to designate non-normative bodies, sexualities and identities that are by definition subversive and dissenting; while 'queering' was often seen as a transgressive practise of denaturalising and challenging the heterosexual order.

Analysis of the relationship between queer sexuality and the nation has predominantly focused on the ways in which gays, lesbians, bisexuals and transgenders were excluded from citizenship, national belonging and/or mobility across national borders (Alexander 1994; Luibhéid 2002; Puri 2004); or on the ways they could queer the nation, for example through various practices of citizenship such as marriage, military service, or consumption (Bell and Binnie 2002; Berlant 1997; Cooper 1995, 2002; Gross 2000; Richardson 1998, 2000).[2] Theoretical debates on these new forms of sexual citizenship mostly focused on whether – and to what extent – queer-

1 This construction has not changed but was definitely intensified and refigured as global after the 9–11 bombings. On the relationship between the US 'war on terror' and Israeli warfare in Palestine see Gregory (2004a). On the relationship between American and Israeli 'exceptionalism' in the context of 'war on terror' and national security see Puar (2007).

2 The Pride Parade, discussed in the previous chapters, can be read as another practise of citizenship.

ing the nation is transgressive or mainstreaming.[3] These debates, however, rarely accounted for the queer sexiness, violence and hatred embedded in nationalism – in particular, if it is a nation in the midst of an inter-ethnic conflict, colonial struggle or war. Recent work on critical queer studies positions these very issues at the centre of their analysis. 'A renewed queer studies', as Eng, Halberstam and Muñoz write in their 'What's queer about queer studies now?', insists on a broader consideration of the late twentieth-century global crises that have configured historical relations among political economies, the geopolitics of war and terror, and national manifestations of sexual, racial and gendered hierarchies (Eng et al. 2005: 1).

Puar in her discussion of queer terrorist corporealities further suggests that today's accounts of queerness should move away from queerness as identity and 'queering' as a transgressive practice and instead 'underscore [its] contingency and complicity with dominant formations' (Puar 2005: 121–122). My discussion of the Soldier and the Terrorist as two figures that are always intertwined, follows precisely this call. Looking at their complex figurations that merge queer immigrants' sentimentality, right-wing nationalism and anti-Arab hatred, I want to map the relationship between violence and queerness, hatred and belonging, contested borders of, and 'homecoming' to, the nation.

One of my aims here is to unpack and challenge the normalisation of militarism and warring masculinities among many Jewish-Israeli queers who embrace the army once it is potentially queered by the presence of same-sex desires;[4] my writing also works against the discourse of security and 'war on terror' that produces gay patriots versus beastly terrorists and 'us' versus 'them'. Yet I also want to offer a more complicated analysis of queer

3 Richardson (2000), for example, points out that UK debates about gay marriage 'buy into' the dominant discourse of rights, and create a new regime of sexuality. Berlant (1997), on the other hand, shows how the nation can be creatively transgressed by the queer subject.

4 Such an embrace is of course always mediated by gender and race, as Kadish (2001) shows in her discussion of Israeli lesbians, and as Yosef (2004) notes with relation to *Mizrachi* gay men. For a detailed discussion of normalising Israeli militarism through queerness see Gross (2000), Yosef (2005) and Walzer (2000).

immigrants' nationalism that takes into account both the sexualisation of violence *and* the location of the one who does the sexualising. What kind of bodies are mobilised to constitute the Russian-speaking 'homecomers'' sense of belonging, and how are they mobilised? How are Israeli and US discourses of defence and the 'war on terror' interpreted and taken on by the Russian-speaking queers? What is the role of the Israeli GLBT movement in immigrant's positioning as sexual and national subjects? And lastly, what kind of promise does the national and military violence carry for the immigrants?

Arrival 1

Julie Mostov in her work on former Yugoslavia notes 'the seductive force of national mythology for men' (Mostov 2000: 102) by showing how the politics of national identity eroticises the nation by representing it in sensual female images. Many other feminist scholars note that nations are often imagined as female bodies that can be erotically desired, nourished, protected, fertilised and penetrated. Specifically, post-colonial theorising of nationalism and settlement shows the centrality of sexualised imagery and desire for colonial projects. Anne McClintock, for example, points out that the European colonial enterprise imagined distant lands as (erotically) possessed by the colonial pioneers (McClintock 1995). Raz Yosef (2002) similarly emphasises that the notion of 'virgin lands to be penetrated' is central in the early Zionist imagery. Reflecting on Edward Said's (1979) idea that 'Eastern land is feminised and represented as available for the European man' (2002: 557), Yosef suggests that the feminised is not necessarily feminine, and that in early Zionist cinema Jewish settlement was often imagined through sexual encounters with homo-passive, feminised Arab men.

But what if the journey to the colonised land is imagined not (only) through subordination and feminisation of the colonised but (also) through homoerotic adoration of the colonisers? I begin my discussion with a narrative of Jewish immigration to Israel as a gay fantasy in which the sexy masculinity of the colonisers – Jewish-Israeli men and later, more specifically, soldiers – comes to constitute the nation. Rapoport and Lomsky-Feder in their analysis of immigration and Israeli nationalism note the seductive force of national homecoming (Rapoport and Lomsky-Feder 2005). But how is homecoming sexualised? What are the colonial desires of queer newcomers when they dream about sexy Israelis?

> 'Oh how many wonderful discoveries'
> Israeli men. Who could have thought that in such a small country one could meet an endless variety of faces, types and temperaments. The appearance and manners of Israelis sometimes differ so much that it seems that they are residents of different planets. For many of us this was our main discovery in the Holy Land. Blond and dark, bright, tall, suntanned, blood and milk.[5] Tough and rough *kibbutzniks* and swinging night-clubbers. Soldiers, who overcome the hardship of the army life with humour and courage, and successful yuppies. Popular top-models and restless travellers who have visited half of the world with a backpack. Obstinate youngsters who refuse authority and break all the rules; and the mature Jewish 'machos' who have passed through fire, water and glory. Delicate youth with a classic European education from prestigious neighborhoods of North Tel Aviv; and loud, temperamental Mediterraneans. *Sabras*[6] and newcomers. Straight and gay. 'Blonde imps' whose parents came from Germany and Poland and the tanned offspring of immigrants from Yemen and North Africa.
> Look closely at these faces, pay attention to these bodies, tanned under the hot Middle-Eastern sun. And you will understand what makes our hearts throb. What makes us hurry at night to a date hoping to meet another Prince. In the gallery of 'Israel Beauty' you will see Israeli Man through our eyes.
> (http://www.aguda.org/gallery/, saved March 2004)

This poetical adoration of Israeli men is the opening of the on-line gallery, which was part of the non-interactive section of the queer immigrants' website.[7] The gallery, tellingly entitled 'Israel Beauty' (see Figure 4),

5 'Blood and milk' is a Russian colloquialism describing the beauty, physical strength and heroism of young warriors.

6 Israeli-born Jews.

7 All of the non-interactive sections of the website discussed in this book, were published between 2001 and 2004 although the exact dates of their publication were not always

positions the Russian-speaking immigrants as thrilled gay voyeurs, and constructs their immigration as a journey of erotic discoveries, attractions, hopes and promises. The narrative of immigration to Israel as discovery and hope (and implicitly also transformation – once the 'Prince' is met) resonates with the way Jewish repatriation to Israel is constructed in the Israeli ethos as, at the same time, a journey of homecoming to the land, hope for Jews as a nation, and a process of individual (moral, spiritual) transformation (Golden 2002; Rapoport and Lomsky-Feder 2005). Jewish immigration to Israel, called in Hebrew *Aliya* ('ascent'), merges one's personal journey with the hope for national future.

The national aspects of immigration to the Holy Land of wonderful discoveries at first seems to be absent from the narrative of gay excitement. Israel is described first and foremost as the land of attractive men. Yet I would like to suggest that the connection between the national and the sexual is figured here through metonymic substitution: the journey of nationalised immigration becomes the journey of erotic possibilities. Tellingly, all the men described in the opening are Jewish. The mixture of ethnic backgrounds, life-styles, ages and geographical locations described in the gallery figures the Jewish-Israeli collective as a multi-faceted and multicultural, colourful society. It does so by conjuring up many (stereotyped) faces of Israeliness – *kibbutzniks*,[8] soldiers, backpack travellers[9] – and by presenting the class and ethnic make-up in a form of a pick-and-choose diversity. Such figuration of Israel's 'diversity' is in itself a technology of deracination (Castañeda 2002), where internal colonisation (Shohat 1997), racism, and class and ethnic formations become a display for multiple sexual choices and tastes, a display, emptied of histories, tensions and conflicts. But this diversity, importantly, also conceals Israeli exclusionary politics in which non-Jewish residents (such as migrant workers from Asia, Africa and Eastern Europe) often become invisible; and Palestinians – both Israeli

available; they remained on-line until 2006 when they were archived and later removed from the site altogether.

8 People living in or coming from a *kibbutz* – a collective community, traditionally agricultural and sharing means of production and other possessions.

9 Many young Israelis take a 'gap year' after completing their compulsory military service, and go as backpack travellers to the Far East, South East Asia or Latin America.

citizens and residents of the Palestinian Authority – are usually defined as hostile outsiders or as enemies from within.

In the metonymic link between sexual attraction and national homecoming, gay subjecthood is figured as Israeli *and* Jewish. As recent arrivals, struggling to define their place in Israeli society, Russian-speaking queers in this poetic text imagine their belonging through sexuality: the conjunction of Jewishness, the land, the politics of immigration and erotic beauty makes sexy Israeli men synecdoches for the nation itself. Attraction towards the nation and its men becomes one, and the immigrants become Israelis through homosexual fantasies. The reactions of the immigrants towards Jewish-Israeli men, narrated in the gallery opening, are radically different to the way Palestinians and Arabs are presented on the site. The latter are tellingly absent in narrations of Israel as place, country and society; and if/when mentioned they are usually referred to as terrorists. In some of the discussions they also appear as patriarchal, heteronormative and homophobic. Heterosexualising Palestinians and queering Israel work in tandem to mark 'Palestinian gays' as unimaginable subjects. On the only occasion in my ethnography (discussed below) when such a subject was mentioned, his arrival was seen as a threat, both political and ontological. He was immediately and passionately refigured by the Forum participants as a terrorist through suspicion, hostility and hatred as well as through mobilisation of orientalist 'knowledge' of 'the Arabs'.

Arrival 2

In March 2003 a leading Israeli newspaper *Haaretz* published an article on Palestinian gay men hiding in Israel, fearing persecution at home. They were about to be deported, and the Israeli Association of GLBTs was appealing on their behalf, trying to prevent the deportation.[10] The

10 The mobilisation of the Association on behalf of the Palestinians is both admirable and not unproblematic, however it is not my aim to analyse their politics here. For an excellent

article, entitled 'Gays? Palestinians? Who Cares!', described in detail the dangers and suffering of one young man who ran away from his family in Gaza, and after hiding in the West Bank and in Arab villages in Israel, arrived in Tel-Aviv seeking support from the Association. From the point of view of Israel his stay was illegal[11] and any encounter with the Israeli police brought the threat of deportation. Until recently, the article noted, the Association was able to issue special papers that Palestinian gays could show the Israeli police in case of arrest. Due to the changes in policy these documents were no longer accepted. The Association has been fighting the decision to deport several gay men back to the Palestinian authority, while the police, the security services and the Ministry of Internal Affairs have insisted on their deportation.

The translation of this article into Russian soon appeared on the website. Titled 'Deported to Execution', it was published in the *Community* section which was dedicated to the Israeli queer community. The translation was illustrated by a photograph of a Palestinian boy in front of political graffiti (see Figure 5). The visual technology of sexing/nationalising, deployed here, contrasted radically to the way Israeli men were depicted in the gallery. There they were shown mostly in close-ups, focusing on faces and/or torsos thus emphasising their personhood and/or sexual attractiveness. At times displaying homoerotic affection, and at times looking seductively at the camera, they were always at the centre of the picture. Positioned as synecdoches of the nation – they were it's 'beauty' – they were never reduced to their national location. Here, on the contrary, a small body almost disappears in the background of the Palestinian national flag. The faceless figure of a little boy reflects the opening of the article:

---

critique of the ways Israeli queer activists orientalise Palestinian queers and depict them as either victims to be saved from their own society or as impossible subjects, forever 'locked' in their culture and religion and essentially incapable of moving into 'real' Western gayness, see Ritchie (forthcoming). Importantly, Ritchie also gives voice to the experiences of the Palestinian queers themselves, including their own view and experience of Israeli racist politics.

11 Palestinians from the West Bank and Gaza need special permits in order to enter Israel. The issuing of permits is based on a complex bureaucratic system that serves as yet another form of colonial control (Kirstein Keshet 2006).

> When the first Intifada broke out, T [the man described in the article] started school. Together with his classmates he hung out in front of foreign journalist's cameras, showing them with pleasure two V-shaped fingers.[12] What could there possibly be in common between him and the Jewish state? (http://aguda.org/community/pales/php, saved March 2004).

The original Hebrew article (Levi-Barzilai 2003) is ambivalent in its depiction of the Palestinian gay man. On one hand, it frames his story within the Palestinian national struggle, resistance to Israel and antagonism towards the Jews. The article provides a detailed description of Israeli security concerns that inform the decision to deport this – and any other – Palestinian man. On the other hand, the journalist is clearly sympathetic towards the man; and also gives voice to the Israeli GLBT Association that fights the deportation and condemns the cruel policy regarding gay asylum seekers (but not regarding all other Palestinians!).

The opinions of the Russian-speaking immigrants, visiting the website, were not as sympathetic. In the discussion of this article that took place on the Forum shortly after the translation was published, they did not express any support for or consideration towards the Palestinian man. 'This country is run by stupid thieves', wrote one participant, Will. 'Here they have such a great case that can be used in propaganda against the [Palestinian] Authority, but instead they just f*ck[13] around'. In the unfolding discussion Will and others pointed out that the fact of anti-gay persecution in the Palestinian Authority could work to Israel's political benefit. Rather than addressing the gay man himself, they discussed what the state should have done with him, in order to serve national interests. 'The Ministry should not deport him', proposed another person, Pavel, 'but not out of mercy but rather in order to use him as a "bargaining card" in the ideological warfare against the enemy'. It is not clear what kind of 'bargaining card' Pavel refers to, yet his suggestion clearly reflects the discourse of calculations often used to discuss Israeli policy in which Palestinian prisoners, territory and resources are used as bargaining tools in political negotiations.

12 A sign of Palestinian resistance.

13 My translation maintains the self-censorship of the original spelling.

Some participants specifically addressed the man as first and foremost a terrorist, actual or potential:

> <Serno>: I of course feel sorry for gays, and for Palestinian gays, too. On the other hand, one can understand the Israeli side, too. If they [Palestinian gays] were not caught 'in action', some of them would have been *shahids*[14] or *Hamas*[15] members.

Serno was confronted by another participant, Alex, who asked: 'Why do you immediately link the two topics, Arab terrorists and Arab gays?' 'Alex, the two can not *not* be connected', responded Pavel, and continued:

> <Pavel>: And what if he pretends to be gay? And what if his family or his lover in Gaza or Nablus is caught and he is 'offered' to ransom [them] in blood (mainly ours)?

Pavel evoked two different scenarios of the Palestinian man's assumed reasons for being in Israel. In both he is constructed as hostile and dangerous, as a terrorist-rather-than-gay or as a terrorist-because-gay. According to the first scenario, he pretended to be gay in order to enter Israel. This scenario repeats the paranoid Israeli narrative of Palestinian terrorists who claim to be labourers or sick people who come to Israel seeking work or medical care. In the second scenario the man is seen as possibly involved in same-sex relations; in which case, given the assumed homophobia of the Palestinian society (as it is narrated in the article), he is forced into becoming a terrorist in order to ransom his family's shame. The second scenario resonates with a response posted by another participant, Gabriel:

> <Gabriel>: What Pavel says makes sense. We of course should not make generalisations. But it is a well known fact that there were several women-*shahids* who decided to become suicide bombers in order to save the family's honour, for example, in the case of adultery or out-of-wedlock birth etc. It is very possible that a Palestinian gay 'caught in action' could do the same. On the other hand if the General Security Service checked these people and they have been in Israel for a long time it is cruel to throw them out to certain death.

14 Martyrs, Arabic.
15 Palestinian militant party.

Gabriel's caution against generalisations, as well as his opposition to cruel deportation – if the man is approved by the security service – seems to differ from Pavel and Will's cold calculations coupled with hostility towards all Palestinians. Yet the two positions have more in common than it first seems. Both act as a form of virtual checkpoint (Ritchie, forthcoming)[16] that blocks the arrival – physical or imagined – of the Palestinian queers. Both speak from within the Israeli collective, as those who not only belong but have the privilege and the entitlement to decide the fate and to 'manage' the life of the other (Hage 2000). Both, importantly, take the position of knowledge and expertise, the knowledge of who the gay Palestinian 'really' is, or of the reasons why women become suicide bombers. After a sexualised outburst of hatred (which I discuss below) Will posted a long intellectualising message in which, citing Freud and Olga Fredenberg (famous Russian theorist of mythology and the collective unconscious), he declared Islam as a *Thanatos*, the deadly drive that destroys world civilisation.

This position of 'knowledge' has many national and international links: to Israeli warfare narrated through the colonial knowledge of 'the Arab'; to Israel's imperial big brother, the US (Gregory 2004a), whose military strategists in the Middle East used among other sources an anthropological study 'The Arab Mind' (Puar 2005); to the Israeli journalist speaking knowledgably about 'Muslim sexuality'[17] in the article about persecuted Palestinian gays in Gaza.[18] Importantly, some of the participants, like Will and Pavel, locate themselves as *more* knowledgeable than the GLBT Association and the Israeli authorities and security service: they recommend

16 In his poignant analysis of Palestinian queers in Israel Ritchie (forthcoming) suggests that the main metaphor that structures their lives and experiences is not that of the closet but that of the checkpoint, where the Israeli queers constantly inspect the Palestinians – their lives, bodies, and selves – deciding who is allowed into Israeli/Western queerness, when and how.

17 Her own 'knowledge' is most probably shaped by the information and analysis provided by the Israeli human rights activist Shaul Gonen, who acts on behalf of the Palestinian gay refugees and is extensively cited in the article. For an excellent analysis of Gonen's – and other Israeli queer activists' – orientalist 'knowledge' and 'expertise' see Ritchie (forthcoming).

18 The similar stance can be found in media discussions of Abu-Ghraib, see Puar (2005).

what should have been done with the gay man and criticise the handling of the case. They take the position of the 'nationalist manager' (Hage 2000: 42): the one who cares more and knows better, and is entitled to criticise Israeli policy for not caring enough about national interests, or rather, not having a broad enough strategy to defend them.

In that sense, their stance of orientalist 'knowledge' and of wannabe policy-advisers within and without the GLBT community, also resonates with the Islamophobic discourses of the Russian-speaking immigrant media and literature. Dmitrij Shumsky in his reading of the discursive practices of the immigrant elite locates the cultural origins of their racism in a 'Janus-faced' Russian orientalism (Shumsky 2004, 2005). Using Said's (1979) theory of orientalism, Shumsky points out the historically ambivalent position of Russia as 'oriental' in the eyes of the West, and 'Western' and orientalising towards its own others in the East. On their arrival in Israel, Russian immigrants are marginalised by Israeli society, and in order to negotiate their place in the Israeli social hierarchy, immigrant intellectuals employ an orientalist perspective towards Arabs and Jews of Eastern origin. Their orientalism locates them within the Jewish-*Ashkenazi* elite. An anti-Arab and anti-Muslim stand, frequently displayed in Russian-Israeli media and literature, also links the immigrants to the globalised West fighting the evil of Muslim terrorism. Discursive practices of immigrant intellectuals mark their ambivalent position as a Russian-speaking elite vis-à-vis the Israeli centre: their orientalism links them to Israeli hegemonic identity as Western, *Ashkenazi* and Euro-centric. At the same time they do not make an alliance with the *Ashkenazi* Israeli elite, on the contrary, some of the Russian-speaking intellectuals see their orientalism as a challenge to the Israeli establishment, and as a sign of their differentiated and separatist identity that is marginalised and yet morally and politically superior (Shumky 2005). In a study of Russian-speaking university students and orientalism, Lomsky-Feder et al. (2005) further emphasise that immigrants are not passive bearers of cultural discourses but active agents in cultural and political encounters. They suggest that immigrants can combine, deconstruct and navigate the orientalist and racist discourses of both Russia and Israel, and use them strategically in their performance of homecoming (see also Rapoport and Lomsky-Feder 2005).

The orientalism of the queers indeed can be seen as performance of homecoming, national, ethnic, classed and sexual. In figuring the Palestinian gays as terrorists, the participants of the Forum – Will, Pavel and Gabriel (and some others) – navigate virtuously between Russian intellectualism, Israeli politics and visions of 'the civilised world' fighting against terror. They claim their place within the Russian-speaking community of immigrants constituted here through intellectualising.[19] They also perform their entitlement to the country through 'nationalist management' (Hage 2000) of the Palestinian other both in the queer spaces and in the space of the nation as a whole, thus effectively merging the two. And lastly, they map the 'civilisation' as Western and anti-Islamic by necessity, thus refiguring the state's anti-Palestinian violence as defence, and their own Islamophobic hatred as love, care and expertise. The participants' knowledgeable self-positioning as queers (who know about sexuality), as Israelis (who know about Arabs and Muslims) and as Russian-speaking 'civilised intellectuals' (who know about culture), makes queer anti-Arab hatred invaluable capital in the national and global economy of Western superiority and the 'war on terror'.

Guarding the border 1

The two stories of gay arrival – of an excited repatriate and of a fleeing refugee – mirror each other in the trajectory of their movement across national and sexual borders. Yet the mirror linking the two stories is Alice's looking glass: the two are figured in relation to each other through reversals. Jewish

19 Paradoxically, they align themselves to the orientalist discourse of the Russian-speaking cultural elite which is not only vocally racist and nationalist, but also fiercely homophobic, as I have demonstrated in Chapter 1. Tellingly, the same rhetorical, discursive and affective technologies used by immigrants' literature and media to figure the Palestinians outside of the domains of both civilisation and humanness, are often deployed against queers. I will return to discuss the links between the two in the concluding chapter of the book.

newcomers arrive to a national and sexual home, but Palestinian men are refused refuge. These reversals as a 'practice of figuration' (Haraway 1997: 9) also operate through the affective presence of soldiers and terrorists in on-line texts and images: the former, as I demonstrate below, become the object of love, while the latter generate hatred. Ahmed in her discussion of the politics of emotions notes that narratives of hate can work through conversion: 'hate is renamed as love, a renaming that "conceals" the ambivalence that it exercises (we love rather than hate)' (Ahmed 2004: 123). This conversion, I would like to suggest, also constitutes the border through the encounter of the two figures: the loved and the hated. I want to return to the images of 'Israel beauty' to look more closely at the expressions of immigrants' love for the nation and the way it works through both loveable Israelis and hated Arabs.

Among the twenty-two albums of the 'Israel beauty' gallery described at the beginning of this chapter, the topic of the Israeli army is the most popular. While most thematic albums appear once, and one appears twice, the Army theme has four albums.

> Unbeatable and legendary Israeli Defence Forces! We love you not only because you protect our borders and 'waste' terrorists in the latrines. We love you first of all because your soldiers are the most attractive and charming, the most courageous and beautiful. Israel is indeed a great place for fans of uniform (http://www.aguda.org/gallery/index.php, saved March 2004).

This is the opening that accompanies the first three albums of 'The Israeli Army' photographs. Repeating the theme of erotic excitement that appears in the introduction to the gallery, this text describes the immigrant's love for the Israeli Army: hatred of Arabs is transformed into the protection of borders and the killing of terrorists.

The images and the text work together in the figuration of soldiers as eroticised, merging sexual and national feelings. Patriotic feelings of love and hate are also framed within the queer discourse of the army as masquerade, and of uniform as sexual fetish, making Israel and its 'civil militarism' (Kimerling 1993) – militarism as a taken for granted framework and as a collective state of mind – a 'great place' for queer sexual play. In this short declaration of immigrants' feelings, the figuration of the Soldier links together not only love and hate, but also politics and play, state terror and physical beauty, brutality and poetics. The photographs themselves (see Figure 6) simultaneously evoke erotic invitation, homosocial collectivity and tough masculinity in action. These images seem to carry a promise: of masculinity, of brotherhood, of the Jewish nation.

Adoration of military masculinity is not unique to Russian-speaking immigrants or to the Israeli context. As Mosse (1985) points out, the cult of warrior masculinity and the obsession with the male muscular body characterised many political regimes, from Rome to Nazi Germany and post-revolutionary Russia of 1920s–1930s; it was not only homosocial but also explicitly homoerotic. The figure of the Soldier as a gay icon should however be examined within the specific context of the Zionist-Israeli national project. As several scholars of Israeli nationalism have shown, this project is historically intertwined with the construction of the 'new Jew – the muscle Jew' (Boyarin 1997; Mayer 2000a; Kadish 2001). This construction goes back to the 19th century European anti-Semitic discourse of Jewish men as weak and effeminate, the discourse that influenced 19th century Zionist writers (Glusman 1997). They linked 'weak' masculinity to the weakness of the Jewish people living away from the (national) land; and envisioned that settlement in Palestine and working the land would recover both the Jewish body and the national spirit (Mayer 2000a). The new Jew – a muscular warrior and a rough macho – has since then became a national symbol, embodying the racialised dream of superiority over his Arab enemy and his Jewish others: the effeminate Jew of the European Diaspora as well as the racialised *Mizrachi* Jew from North Africa or the Middle East (Yosef 2004).

The sexuality of the Jewish warrior has been at the centre of queer readings of Zionism and Israeli masculinity. Michael Glusman, for example, suggests that the Zionist dream of the nation-state in Palestine was not only about national and gendered redemption but also about (hetero) sexual redemption from the effeminacy of the Diaspora Jew (Glusman 1997). The constitution of the 'new Jew' in a healthy, muscular – and heterosexual – body was inseparable from the desire to be able not only to defend the nation but also to reproduce it.

The anxieties about effeminising and its link to homosexuality might suggest that Israeli militarism is always necessarily heterosexual, and that gays are excluded from national identity and citizenship. The research on Israeli queer identities and culture, however, shows that not only that gays (and lesbians) are allowed – and indeed serve – in the military, but that the Soldier often serves as both an ideal to look up to *and* an object of queer desires. For example, most Israeli gay men adopt and/or subvert the figure of the Soldier, but rarely reject it. Recent films by Israeli gay film-maker Eitan Fox, widely and excitedly accepted by many gays and lesbians (Yosef 2005) address the Israeli Defence Forces as a site where gay men can prove their national belonging, and at the same time challenge the exclusive heteronormativity of the army experience. Similarly, Ruti Kadish in her ethnography of the Israeli GLBT community points out that the warrior/soldier always remains a point of reference in negotiating sexual citizenship and nationhood for gay men (2001).[20] In her discussion of the community's identity politics she cites an essay published in the nationwide free distribution GLBT newspaper: 'Let's prove that we, too, can serve in *Golani* [elite infantry/combat unit] and shoot Arabs between the eyes' (Kener in Kadish 2001: 17). The author of the essay proudly emphasises the participation of gay men in violent military acts towards Palestinians as a proof of their national loyalty. Shooting Arabs between the eyes becomes a promise of national masculinity unthreatened by effeminising; at the same time it figures as a guarantee of gay men's citizenship. For queer immigrants, it seems, military violence carries a particularly tempting promise of belonging through masculinity and homonationalism (Michaeli 2004; Puar 2007); the body of the sexy Soldier becomes a ground from which they can claim their belonging as both immigrants and queers.

But the adoration of Israeli soldiers by the queer immigrants does not simply reproduce the figurations of normalised violence that constitute Israeli queer militarism. Rather, the Soldier is refigured as both a site of national and immigrant sentimentality, merging Israeli topography with

20 Kadish also notes that many Israeli lesbians follow the national ideal of female citizenship-as-motherhood.

Russian and Soviet imagery, evoking very particular associations among Post-Soviet readers. 'Protecting our borders', for example, is a common expression that was used in Soviet patriotic pathos to describe border police who guarded the sleep of Soviet citizens day and night. Exercising violence against 'terrorists' is also linked to another context: that of the violence and abuse inside the Russian/Soviet military and criminal system.[21] As discussed in Chapter 1, the latrine in Russian and Soviet criminal culture is symbolically association with humiliation, beating and sometimes also homosexual rape. To 'waste someone in latrines' is an expression that originates from criminal slang and refers to the brutal and humiliating killings often perpetrated by gangs. Importantly, 'wasting in the latrines' also means killing someone in his own home/territory, or killing on the spot. In the context of Israeli warfare this trope includes frequent military raids on Palestinian homes, 'searching for terrorists' often bringing death and destruction; and also to the so called 'targeted killings' – Israeli extra-judicial executions of Palestinian military leaders in the West Bank and Gaza.

The declaration of love for the nation is repeated in three photo albums. In the forth album another text is introduced:

> We continue the army theme in our gallery of Israel Beauty. Today, in these April days of 2002, more now than ever ... Soldiers of the Israel Defence Forces protect our homeland from the enemy. Young beautiful lads risk their lives so that we can sit in cafés, dance in night clubs, ride buses and walk on the streets of Israeli cities without fear of terrorists.
>
> Oh mean war, what have you done!
> Our streets have emptied and became still
> Our boys raised their heads
> Adults before their time
> Lingered a few minutes in the doorway
> And left, soldier after soldier ...
> Good bye, dear boys! Dear boys
> Come back, if only you can.

21 On the phenomenon of *dedovschina* (hazing) in the Soviet army, see, for example, Belanovsky and Marzeeva (1991) and Olejnik (2003). On sexual violence in prisons see Healey (2001).

No, don't you hide, be brave
Don't spare the bullets and grenades
Have no mercy on yourselves, but still
Try to return.
(http://www.aguda.org/gallery/army4.php, saved March 2004)

The types of photographs displayed here are similar to the three other albums. The textual framing, on the contrary, shifts from soldiers as courageous perpetrators to soldiers as victims of a war that was imposed on them. In the previous text the queer narrator (and his assumed readers) referred to military actions that took place 'out there', in terrorists' homes. Here the narrator(s) and their audience are themselves described as being under threat. Their own homeland is in danger. The short and dramatic text induces patriotic sentimentality through complex rhetorical technologies: by using the language of public speeches tied to significant events ('in these April days of 2002');[22] by repetitive evocation of collectivity (we, ours); and by metonymic shifting of times and places. The poem used here is part of a famous song by a well-known Soviet bard Bulat Okudzhava. The song describes young Russian soldiers who perished in the Second World War, or the Great Patriotic War, as it was called in the Soviet Union. In line with Soviet patriotic narratives, the poem emphasises the youth and vulnerability of the soldiers (many men concealed their real age and left for the front before they turned 18), together with their bravery.

The figuration of 'us' in 'Israeli Army-4' works though a complex metonymic sticking (Ahmed 2004) and transformations. The 'we' of the queer narrator(s) of the website ('we continue the army theme') transforms into the 'we' of Israelis in cafés, buses and night clubs – loci of frequent suicide bombings and symbols of endangered Israeli civilians; and into the 'we'

22 In April 2002, following a suicide bombing in the Israeli seaside town of Netanya in which almost 30 civilians were killed, the Israeli army invaded the Palestinian town of Jenin from which the terrorists allegedly came. The ensuing battle was a prelude to Israeli military re-occupation of the West Bank and Gaza, parts of which had been under Palestinian rule since the Oslo agreements. From an Israeli perspective, this was a time of growing terror, claiming many Jewish victims. Harsh military response was perceived by many Israelis as a struggle for survival.

of Soviet people during WWII. Evoking the sentimental legacy of Soviet patriotism and the context of the Great Patriotic War, the song cited in the gallery constitutes a metonymic link between Nazi Germany and the Palestinians, despite the fact that neither is explicitly named in the text. This link erases the distinctions between countries and epochs, as well as between Russian-speaking immigrants and other Israelis: all seem to face the same enemy – the Terrorist – that threatens to penetrate their homeland.

Guarding the border 2

In the discussion of the Palestinian gay man, presented earlier, one participant's remark about the cruelty of sending gay men to certain death generated the following exchange:

> <Provocateur>: Instead of feeling sorry for the (poor) Arab you'd better think how to throw them all out of the country.
>
> <Madhatter>: And to hang all provocateurs.
>
> <Provocateur>: Why would you hang me, I am not an Arab and don't lick their asses.
>
> <Bobby>: What, the mean and lusty provocateurs have something against reaming cute brown Arab boys with almond asses? 😄 Or do they prefer to lick their own racist balls? (sorry for being rude) ☹
>
> <Provocateur>: Arab boys in principle cannot be cute. It's even hard to call them humans. Sex with an Arab is bestiality.

Such exchanges of snappy messages and insults are far from uncommon on the Forum. The community's club (discussed in Chapter 6) and Israeli politics, feminism and on-line anonymity, economic reform and sexual morals – these and many other issues often turn discussion threads into heated on-line fights, known in cyberculture as flaming or 'flame wars'. I turn to the detailed discussion of flame wars in Chapters 5 and 6. In Chapter 6 in particular, I will demonstrate that flaming often works choreographically, slipping between genres and moving between serious debates and personal attacks, flirting and litany, playfulness and injury. Here I focus on only one example of flaming, around issues of race and sexuality. I want to concentrate specifically on the *slippery transformations* that turn racist hate speech into boundary-making work legitimising (some) violence; into an on-line provocation; into a sexual tease; into carnivalesque imagery of homosex; into bestial dehumanising. These transformations, I argue, are a technology of refiguration that marks some violence as legitimate and desirable, both politically and sexuality, while also making this violence undeterminable – is it 'only' a joke? 'Only' a sexual tease? 'Only' an on-line game? – thus allowing the perpetrator to escape its consequences and any responsibility.

In the dialogue presented above, the participant bearing the nickname 'Provocateur' suggests that not just the gay asylum seeker but all Palestinians should be thrown out of Israel. His nickname hints that his main aim might be simply provocation. Indeed, later in the discussion thread someone suggests that Provocateur's appearance is a purposeful disruption; he wrote that 'internet provocateurs post clearly enraging messages and then enjoy watching a stirred ant hill'. The pleasure one can derive from on-line provocation reflects the fact that flame wars are seen by many on the site as enjoyable rather than disruptive.[23] But what about the pleasures of racism?

The idea of 'throwing them all out of the country' echoes many aspects of Israeli colonial nationhood that aims to keep Israel as a Jewish state, demographically, politically and culturally. Interestingly, Provocateur's violent fantasy inverts the trope often used by Israel to justify its actions, claiming that it has to defend itself against the Arab enemies that dream of throwing all Jews into the sea. The flaming exchange starts when Provocateur's call is confronted by another participant, Madhatter. Madhatter tosses the call for violence back at Provocateur by making the latter part of

23 For more details on how on-line fights are enjoyed by many participants, see Chapter 6.

an imaginary collective – 'all provocateurs' – subjected to persecution (this tactic resembles the substitution of queers for Jews in anti-homophobic writings of the RFAHD members, discussed in Chapter 2).

In response, Provocateur reinstates his limits of legitimate violence: it should be exercised (only) against Arabs and those who support them. In the context of this discussion it may mean the Israeli GLBT association petitioning on behalf of the Palestinian gay man, or Gabriel who 'felt sorry' for him when questioning the cruelty of deportation to likely death. Those few participants of the Forum who expressed support for the Palestinians or who criticised Israel's military violence quickly became targets of vicious verbal attacks, threats and/or silencing. Provocateur's reference to 'Arabs and those who lick their asses' should be read within this context of violence against those who dare to voice compassion or solidarity – rather than hatred – towards those defined as the enemy. Yet the sexualised imagery embedded in his hateful language also evokes notions of queer sex. Indeed, Provocateur's words are picked up by Bobby who forces out their literary meaning: 'licking one's ass', a rude and derogatory Russian metaphor for 'pandering to' or 'supporting', becomes a homosexual act of reaming. In the same move, Arab terrorists become 'cute Arab boys with almond asses', an orientalist fantasy of feminised men available for the Western homoerotic enjoyment (but not entitled to gay subjecthood!). The fantasy about sexy 'boys' also recalls the picture that illustrates the article: a little boy swallowed up by a Palestinian flag. In the next line of the flaming dialogue the refiguration of race and sexuality takes another turn: the orientalist fantasy is rejected and Arabs are denounced as animals.

Hatred, suggests Nitza Yanai in her analysis of anti-Arab hate speech in Israel, is a form of ambivalent knowledge that constitutes both the colonised and the coloniser (Yanai 2002). Reflecting on Bhabha's discussion of colonial ambivalence, Yanai points out that 'colonial power relations are constituted on both desire and hate, mastery and defiance, pleasure and agony, knowledge and fantasy, and are never simply split between oppression and submission as two opposing essential entities' (Yanai 2002: 74). 'Desire and hate, pleasure and agony, knowledge and fantasy' characterise the ways the Palestinian gay asylum seeker is refigured once as a liar and once as a terrorist, once as a cute boy and once as an animal. Hate, here, works between attraction and the fear of proximity (Ahmed 2004), between fascination and repulsion. Yanai's interviews with Jewish adolescents show that they depict Palestinians with ambivalence, constantly questioning: are they/can they be like us? Discussion of the case of the Palestinian gay man's refuge that takes place on the queer website locates him in proximity with Russian-speaking immigrants. For both, coming to Israel is intertwined with the discourse of Western gay liberation, both cross the border as queer subjects. For Russian-speaking immigrants, Israel is figured as a land of erotic possibilities and of queer belonging. This narrative of promise is inseparable from the racialised homecoming-for-Jews-only. A Palestinian queer searching for similar promises raises a question, unbearable within the regime of warring Israeli nationalism: are they – can they be – like us? The ambivalence of hatred results in either complete rejection (they are not really gay; sex with Arabs is bestiality), or in hypersexed fantasy of racial domination transforming a man caught between deportation and persecution into a cute brown boy.

But how are we to understand the sexiness of such a violent fantasy? What is so appealing in the conjunction between nationalism, racism and queer imagery performed in a queer space? How do expressions of hatred so often slip into references to non-normative sexual practices, homoerotic hints, and flirtation? Is it because the object of hatred – the Palestinian-Arab-Muslim-terrorist is always already queer, or in Puar's words, because 'queerness is always already installed in the project of naming the terrorist'? In her discussion of terrorist corporealities Puar notes that

> [T]he depiction of masculinity most rapidly disseminated and globalised through the war on terrorism and terrorist masculinities: failed and perverse, these emasculated bodies always have femininity as their reference point of malfunction and are metonymically tied to all sorts of pathologies of the mind and body – homosexuality, incest, pedophilia, madness and disease (Puar 2005: 127).

Puar's discussion of terrorist corporealities provides an important insight into the ways the terrorist's masculinity is figured as 'failed and perverse'. Depicted on the Forum as a beast or a boy, the figure of the Terrorist illuminates the human and the man – the soldier-hero who kills terrorists 'protecting our borders.' The two figures are constituted as queer, and sexy, but in very different ways. The life – and normalised sexiness – of one is dependent on the death – and perverse sexuality – of the other. Just like in the two narratives of arrival, in the two stories of guarding the border, the Soldier and the Terrorist become distorted reflections of each other. But it is not just the soldiers whose (queer) patriotism is constituted through violence against terrorists. As the following example will show, violated 'terrorist corporealities' also circulate on the Forum in the fantasies of (queer) torture.

In May 2004, when Western media was galvanised by the publication of the Abu-Ghraib photographs of torture,[24] a new discussion thread was opened by one of the participants. The thread was entitled 'without a trial' and began with a link to a news item about the American soldiers caught in the video. The discussion focussed mainly on whether or not the exposure of the American soldiers' actions – rather than the actions themselves – was appropriate. 'I wonder, who grassed on them?', asked one participant. 'Was it one of them [the soldiers], or someone from the outside, who first watched the porno, and then ran to report [them]?' Many of the participants justified the soldiers' actions, presenting them as inevitable and even necessary (sic!) in any war. Some claimed that since Iraqis would have tortured and killed Americans had they captured them, there was nothing wrong in a bit of 'entertainment' for the soldiers. Others stated that those tortured must have been 'bandits that deserved it'. Some have questioned the very fact of torture and sexual abuse:

> <Lena>: I don't think anyone fucked them... who needs their hairy asses?) When you look at the photos you see that no one abuses no one... well, they undressed them, so what?)) They had a medical examination)) so they put them together ... for the background ... soldiers need to have fun too :) you could see how they posed and smiled....it is their booty...they [the photos] simply got into the wrong hands ... that kind of photos probably exists in Israel as well.

24 For a detailed discussion of these photographs see Bhattacharyya (2008), Gordon (2006) and Puar (2007).

Here again, just like in the case of the figurations of the Palestinian gay man, Iraqi prisoners are virtually – and queerly – dissected. They became 'asses', hairy and bestial, funny toys, the soldiers' booty; anything but tortured *human beings*. This synecdochic dismantling – a cyberfantasy that replays the violence of actual torture time and again – appeared next to the links to Israel. The 'so what' about Iraqi torture by association implied the presence – and the taken for granted acceptance – of torture in Israel. But it was not only the notion of the parallels between Israel/Palestine and US/Iraq. The Israeli torture was not simply justified, it was fantasised about.

> <Bagira>: And do you remember that scandal we had a while ago about using torture with Palestinian prisoners?!?! Our poor 'brothers' were tortured in Israeli prisons... and have the leftists thought that beating the information out of those bastards would prevent acts of terror?? If it would prevent one terrorist act let them put burning metal rods up the asses of thousand Arabs, to make them loosen their tongues. Well, I got distracted from the Iraqi topic, haven't I?)) Well, my point is that with goats one has to speak goat's language... This way they get it faster.

Bagira refers to a recent case of the Public Committee Against Torture in Israel that protested the use of physical torture against Palestinian prisoners, defined as 'security threats'. She mocks the 'leftists' (the Committee Against Torture and other left-wing organisations involved in the case) and glorifies the torture; humanising the Palestinians and compassion towards victims of torture is at the centre of her sarcasm ('our poor "brothers"' she refers to them). But what is most important here is not just Bagira's acceptance and justification of torture as a political act, but also the fact that the material practice of torture and the cyberfantasy and threat thereof is a practice of figuration that figures the Terrorist. The act of torture, in other words, is constitutive of the terrorist: the tortured *become* terrorists at the moment the torture is justified. But the act of torture also constitutes the torturer who becomes the ultimate carer for the nation – the privileged 'nationalist manager' (Hage 2000) – through inflicting suffering on the enemy.

Just like Will and Pavel, described earlier in the chapter, Bagira speaks knowledgeably on Iraqis and Palestinians; just like Will, Pavel and other wannabe political advisers she reflects on what should be done with terrorists. Her fantasy is extremely brutal, and at the same time queer, both because 'torture of the anus seeks to simulate anal sex and, thus, arouse the spectre of homosexuality' (Puar, 2005: 135) and because of the beastly, 'perverse and malfunctioning' body of the Terrorist. And like many other instances of hate speech on the website, Bagira's posting, and in particular her reference to penetration with metal rods, dances on the slippery ground between righteous brutality and playful, sexy entertainment that at the same time gestures towards male-to-male anal sex, a fantasy of female-on-male domination and penetrative power, and the lesbian sexual practice of using dildos. The playfulness is picked up by another person, Mashen'ka, who initiates a dialogue of collective queer fantasy. 'I wonder', she writes, 'would the rod be lubricated before use? :)'. Her question, accompanied by a 'smiley' (an internet sign indicating a smile), shifts the focus from Bagira's description of torture to a queer 'inside' chat about anal sex and lubricants. 'No, Mashen'ka, it would be not', replies Bagira. 'It can slip in smoothly by itself)))'.[25]

The soldier and the terrorist

In the two figures described in this chapter, nationalism, orientalism, the global war on terror, sexuality and immigration are intertwined in multiple and complicated ways. Immigration to Israel is narrated as erotic discovery, and warring Israeli masculinity figures the Soldier as the quintessence of charm and beauty. Palestinian gay men are figured as 'Arab terrorists',[26] and violence against the former becomes a source of queer pleasure and at

25 Adding smileys in the context of extremely violent messages creates an uncanny sense of ambivalence (Is she joking? Is she serious?). I return to a detailed analysis of the uncanny joking and laughter in the context of on-line violence in Chapter 6.

26 Notably, while men as well as women cross the borders, in the figuration of the border as the tandem of soldiers and terrorists, women disappear altogether. In the next chapter I

the same time a promise of a safe(r) Israeli home and better Israeli future without the Arabs. The boundaries of the Israeli-Palestinian conflict shape the boundaries of gay political subjecthood, and the boundaries of acceptable speech on the website allow attacks on the 'nation's enemies' and their supporters but reject solidarity or compassion across borders. Violence embedded in and between those figures is always slippery; it often exists in flirtation, can be masked by it, but never disappears.

In the complexity of tropes, feelings, meanings and memories, masculinities become synecdoches of nation and queer desires and sexual practices constitute one's belonging in – and entitlement to – the nation and the violent 'management' of its enemies.[27] Repeated emphasis on queer warriors who protect the borders and terrorists who are trying to cross them takes us away from the discussion of the nation as (re)produced through particular gendered and sexual identities and practices, as the many feminist and queer discussions of the nation have suggested. It positions violence itself – and its slippery transformations! – as the main technology of constituting immigrants' belonging. Male bodies make queer figurations of patriotism and racism; of arriving, border crossing and deportation; of a gay national self and of a terrorist other; of homeland security and of killing the enemies in their homes; of pleasures and fantasies and of rape and torture. The figures of the Soldier and the Terrorist, in other words, become grounds for claiming political righteousness and the privilege to decide who is entitled to life, safety, home and recognition and who is destined for deportation, torture or death. Here the 'nationalist management' in which the national other is figured as merely an object (Hage 2000) is

take a close look at what happens when the border operates on – and through – a female body.

27 It is important to emphasise that the examples of imagined encounters discussed here do not necessarily reflect actual sexual encounters between Russian-speaking immigrants and gay Palestinians. Such encounters are not infrequent; they should be a subject for a separate, undoubtedly important, study. For an interesting discussion of the politics of homosex between Albanian and Macedonian men and the ways the violence of national and ethnic conflicts affect sexual acts, see Lambevski (1999).

transformed into the management of life and death, or what Puar (2007) poignantly calls 'queer necropolitics'.[28]

My reading of the several border stories suggests that the soldier and the terrorist operate in tandem: one is necessary to constitute the other through its distorted reflection. This reflection is what marks the non-existing yet ever present border between Israel and Palestine, a border that is always simultaneously material, semiotic and psychic: the desperate insistence on ontological differences between 'us' and 'them', the absent imaginary line on the map, the 'just a wall' which is so much more than just a wall. But what is at stake here is not only reflection, but also violation, in cyberspace and beyond. For example, in order for the Jewish Israelis to be safe in their homes and cafés, the homes of the Palestinians have to be penetrated and destroyed; adoring, desiring and protecting the (body of) the soldier, and the nation he represents, is dependant on the violation of the body of the terrorist.

The violation itself, and the pain it inflicts, *are* what make the border. Or rather, they become the border. Bodies and worlds materialise through pain, and it is the pain through which 'the effect of boundary, surface and fixity is produced', as Ahmed suggests in her discussion of the politics of emotions (Ahmed 2004: 25). Pain, she continues, 'involves the violation or transgression of the border between inside and outside, and it is through this transgression that I feel the border in the first place' (2004: 27). But what does it mean to feel the border, and who is the one feeling it? Is it the Palestinian man whose existence shrinks to only one option – the terrorist to be caught, killed or tortured? Or is it the queer immigrants who need to inflict pain in order to secure the border between 'us' and 'them'?

The pain, it seems, does not simply produce a border between bodies (or peoples). Physical violation, or the fantasy of it, marks the relation of interdependency between the tortured and the torturer. The latter comes into being through erasing the former. Through destroying the 'enemy' – a suicide bomber whose very body is a threat and therefore has to be

28 I return to a more detailed discussion of queer necropolitics in the conclusion.

dismembered;[29] or a Palestinian gay man whose claim for safety lays a claim on the Jewish national home – the queer Russian Israelis come into being as sexual and national subjects. Their belonging as Russian-speaking Jews, Israelis and queers, in itself unsteady and contestable, is dependant on the work of violence, or in Elaine Scarry's words, '[i]t is only the prisoner's steadily shrinking ground that wins for the torturer his swelling sense of territory. [...] The larger the prisoner's pain, the smaller the prisoner's world and therefore, by comparison the larger the torturer's world' (Scarry 1985: 36).

29 Or taken apart, as a bomb. Notably, in Israeli language of interrogation, the tortured Palestinian detainees are literally called 'the ticking bomb' (which can explode any minute).

CHAPTER 4

Daughter of Palestine

Daughter of Palestine

In December 2003 a new thread appeared on the *Lesbi-Forum* section of the Forum – a space designated for lesbian, bisexual and other queer women. The thread was entitled 'Leaving the underground in Haifa'. It started with a link, posted by one of the participants, to a news item in one of the many Russian-language Israeli news websites. The item told the story of eighteen Palestinian lesbians in Israel and the Occupied Territories. Having met on an on-line forum they got together in Haifa[1] and established the first ever support group for Arab lesbians.[2] 'Damn! ☺ There are more of them in Haifa than of us ☺. This is not right!!!' responded one participant, Nira, evoking the ever haunting Israeli theme of 'us' versus 'them'. It was not really clear, of course, who were the 'us' she referred to: Jewish/Israeli lesbians, or specifically Russian-speaking ones.[3] It was also not clear, whether Nira

1 The largest Israeli city in the north of Israel and also one of the most mixed in terms of Jewish and Arab residents.

2 The organisation, ASWAT, was founded by Rauda Morcos in January 2003. ASWAT provides Arab gay women – lesbians, inter-sex, queers, transsexual, transgender, questioning and bisexual – a place to meet, share ideas, and explore the political context of personal experiences; it has organised support groups in rotation in Haifa, Jerusalem and Tel-Aviv, and provided assistance to individuals in crisis situations, conducted media outreach, and coordinated educational activities. In May 2006 ASWAT received a Celebration of Courage Award from the International Gay and Lesbian Human Rights Commission (IGLHRC). Details of ASWAT activities and publications can be found on their website, http://www.aswatgroup.org/english/ [Accessed October 2008].

3 Nira was one of the organisers of the 'Russian' GLBT group in Haifa, and so she was probably comparing the two 'minority' groups in Haifa's queer scene. But whether she

was really upset or if she was joking. But the distinction between 'us' and 'them', as well as the changing and ambivalent nature of this distinction, framed this thread from the very beginning.

The responses to Nira varied. Some read Nira's words as lamenting the small numbers of Russian-speaking lesbians in Haifa and the north, and indeed Nira further complained that all the good lesbians had left for the 'centre' – Tel Aviv, where indeed most of the queer activities, Israeli and immigrant, take place. The discussion, just like many other threads on the *Lesbi-Forum*, quickly turned into an exchange of short and witty postings and flirtation. Then another person, Hal, wrote: 'Instead of helping all you do is talk talk talk'. 'And how do you suggest helping Arab lesbians?', asked Nira. The posting that followed Nira's question resulted in a dramatic shift of the tone and style of the thread, which made it particularly interesting for my discussion of borders and crossings. Here is that posting:

> <Daughter of Palestine>: Cool topic. 2 Labris: There is no need to help Arab lesbians, because:
> 1. Among the Arab people there are no lesbians
> 2. These are Jewish women pretending for ☺ chic
> 3. Even if there are any, just shout LESBIAN in a crowd of Arab women, and whoever turns around.... ☺
> 4. I want a Jewish woman
>
> <Nira>: ohmygod! ☺))))))))))))) What I like about you is your sense of humour. ☺))) Daughter of Palestine ☺))))))
>
> <Tornado>: How lovely, it turns out that our Arab friends read Russian. Simply incredible! ☺

---

meant it or not, Nira's response also resembled the constant Israeli paranoia about the Arabs outnumbering the Jews, whether by means of reproduction and numerous children, or the marriage between Palestinians who are citizens of Israel and those who live in the Palestinian autonomy, or the debates on the Palestinian refugees who, if granted the right to return, would 'put an end to the Jewish majority'.

Unlike Nira, Hal and Tornado – veterans and frequent participants in the Forum – 'Daughter of Palestine' was a new character[4] and her response in this thread was her first message on the Forum. From the moment of her appearance Daughter of Palestine was figured as a pretender: Nira laughed her off as a good joke, and Tornado was doubtful that an Arab could read Russian. Both seemed to suggest that Daughter of Palestine was someone else, passing as a Russian-speaking Arab/Palestinian. As the thread progressed, the theme of pretending and passing returned again and again. Much of the discussion concentrated around who Daughter of Palestine 'really was'. Some related to her postings as a game of words and flirtation; others insisted on creating explanations for her contradictory appearance; while others attacked her or defined her presence as a political provocation undesirable on the Forum. Daughter of Palestine was indeed a controversial and a contradictory figure, and a very unusual one. The thread with her participation stood out among hundreds of other Forum discussions collected during my fieldwork. First of all, it was one of the only two occasions where Palestinians figured as possibly queer subjects (the other occasion was the Palestinian gay refugee discussed in the previous chapter). Secondly, this was the only case where a (putative) queer Palestinian had had a presence and a voice of her own – as opposed to being an object of debate, management, attack or fantasy. And thirdly, and most interestingly, her figure conjured up the many complexities, contradictions and ambivalences that constituted queer immigrants' own racial, sexual and national belongings.

The profile of Daughter of Palestine, the participant, marked her as a simultaneously disturbing and hilarious figure. Here is what the profile – a set of details configured at registration that then appears with each message posted by a person on the site – looked like:

4 This does not necessarily mean that she is a new participant, as she could have been one of the regular participants writing under a new name.

DAUGHTER OF PALESTINE *Date of registration*: December 2003 *Lives*: Occupied Palestine	Cool topic. To Labris: There is no need to help Arab lesbians, because: 1. Among the Arab people there are no lesbians 2. These are Jewish women pretending for ☺ chic 3. Even if there are any, just shout LESBIAN in a crowd of Arab women, and whoever turns around.... ☺ 4. I want a Jewish woman ** When I see Katiusha, my heart beats against my fly

Her name evoked images of collective struggle where kinship is politicised and narrated through the nation, and individual names are replaced with one's political attachment (Daughter of the revolution, Daughter of Palestine, etc). In line with the name, her place of residence – 'Occupied Palestine' – signalled opposition to Israeli topography and Occupation, and further strengthened the political connotations of the name. Her signature, 'When I see Katiusha, my heart beats against my fly' on the other hand, was not related to the Israeli-Palestinian conflict. It was playful and explicitly sexual. It is a Russian slogan, a euphemism for an erection and a somewhat rude popular rhyme of a (hetero)sexual nature. On the GLBT forum such a slogan inevitably reads as a queer act, and suggests that the speaker that inhabits this figure – Daughter of Palestine – uses female gender and therefore is marked as a woman, and is most probably a lesbian or a bisexual (although there were several participants who defined themselves as completely heterosexual, interested in relations with women). But was Daughter of Palestine indeed a queer – a lesbian or a bisexual? 'There are no lesbians among the Arabs, these are Jewish women pretending', she wrote in her very first message and then added 'I want a Jewish woman'. Was she signalling that she herself was a Jewish woman pretending to be a Palestinian performing cross-racial desire? Or was she a Jewish woman passing as a heterosexual Palestinian who polices and denies Arab queerness? Was she a Palestinian woman passing as a Russian? Russian-Jewish? Russian-Israeli? Or was she none of these? And most importantly, (why) does it matter?

Scholars of Internet and cyberculture have long been obsessed with questions of on-line passing. The first generation of cyberstudies approached cyberspace excitedly and uncritically and depicted it as the ultimate postmodern space where the signifiers are completely divorced from the signified and anyone can pass as anyone (Silver 2000). Later works addressed on-line interactions more carefully, focusing specifically on how identities are formed and navigated. But as Lisa Nakamura and others (Nakamura 2002; Tal 1996) noted, theorising of passing in cyberspace has predominantly focused on gender cross-dressing and the ways the very binary of gender were blurred. Racial passing has gained less scholarly attention. In her own study of LambdaMOO,[5] a collective space of gaming and socialising, Nakamura (2002) noted that many players described themselves in fantastic terms, such as a 'human size pickle' or a 'pot-bellied pig'. Race was not a category stated in one's profile (unlike gender), however some players presented themselves in terms of appearance (blue eyes, blond hair) signalling their whiteness. Those players who chose to describe themselves as Asian, African American or Latino were often seen as disturbing the playful atmosphere of the collective, by introducing divisive political issues.

The appearance of Daughter of Palestine, a participant fluent in both the formal and informal language of the Forum, can be seen as another example of such 'disturbing' performance. Her presence seemed to challenge the undeclared boundaries of speech, of things that should not be said or, if noted, should be addressed only in a particular way. My own first response to her appearance was excitement. I was reading this thread as it unfolded in real time, and after endless examples of anti-Arab hate speech, on the one hand, and silencing of pro-Palestinian or anti-nationalist voices on the other, I was glad to see this figure, and gave little thought to who might be inhabiting it. At the time, I thought of this Daughter of Palestine as the only alternative to the undeclared nationalist consensus on the Forum. But as I returned to re-reading the archived text of the discussion again and again – the figure of Daughter of Palestine has haunted me

5 The oldest on-line community of the MOO (Multi-user domain, Object Oriented) founded in 1990 in Washington State.

since the moment I started this research – I saw that the forms of passing through which she was figured in the discussion, as well as their possible meanings and effects, were much more complicated. How was Daughter of Palestine read by other participants? Could her appearance really challenge the regime of silence? Could it refigure the Palestinian queer as someone other than an 'impossible subject'? Or was it appropriated into the dominant figurations of orientalism and nationalism?

Passing and other forms of border crossing such as hybridity and mimicry have been extensively discussed by scholars in relation to identity categories and power relations. These discussions point to the fact that there is no authentic identity (Butler 1993; Garber 1992; Bhabha 1994); that passing can subvert and denaturalise orders of gender, sexuality and race; yet at the same time the lived experience of passing is always embedded in power relations, and is always about survival – social, cultural, mental and physical (Muñoz 1997). Other scholars noted that the analysis of passing, hybridity and other practices of border crossing or living in borderzones always demands contextualisation and that not all forms of passing are equally subversive or equally accessible (Bardenstein 2005; McClintock 1995; Lavie and Swedenburg 1996; Lavie 1996). For example, Carol Bardenstein (2005) in her discussion of cross-casting in Israeli-Palestinian cinema notes that there is a spectrum, a continuum of social identities around which the boundary crossing occurs. Some of these crossings reinscribe fixed identity categories and hegemonic narratives; others can substantially and even radically subvert them; and yet others occupy a middle ground. Interestingly, Bardenstein notes that most of the instances of cross-casting and role-switching occur between those close to each other on the spectrum, usually *Mizrachi* Israelis and Palestinians with Israeli citizenship. These instances bear a transgressive potential, because of the visual (as well as cultural and linguistic) closeness of the two groups threatens the hegemonic logic of separation between Jews and Arabs.[6] But as Bardenstein emphasises, 'the boundary crossings in these films are generally transposed

6 For a discussion of this closeness and moving accounts of Arab/*Mizrachi* (mis)readings see Lavie (1996).

back into the more reductive binaries of Arab/Jew and Palestinian/Israeli' (2005: 103).

It is these relations between a spectrum of passings and a range of their possible effects *and* the 'transposing back' into reductive binaries and violent separations that interest me here. In this chapter I will look at Daughter of Palestine not as an individual participant with particular actions and intentions, but explore Daughter of Palestine as a figure that 'collects up the people' and 'embodies shared meaning in stories that inhabit [its] audiences' (Haraway 1997: 23). My aim is to examine the social and psychic mechanisms of figuring Daughter of Palestine through various forms of passing and border crossing; by doing so I will also be able to trace the ways the borders – of queerness, of ethnicity and race, of national entitlement and of humanness – are figured through her. Ahmed in her critical account of passing asks:

> How are differences that threaten the system recuperated? How do ambiguous bodies get read in a way which further supports the enunciative power of those who are telling the difference? In what ways is 'passing' implicated in the very discourse around tellable differences? How are social identities fixed and secured? To simply focus on strategies or tactics of destabilisation, transgression, mimicry, rupture, hybridity, breakage, travesty, masquerade, iterability, performativity, citationality, camouflage (one must note the proliferation of such terms which celebrate and affirm the structural possibility of displacement from social norms), is to forgo an analysis of the complex social and psychic mechanisms for dealing with such tactics (such as designating them as undesirable outcomes of the loss of social and familial security) (Ahmed 1999: 89).

Informed by Ahmed's insistence on examining the ways threatening differences are recuperated, sometimes precisely through the very notion of passing, I approach on-line passing and outing as performance of borders. In other words, I look at the ways imagined borders between places and identity categories are questioned *and* reinforced, and how passing becomes the very tool of materialising – and guarding – the borders it aims to cross. Continuing the theme of border anxieties and border violence, discussed in the previous chapter, I also explore sexual, racial and national borders as threateningly ambivalent. If the Soldier and the Terrorist were two figures that clearly marked the border (to be crossed or protected), Daughter of

Palestine is a figure that makes both easy crossing and unproblematic protection impossible.[7] In the sections that follow, I will look closely at three aspects of her passing and of the attempts to 'out' her or establish who she might be. These are language, sexuality and politics.

Ahmed notes that passing cannot be understood, and should not be theorised, as a logic of the subject. Instead, it should be considered as 'taking place through encounters with others' (Ahmed 1999: 94). I address language, sexuality and politics as sites of such encounters. And rather than focusing solely on the one who passes, I will look at those who read the passing person – those who take the position of authority through telling or claiming to know 'the truth' – paying particular attention to the ways their authority can be both undermined and reinforced.

Passing through language

The language of passing, both phenomenological and theoretical, is structured around the notion of visibility and the intimate connection between seeing and knowing (Schlossberg 2001). Note for example the ideas of political (in)visibility, the anxiety caused by hybrid and ambiguous bodies whose 'difference' is hard to see (Ahmed 1999; Haritaworn 2009), or the idea of surveillance as (self)discipline. But how is the regime of visibility translated into text-based cyberspace? What are the textual markers that allow passing or detection? Brenda Danet in her discussion of gender in multi-user domains of the mid-1990s puts forward the idea of text as mask: in the absence of visual clues words act as markers of one's gender (Danet 1998). She shows that participants use gendered pronouns and

7 Throughout the chapter I show that the relations between symbolic and material borders are complex and multi-layered; but it is important to remember that there is always a difference between crossing and passing in cyberspace and actual physical movement across state borders and/or military checkpoints.

conversational styles to virtually cross-dress; but some also invent gender categories other than male and female, turning gender categorising into a carnival. Danet's combination of Goffman's idea of the presentation of self (Goffman 1956) with the Bakhtinian (1968) analysis of the carnival is useful in understanding passing in textual environments. The notion of masquerade also accounts for the playful nature of many on-line communications and, following Bakhtin's reading of the medieval carnivals, it opens up a theoretical space to reflect on the effects of such a masquerade on social relations of power and domination. Yet at the same time Danet's use of 'text' is simplistic, because she reads language only within the framework of gender;[8] and instrumental because she approaches language as an unproblematic tool of communication rather than as a contested terrain of (dis)identification, power and haunting violence.[9]

As the following discussion will show, language operates not only as a *tool* of passing. Rather, it can itself become a terrain, a metaphysical space through which one has to pass. In the discussion thread that unfolded after the appearance of Daughter of Palestine, language at times seemed lighter than words, because the meaning of a word would shift from one posting to another and back again. Other times it felt thicker than air because, disembodied as it was, it blocked the passing better than any physical border.

'How lovely', wrote Tornado when Daughter of Palestine first appeared on the Forum, 'it turns out that our Arab friends read Russian. Simply incredible! ☺' Tornado's reference to Palestinians as 'our Arab friends' sounds at the same time sarcastic and brutal: in the realities of today's Israel, Jews view Arabs as anything but friends; the reference to 'our friend' signals suspicion, if not hostility. Suspicion, as a first and immediate response to someone who might be an Arab, is part and parcel of the Israeli reality of Occupation and military rule and the ways the Palestinians are figured by it. Suspicion is a practice of figuration that cuts across media discourses,

8 For more critique of gender as the main category of analysis in cyberstudies see Gajjala (2001).

9 As, for example, I demonstrated in Chapter 1.

political thinking and everyday encounters at checkpoints.[10] Palestinians are constantly suspected of being terrorists, to the point where suspicion no longer acts as surveillance because a Palestinian is always *already* figured as a terrorist. The Palestinians – or the Arabs, as they are usually referred to by Israelis, in the persistent denial of their national identity – are constantly and repeatedly figured as liars and trespassers. The IDs they show at checkpoints are considered as probably fake; they lie about the sick and pregnant who in reality carry guns; they lie when they hide terrorists from the Israeli Army; gay men lie about their sexuality; Palestinian leaders lie about the evils of the Israeli Occupation that is not an occupation at all (or if it is, it is the most humane occupation ever); and Palestinian people lie about 'Palestine' as a nation that in fact has never existed. Suspicion, in other words, exceeds beyond the idea of inspection or control: it becomes a technology of governance through denying:[11] denying passage, dignity, sovereignty and basic humanness.

It is within this regime of suspicion that I read Tornado's remark not just as sarcastic but also as violent: my reading extends Tornado's actual intention, whatever it may have been, into the broader figuration of the suspected Arab. When Daughter of Palestine challenged her ('Well, no one is surprised that in Israel Jews speak Russian ☺. Arabs, similarly, have been all across Mother Russia ... ☺'), Tornado persisted: 'Yes, but being so fluent in Russian ... If only Stanislavski were here. ☺' Stanislavski, the well-known Russian director and theatre theoretician, is famous for his phrase 'I don't believe you' (or, in a more literary but less accurate translation, 'I am not convinced'). According to Stanislavski's School of Acting, the actor must really feel what the character feels, rather than simply pretend. In rehearsals, he used to exclaim 'I don't believe you' if someone's acting was not convincing. Tornado's reference to Stanislavski is a way of saying that the 'game' played by Daughter of Palestine is not convincing. In the same move, this

10 For a detailed discussion of the checkpoint as a metaphor of Palestinian queerness, see Ritchie (forthcoming).

11 I am not suggesting that the passage at checkpoints is *always* denied; rather, I am referring to the situation where it can always *be* denied, any time and for no reason.

reference of course performs the collective 'we' of those who understand Tornado's metaphoric speech, as well as sharing her unpronounced disbelief. 'If only Stanislavski were here' becomes a silent speech act that constitutes Daughter of Palestine as an unconvincing pretender.

In the face of this refusal to allow her to pass, Daughter of Palestine of course does not remain passive. She responds: 'Even Ariel Shaaron is not here ☺ And I can also read Schiller without a dictionary ... no problem ☺'. Reading Schiller without a dictionary is a popular Russian euphemism of one's fluency in German, metonymically used to describe a person who is fluent in foreign languages. Here it is evoked to explain Daughter of Palestine's fluency in Russian (as well as in other languages). Showing off about her knowledge of languages, she also demonstrates that she understood Tornado's clever speech acts, and can paraphrase it just as cleverly. The absent Stanislavski who would have declared the performance unconvincing becomes Ariel Sharon who would literally and not metaphorically prevent the Arabs' passing. But the name of Sharon is misspelled (as Shaaron), probably accidentally, and the misspelling picked up by Tornado, who writes:

> <Tornado>: And Shaaron – is it your new Arab leader? The name with the double 'a' is too Arabic ☺.
>
> <Daughter of Palestine>: ☺ Well f*ck knows who that Sharon is. ☺. Here, on the other hand, we have a neighbour, Iosif Moiseevitch, and he is Russian, sort of. So nothing surprises me anymore... Not the double 'a', nothing... ☺

Daughter of Palestine's quick and witty responses turn the conversation on its head and make the Russian speaking Jews/Israelis, and not the Arabs and Palestinians, the subject of examination and suspicion. Her earlier response to Tornado ('no one is surprised that in Israel Jews speak Russian') disrupts the connection between nation, location and language that Tornado tries to use: some Jews in Israel speak Russian, rather than Hebrew. In the context of surprise-as-suspicion, Daughter of Palestine's remarks can in fact be extremely painful to many immigrants: the Russian language of the immigrants is *not* a non-surprising fact. It is a marker of difference. The Israeli national ethos, built on the 'revival' of the dispersed

Jewish people in the land of Israel, positions Hebrew at its core.[12] Modern Hebrew, revived by European Jewish settlers and pioneers in the 20th century (Lavie 1996; Seidman 1997), lies at the heart of the Zionist idea of repatriation and acculturation. All new immigrants are taught Hebrew in special language schools, and are expected to gain full language skills within a few years of their arrival. Until recently newcomers were also expected to cease using their mother tongues in favour of Hebrew. In the Israel of the 21st century the situation is changing, and the use of the Russian language has become more acceptable.[13] And yet, 'in Israel Jews speak Russian' can be read as another painful reminder of the immigrants' otherness, or of their impossible passing as 'proper Israelis'.

Then Daughter of Palestine mentions the lack of surprise once again, this time referring to the (impossible) passing of a Jew as a Russian. Iosif Moiseevitch is a (stereo)typical name of a Russian Jew. In Russian, full names contain the name of the father. Here, the name means Iosif (Joseph), son of Moisej (Moses). Both Iosif and Moisej were very common names used by Jews in Russia, although in the Soviet period many chose to Russify their names by replacing them with Russian equivalents (Moisej, for example, became Michail). Names played a central role in the history of the passing – and detecting – of Soviet Jews. Another indicator was passport registration. Until after the fall of communism one's nationality was registered in one's passport. When registering for a passport at the age of 16, a person of mixed parentage could choose the nationality of either one of the parents. Many Jews from mixed families were particularly encouraged to register as Russians. 'Iosif Moiseevitch the Russian' embodies this history of passing, the passing that was never really possible, because Jewishness always remained detectable, if not through visual signs of racial difference, then through a name.

Sharon turning into a 'new Arab leader' by acquiring an extra 'a' and Iosif Moiseevitch who becomes a Russian by acquiring a word in his passport both are framed by Daughter of Palestine as a joke. Accompanied by

12 The revival of modern Hebrew is attributed to Eliezer Ben-Yehuda who is one of the key figures in Zionist mythology (Seidman 1997).

13 Since the 1990s dozens of Russian-language newspapers have appeared in Israel; and since 2002 there are also two Russian-Israeli TV channels.

'smileys' they make passing seem very easy – just one letter, just one word – and at the same time impossible.[14] For Tornado a Russian-speaking Arab is a fake, as impossible as Sha(a)ron the Arab leader. This impossibility is established by a Russian-speaking Israeli who becomes an authority on both the Russian language and Arabs. But this authority is undermined by Daughter of Palestine who refigures the relationship between the 'nationalist manager' (Hage 2000) and its racial other: she makes the Russian-speaking Jews (in Israel and elsewhere) into doubtful subjects. She shakes their position as authentic and therefore having the authority to determine the identity of the other: they are figured as neither 'real' Russians, nor 'real' Israelis. But in doing this, Daughter of Palestine herself remains an ambiguous figure – maybe a Russian, maybe an Arab, maybe neither, maybe both.

Her dialogue with Tornado constitutes passing as inevitably violent: whether in its immediate effects, or in the suspicious response, or in the history embedded in it. Violence here circulates in the ping-pong of the detector and the detected. Later in the thread, for example, another participant makes an attempt to claim the authority and 'out' Daughter of Palestine, this time by imagining her biography:

> <Fluffy>: Hey, are you all serious? Isn't it clear that this Daughter of Palestine was born in Russia and lived there until she was a grown up. The mentality is all over the place. You can learn Russian, but you can't pick up the manner of communication in that language. And she is in Israel because she must have married some Arab, who was studying in the University of International Friendship.[15]

After many exchanges between Daughter of Palestine and other participants, that seem to shake the very possibility of telling the difference (can Arabs speak Russian? Can Jews be Russians? Can Sha(a)ron be an Arab leader?), Fluffy's posting seems desperate to establish a tellable story, an explanation of who Daughter of Palestine 'really' is. Like Tornado, Fluffy positions language at the centre of her 'detecting', yet she distinguishes between speaking a language – something that can be learned

14 I will return to discuss the complexity and the ambivalence of on-line jokes in Chapter 6.

15 The University of International Friendship was established in Moscow specifically for overseas students from developing countries, supported by the Soviet Union.

– from 'mentality' and cultural capital that are figured as given, authentic and beyond pretence. The mentality is intimately tied to biography that acts as a clue, sticking together territory, nation and language and cultural sensibility. Based on Fluffy's assessment of Daughter of Palestine's use of Russian, her Palestinianness is denied and she is 'outed' as a Russian woman married to an Arab. But Fluffy's narratives did not only create a biography for Daughter of Palestine. She also created the trajectory of Daughter of Palestine's movement: having married an Arab man, she arrived in Israel. When challenged by Nira ('Fluffy, who told you that she lives in *Israel*? ☺', emphasis mine), she wrote: 'No one told me. If you look carefully, you will see that she wrote that she lives in "Occupied Palestine"'.

Fluffy's insistence on knowing the truth – as well as being able to tell it – points to the ambivalence of the ability to tell, as well as that of the language itself, on which the telling is based. Fluffy rejects Daughter of Palestine's Palestinianness, yet reads the 'location' in her profile as true (rather than as a lie or pretence). But the location is refigured at the moment it is read: 'occupied Palestine' becomes 'she is in Israel'. This refiguration can be interpreted as both acknowledgement and denial of the Palestinians' rights to their land. While for the Israelis the term 'Occupied Territories' usually refers to the West Bank and Gaza held under Israeli military rule since 1967, many Palestinians address both these territories, as well as the Israeli borders established in 1948, as 'Occupied Palestine'. Thus Fluffy could be acknowledging this Palestinian discourse. Yet her explanatory biography claims the status of truth both about Daughter of Palestine and about geography, where 'Occupied Palestine' is nothing but 'she is in Israel'. This act of (re)naming – and more broadly, of refiguration – becomes a speech act that performs the Israeli ownership of the land.[16]

16 Renaming places is a common practice of colonial regimes, a practice that has been widely used in Israel throughout Zionist settlement there. Many of the Palestinian towns were given Biblical names to mark the Jewishness of the land; others were renamed by slightly modifying the original Arab name. Israeli landscape, both in the Occupied Territories and within the 1948 borders, bears marks of erasure, demographic as well as symbolic: renaming and repopulating work hand in hand.

Passing through sexuality

How are we to understand Daughter of Palestine's first posting ('There are no Arab lesbians, there are Jewish women pretending [...] I want a Jewish woman')? What are the effects of such declarations about sexuality within the context of this thread where 'Jew' and 'Arab' are destabilised as readable categories of identity, and yet constantly constructed in opposition to each other? What interests me here is not to ascertain whether Daughter of Palestine is a queer Jewish woman pretending to be a Palestinian, a straight Arab woman pretending to be queer, or something else altogether. Rather, I am interested in the very themes of pretending, passing and disclosing in relation to figurations of 'Arab sexuality'. Based on a discussion of two episodes from the thread, I want to look into how this sexuality is understood within the orientalist framework of something repressed and hidden (to be revealed by the West), or exotic and bestial, particularly in the fantasy of someone passing as 'oriental'.

In her discussion of race in MOOs, Nakamura (2002) found that while introducing the troubling issues of racial otherness and racism was disturbing, some players engaged in racial passing that was accepted and condoned because it was not seen as threatening the order of whiteness. These players, who according to Nakamura's findings were all white, often used stereotypical images of Asian characters such as 'Bruce Lee', 'Miss Saigon', etc. Their 'orientalised theatricality', suggests Nakamura, 'allows them to indulge in a dream of crossing over racial (and gender) boundaries temporarily and recreationally' (Nakamura 2002: 39).[17] At the same their presence – as the only acceptable form of racial otherness – reassures and

17 Importantly, the crossing allowed by the on-line environment is not unique to the Internet: Nakamura specifically notes the historical roots of this fantasy tourism in colonial writings and links her reading to Said's discussion of the construction of the Orient (Said 1979). On-line racial cross-dressings, she emphasises, are based on Eurocentric 'knowledge' and stereotypical images of the Orient as it is depicted in travel writing and later also in cinema and advertisements. For a detailed discussion of orientalism in cinema see, for example, Shohat and Stam (1994).

reinforces these stereotypes by acting. Daughter of Palestine's own presence can be read as such orientalised theatricality (I shall return to it later in more detail). But interestingly, Daughter of Palestine's appearance also became the locus of the orientalist fantasies of other participants: discussing who Daughter of Palestine was, they began fantasising about a sexual encounter with an Arab woman. 'I would never lay an Arab [woman], that's for sure,' wrote one participant, Dolly.

> <Katekins>: yeh? and why so?
>
> <Dolly>: Well they all wear burkas and pretend they are saints
>
> <Katekins>: maybe they do what they can, but if you fondle them gently, and introduce a little tongue, you will discover what oriental passion is, and the burka will be forgotten at once; you just look at their suffering, at their fear of being different and you spit at their backs, but they are just a poor breed afraid of being cursed and rejected by everyone. You should have compassion for their miserable Arab fate.

The exchange between Katekins and Dolly is structured around two discourses of Arab female sexuality: on the one hand it is figured as repressed and therefore unattractive for a lesbian; on the other hand Arab women appear as passionate. Puar, in her discussion of discourses on Muslim sexuality around Abu-Ghraib, notes the shift in the image of the Orient:

> The Orient, once conceived in Foucault's *ars erotica* and Said's deconstructive work as the place of original release, unfettered sin, and acts with no attendant identities of consequences, now symbolises the space of repression *and* perversion, and the site of freedom has been relocated to Western identity (Puar 2005: 125, italics in original).

But in the dialogue between Dolly and Katekins the two types of the sexualised Orient are present at the same time. Oriental female sexuality is figured as both repressed (but can be liberated by a Western lesbian who is compassionate and kindly) *and* inherently passionate. Katekins' fantasy of an encounter with an Arab woman reads as the familiar assemblage of Arab-Islam-burka-repression, circulated within the rhetoric of liberating Muslim women of Afghanistan, Iraq or any other country to be invaded in the name of democracy, as well as in the 'West' itself, as recent events in France, UK and other European countries indicate. In Katekins' posting this orientalist figuration is queered: the 'liberator' is a woman, not a man. Yet the queering only strengthens the discursive violence of orientalism, when the fantasy of 'oriental passion' is presented as 'compassion'. Katekins' notion of compassion might at first be misread as a reference to lesbian solidarity across cultures, but paired with words such as 'poor breed' and 'miserable Arab fate', it is in fact mocking disdain. What's more, in both Dolly's and Katekins' postings, despite their disagreement, the Arab woman is figured as a pretender.

But what about Daughter of Palestine herself? Later in the thread, when one participant, Lupi, suggested that she was a man passing for a woman, Daughter of Palestine responded:

> <Daughter of Palestine>: I can't take off my pants here in front of you all, can I? ☺ You will have to believe my words ☺ We Arabs, are the most honest, Subn Allah ☺.
>
> <Dolly>: ☺ To be honest I never met an honest Arab, no offence, I met kind ones but not honest ones, just liars
>
> <Daughter of Palestine>: 2 Dolly: who is it talking about honesty? ☺ Jews? ☺))
> Lupi, if you are talking to me, please don't distort my nickname, ok? [Earlier Lupi caller her 'little daughter']
> I'm pissed off, my knickers are all wet ☹
>
> <Lupi>: Your knickers get wet because you are pissed off?.. That's new. Are you sure that's the reason?
>
> <Daughter of Palestine>: InshAllah, always ☺
>
> <Daughter of Palestine>: Especially, when I watch the dogs shag, hasn't it happened to you?
>
> <Lupi>: you feel PISSED OFF because dogs shag? Like, 'even the dogs shag, and what about me? I am so pissed off ...'?
>
> <Daughter of Palestine>: My Arab mentality will never meet yours ... unfortunately

In this short dialogue the theme of disbelief and suspicion comes up again and again. Lupi suspects that Daughter of Palestine is a man, and Dolly says – recalling the all too familiar trope of Arabs as liars – that she has never met an honest Arab. As elsewhere in the thread, Daughter of Palestine is quick and clever with her responses. When Dolly uses the image of Arabs as liars, Daughter of Palestine responds with the allusion that all Jews are dishonest, evoking the long history of the anti-Semitic trope of Jews as manipulative and deceitful.

Daughter of Palestine's own words emphasise her alleged authenticity. Arabs are the most honest, she says, and in order to 'prove' her Arabness, she adds phrases that would mark her as an authentic Muslim: *Subn Allah* (or rather, *Subhan Allah*, meaning 'Glory to Allah') and *Insh Allah* (or *InshaAllah*, meaning 'If Allah wills it'),[18] the two Arabic expressions often used by Muslims when speaking in Arabic as well as in other languages. Yet her postings create an eerie feeling of inconsistency, for example, the image of a religious Muslim and a reference to dogs shagging. Since dogs in Islam are considered *haram* (prohibited, impure), Daughter of Palestine's reference to zoophilic arousal marks her character as someone who is not only incompetent (and therefore not really an Arab or Muslim user) but may even be deliberately offensive. In the same move, Daughter of Palestine notes her 'Arab mentality'. In the context of Fluffy's earlier comment on 'Russian mentality' this reads as a sarcastic remark that undermines the idea of essentialised and detectable identity. But it can also be understood as linking Arabness to monstrous sexuality – another orientalist fantasy, in its particularly Russian take. In the Russian context dogs often figure in descriptions of deviant and monstrous sex (note, for example, the story of the Gulag criminals copulating with a dog, described in Chapter 2). When Daughter of Palestine says that her knickers get wet when she watches the dogs shag, the two sexual images stick together and read as Arab sexuality equals bestiality.

18 I have kept the original spelling (*SubnAllah* and *InshAllah*) used by Daughter of Palestine.

This particular moment in the thread positions Daughter of Palestine as someone who employs passing not only to cross racial boundaries 'temporarily and recreationally' (Nakamura 2002: 39) but to specifically inflict violence *because* of its potential to be read as authentic. But the next development of the thread shows that even such a reading is not the only one possible. Several postings after the reference to Arab mentality, Daughter of Palestine wrote: 'Who is using my nickname?? What the hell??!!! Take a look, this fake has already got many messages ... Damn ... envy everywhere ... ☹' She is suggesting that not all the messages that appeared under her name were written by her. Indeed, the list of registered participants showed that there were two users registered under the same name, and their profiles (including place of residence and signature) seemed to be identical.

Two Daughters of Palestine exchanged several angry messages which at that moment appeared completely schizophrenic. When I was reading this exchange in real time there was indeed no way to distinguish between the two users.[19] 'Well if you at least were joking in a smart way ... but you only write stupid ramblings ... ☺', wrote one of them. 'I am going to sleep now and will delete the clone[20] tomorrow', wrote the other. But the next day the 'clone' had not disappeared. Instead it had changed the signature. Reading the archived discussion retroactively it became possible to distinguish between the two nicknames. Once modified on the 'personal profile' page, the signature (or any other personal detail) changes automatically in all the messages written by a given user. So when the 'clone' changed part of its details, it became possible to attribute the postings to either of the two Daughters of Palestine, although this could tell us nothing about who – or how many people – was writing under each of the nicknames. Re-reading of the thread after this modification revealed that the messages on shagging dogs and Arab mentality were written by a 'clone' – the

19 Technically two identical nicknames cannot be registered at once. One of the ways to bypass the system is to use Latin letters for similarly looking Cyrillic ones (several letters of the two alphabets look the same). Graphically the names would appear the same, but the computer system would read them as different.

20 The idea of an on-line troublemaker as a clone, and the notions of sameness and difference the clone evokes, will be further discussed in Chapter 6.

'new' Daughter of Palestine. The clone appeared after the 'old' Daughter of Palestine mentioned her wet knickers. Was it another Forum participant, trying to pass as Daughter of Palestine in order to sabotage her presence? Or were the two 'Daughters of Palestine' – the 'good' and the 'bestial' Arab – authored by the same person, producing what Tal and Lyman (2000) call 'a room full of mirrors', when the imagined 'other' only reinforces the self-image of the one who does the imagining?

Passing through politics

From the moment Daughter of Palestine discovered the 'clone' – this is how she called the other nickname – she appeared to be angry. 'Envy everywhere', she wrote, upset about the loss of her exclusive status. 'Took everything, even my Katiusha!', she exclaimed dramatically, referring to the fact that not only her name but also her signature was stolen and duplicated. 'And who would compensate for the knickers??' she added. Her anger was exaggerated and theatrical; her protests against the cloning walked on the shaky ground where playfulness and violence intertwine.[21] The day after the first appearance of the clone, the following dialogue took place between the two Daughters of Palestine (I reproduce it here in the way in appeared on the Forum, including the personal profile and the – now different – signatures):

21 Such exaggerated theatricality, ambivalent in its playfulness and violence, is not unusual for people engaged in on-line fights. I return to it in my discussion of the flamer in Chapter 6.

DAUGHTER OF PALESTINE *Date of registration*: December 2003 *Lives*: Occupied Palestine	What is that ... not fair ... The Jews here talk about honesty ... but making clones ... that's backstabbing ... betrayal!!! Like Cain and Abel ... ** When I see Katiusha, my heart beats against my fly

DAUGHTER OF PALESTINE *Date of registration*: December 2003 *Lives*: Occupied Palestine	WELL, COME ON, I HAVE FIXED IT ... WROTE THE MARK IN BLOOD ** CLONED DAUGHTER OF THE NEARBY STATE

This short dialogue positions both cloning and differentiation in the chilling context of extreme physical violence. The first Daughter of Palestine defines cloning as 'backstabbing', where Jews act as perpetrators, although it is of course not clear who created the clone and why. Her words frame the relations between Daughter of Palestine and her clone as the relations between 'the Jew' and 'the Arab'. The other Daughter of Palestine claims to have fixed the confusion by writing her signature in blood. Her signature – 'CLONED DAUGHTER OF THE NEARBY STATE' – appears in very big red letters[22] that resemble the cinematic images of bloody writing on walls. Both postings evoke several violent associations: from Biblical murder to stabbings (including the many stabbings of Jews by Arabs in the years of the first Palestinian *Intifada*) to horror films. The exchange between the two Daughters of Palestine appeared within the overall playful tone of the discussion, where they and other participants of the Forum were joking, flirting and adding many smileys to their missives. And yet, one cannot escape the violent context of the two comments and their relationship to

22 Usually the signature is written in a smaller font than the default font of the postings.

the bloody conflict between Jews and Arabs, two peoples who in religious genealogy are seen as cousins, who share a common ancestry and a small piece of land. Passing and cloning, as forms of border crossing and as cyberspace entertainment, are refigured as deeds written in blood, material as well as semiotic. This refiguration is inseparable from the raging violence that is taking place outside of cyberspace but also lives through on-line words and actions. The play with on-line identities, in other words, turns out not to be playful at all – or rather, it has never been playful in the first place. As Bardenstein in her discussion of passing and casting in Israeli and Palestinian cinema notes:

> There is no play whatsoever involved in today's most common enactments of passing in the Palestinian-Israeli context: Israeli passing in undercover units long enough to commit extrajudicial assassinations of Palestinians, and Palestinians passing long enough to detonate themselves and Israelis around them in suicide bombings (Bardenstein 2005: 120).

And while the virtual and the physical backstabbing are clearly not the same, the large red letters – the bloody signature of a clone from the nonexistent state – signal that the performance of violence in cyberspace and the material violence outside of it are always intertwined, reverberating through each other.

The violent context of cloning and passing, and its relations to politics, dominated the concluding part of the discussion thread. 'The most insulting was that she copied Katiusha', wrote the first Daughter of Palestine, and added: '☺ dis we da nat farget ☺'. Her last phrase ('this we do not forget') uses distorted spelling to imitate what is considered in Russia 'the oriental accent', marking people from Russia's own imperial Orient – Caucasus, Georgia and Central Asia (Shumsky 2004). The figure of the 'oriental man' circulates in endless jokes, many of them about Georgian men. These men appear as simultaneously hypermasculine, violent and somewhat ridiculous. Here Daughter of Palestine, angry about her virtual identity being copied, threatens the clone, mimicking an oriental man. Was this supposed to be another sign of her Arabness? Shumsky in his discussion of Russian-Israeli orientalist discourse points out that the images of the Russian Orient often serve as an interpretative framework for reading

Israeli reality. Tracing immigrant media and literary production, Shumsky demonstrates how Russian orientalist knowledge of 'the Georgian' or 'the Bucharian'[23] becomes the way to read the Palestinian Arabs as someone-thing already familiar and knowable. He points out textual similarities in the ways oriental figures of the former Soviet Union and of Israel/Palestine are constructed by immigrant writers and journalists. The interpretative slippage between the Georgian and the Arab – whether it was meant by Daughter of Palestine or not – became clear in the response to Daughter of Palestine's joking threat:

> <Fluffy>: < *The most insulting was that she copied Katiusha. ☺ dis we da nat farget* ☺. >
> See ... with you any little reason – and all of a sudden its 'jihad'. Although more often, there is no reason at all.

Fluffy's response spelled out what seemed to have been in the air from the beginning of the thread. Daughter of Palestine was seen as a terrorist, simply because of her Arabness. In the end of the thread Fluffy warned other participants, saying that Daughter of Palestine 'has to be treated gently. Or else she will go mad, and will decide, in the best traditions of "her people", to take "bloody revenge" on her innocent Jewish neighbour because she was insulted by evil Jewish lesbians!!!' Daughter of Palestine responded to Fluffy's notion of *jihad* in her usual style of half-serious half-joking use of politics: 'and you, if you only could, would immediately start expanding your borders ☺'. But the notion of borders in conjunction with *jihad* transformed the so far playful tone of the discussion. From this exchange onwards Daughter of Palestine ceased being an ambivalent figure, a joker or a possible pretender. She was suddenly refigured as a *real* Palestinian whose identity was no longer doubted. She became the 'true' representative of the Palestinian people or even of all the Arabs: with *you* it is jihad for little or no reason.

23 Buchara is a city in (Soviet) Central Asia, but in the orientalist discourse of the Russian Israelis it often serves as a synechdoche for the whole area.

After Daughter of Palestine mentioned the expansion of borders, one participant, Lady, wrote to her rudely:

> <Lady>: Hey, why do you start here with politics.. This site is not political. You better go and deal with your little Palestinian sistas, they probably don't have a place to go to (without the Russian language, unlike you). Don't make provocations here. If you want to be accepted here, change your nickname and clear your lexicon, or are you looking for a squabble?

Another one told her to stop criticising the Jews and take a better look at herself. And yet another one, Nibbler, wrote:

> <Nibbler>: I didn't quite understand. Daughter of Palestine, are you joking or serious? If you are, so to speak, for the rights of Palestinians, that is for the friendship of peoples, then you should not care who expands borders, and who is with whom. And if you are for Palestine as a political entity, then excuse me, savage Arabs who didn't even have an idea about statehood and lived happily under the Ottoman Empire and the British Mandate, now all of a sudden they also want something? No F*KING[24] way.

It seemed like the mere reference to borders (and to the spectre of the ongoing Israeli-Palestinian territorial dispute) immediately narrowed the space of cyberfantasy and playful on-line chatting. The space of Daughter of Palestine's identity possibilities was narrowed down, too: the reference to politics became an unacceptable provocation, and her nickname itself turned into a border: in order to be 'accepted here', Daughter of Palestine was offered to change it – read, to *disappear* as a Palestinian.

In Nibbler's posting Daughter of Palestine's reference to borders was defined as either illogical or impossible, so in any case irrelevant. If it was a joke than it should not matter, but if it was serious it cannot be accepted. In the first possible interpretation that Nibbler offered, Palestinian rights were refigured as 'the friendship of peoples' – an old communist slogan of internationalism – which is juxtaposed to territorial nationalism, thus denying the latter. In the second, the notion of Jewish territorial expansion

24 Censored in the original.

is read as Palestinian political claim for state sovereignty, only to be rejected. Repeating the trope of savage stateless Arabs, frequently used in Israeli rhetoric to discredit the very concept of 'Palestinian people',[25] Nibbler, just like Will and others discussed in the previous chapter, becomes the 'nationalist manager' (Hage 2000), the spokesperson for the Israeli state, the one who holds both the knowledge about 'savage Arabs' and also the entitlement to determine whether they deserve a state and a say. Nibbler's response simultaneously performs the closure of political possibilities for the Palestinians *and* the closure of identity possibilities for Daughter of Palestine, finally making the link between the two explicit.

An unimaginable figure

Throughout my fieldwork I kept wondering who this Daughter of Palestine might be. Her name and her messages differentiated her from the rest of the participants. They stood out in the general tone of the discussions that ranged from sentimentally patriotic to militantly nationalist. Daughter of Palestine presented – albeit jokingly – the Palestinian point of view that was very rarely voiced on the website, and when voiced, often mocked, attacked or even threatened with banishment from the Forum altogether.[26] Maybe Daughter of Palestine was one such participant, who wanted to oppose the Forum's racism and nationalism but did not want to use their nickname for fear of being attacked and even expelled from the site? Understood as such, her passing can be read as an act of political resistance. Her last posting definitely contributed to this possibility. When attacked by Fluffy, Nibbler and Lady at the end of the thread, Daughter of

25 This trope, supported by academic 'knowledge' and expertise, is that there is no such a thing as a Palestinian people, only Arabs.

26 My friend Rita, briefly introduced in the prologue, was indeed threatened with expulsion when she posted information about an anti-war demonstration, organised by a group of Israeli queers at the time of the US invasion of Iraq in 2003.

Palestine abandoned her playful style and wrote a long serious response. She emphasised that every forum is political in one way or another. She stated that Arabs were not savages but contributed greatly to culture and science. She wrote that she objected to attacks on any nation, and openly confronted people's aggression and racism.

This response could be seen as a self-outing of sorts, revealing Daughter of Palestine's intentions, removal of masks, and 'leaving the stage'. And yet, her other postings suggested that her intentions may have been simply provocative and that Israeli-Palestinian politics were nothing but a convenient topic with which to stir up the Forum. Clearly, the reference to Palestine, Jews, Arabs and borders is an inflammatory tool (this in itself is of course telling in relation to the boundaries of belonging in this particular on-line space). Or maybe she was, in Bardenstein's words, 'toying with or blurring fixed identity categories and hierarchies, but in modes that are largely ephemeral or quasi-utopian, leaving dominant social categories and hierarchies securely in place' (Bardenstein 2005: 100).

However, what really interested me in this chapter was not so much the intentions of the person writing under the nickname of Daughter of Palestine, but rather the effect of Daughter of Palestine as a figure and the ways this figure became a ground for various claims – of authenticity, of knowledge, of culture and of national subjecthood. Daughter of Palestine's ambiguity and her passing through language, sexuality and politics did a complex work of mapping the contested relations between cyberspeech and recognition; between race and desire; and between cyberfantasies and the materialities of nationhood and colonial occupation. Most importantly, figuration of Daughter of Palestine through passing and detection mapped yet another way in which belonging can work though violence: those inspecting and claiming the authority to stop or let through constitute their belonging through violence towards those who are denied passage, or subjected to a possibility of such denial. Similarly to the Soldier and the Terrorist, discussed in a previous chapter, the story of Daughter of Palestine's passing points to the ways queer immigrants' belonging is intertwined with – and dependent on – racial and national violence, where inflicting violence on the 'enemy' performs one's own entitlement to the nation. However, Daughter of Palestine's ambivalent figuration, and the inability to stop her, also point to the performative failure of border violence, where neither the national self nor the national other can be determined and 'managed' with certainty.

Following the ways Daughter of Palestine was figured through various forms of border crossing, as well as the ways various borders were figured *through* her, this chapter pointed to the double meaning of passing: passing as identity, visibility and recognition and passing as the crossing of borders, symbolic as well as material. The two are closely related and their relations are always unstable and changing. The two forms of passing do not simply reproduce each other (for example, the management through suspicion deployed by the Forum's participants towards Daughter of Palestine resembles, but is not the same as, the management through suspicion exercised by a soldier towards a Palestinian man or woman crossing a checkpoint). Rather, they reverberate through each other, leading to multiple, complex and at times unpredictable effects.[27] For example, a subversive performance in cyberspace can threaten or even undermine the authority of colonial knowledge, but can simultaneously intensify border anxieties and nationalised hatred; the performance of borders by a marginalised immigrant newcomer can both open up and close down the possibilities of cyberidentities and can lead both to diasporising the nation and to tightening the definitions of national belonging. In other words, the two forms of passing can both challenge and reconfigure the borders of race, culture, sexuality and nationhood, in cyberspace and beyond.

'Passing takes place through encounters with others in which there is a crisis of reading, a crisis that hesitates over the gap between an image that is already assumed and an image that is yet to be assumed', writes Ahmed in her discussion of passing (Ahmed 1999: 94). My discussion of Daughter of Palestine's figuration on the Forum indeed demonstrates that on-line passing and its readings, as forms of boundary work, are always about encounters with others. But although these encounters took place in the textual domain of cyberspace, this chapter pointed to the fact that the *violence* of passing is never just about the reading. Suspicion as an affective

27 I return to discuss reverberation and its effects in the conclusion.

regime and as a technology of governance (and self-governance), words that stop or wound, signatures written in blood, and most importantly the material-semiotic-psychic nature of borders themselves, show that passing is much more than the crisis of reading.[28] The unidentifiable that emerges from the gap is about the haunting (but very real!) violence of borders in Israel and Palestine.

Gordon's (1997) notion of haunting, discussed in Part I, is particularly useful in describing the effect of Daughter of Palestine's presence on the participants of the Forum (and on me as a researcher). For example, one thing that was left unmentioned in the thread I discussed – yet remained absently present – was the raging military violence that underlies today's dichotomy of Jews and Arabs as categories of identity. Warring brutality, so explicit in the figures of the Soldier and the Terrorist, followed Daughter of Palestine like a shadow but was never expressed in words. Another shadow was her name itself. 'Daughter of Palestine' was the name given to the first Palestinian female suicide bomber, Wafa Idris, who killed herself and one Israeli man and injured about a hundred others in January 2002 (about two years before the Forum discussion). After her death Wafa's mother referred to her as the Daughter of Palestine, and this title was reproduced again and again in newspapers and websites. Although her story and her naming were widely circulated in the media of that time, Wafa Idris was of course not the first nor the only one named 'Daughter of Palestine'. For example, Hanan Ashrawi, a Palestinian politician and intellectual, used the name 'Daughter of Palestine' in her poem, addressing Areej Al-Jabali, an 18 year old girl killed in Hebron in 2001 by the Israeli Army (Ashrawi 2001). The name also circulated in the Russian-language internet when around 2002 a Russian-speaking woman, Marina Strukova, published a poem, entitled 'Daughter of Palestine', in an on-line newspaper, *Zavtra* (Tomorrow, Rus.) (Strukova 2002). The poem glorified a woman *shahid* who bypasses Israeli soldiers at a checkpoint in order to blow herself up in the streets of Tel Aviv. Was 'Daughter of Palestine' that came to the Forum the ghost

28 Undoubtedly, the lived experience of the one who is being (mis)read is also about much more than words.

of intertextual travel? Was she a reminder of the on-going bloodshed in Israel/Palestine? Was she fooling the Forum's participants like the *shahid* woman fooled the Israeli soldiers? The impossibility of reading her and the insistence on reading her nevertheless also resemble the hyper-theatrical but ever failing work of Israeli military checkpoints (Kirstein Keshet 2002): soldiers at the checkpoints inflict humiliation and abuse on an everyday basis but do not prevent suicide bombers, although they use the latter to justify the former.

The detective work of reading – at the checkpoints and in cyberspace – is also haunted by many indefinable, unnamed or unimaginable possibilities, such as for example of a Jewish woman who lives in Palestine and/or identifies with the Palestinians, or a person who is both Jewish and Arab. But maybe the most unimaginable, and therefore the most terrifying possibility seemed to have been the idea of a Palestinian *subject.* Not the national object to be inspected and managed, not a terrorist, not a demonised suicide bomber or a religious fanatic, but a person, virtual yet almost real, complex and contradictory, flirty and funny, speaking up and speaking back, someone who is human[29] and possibly even queer. These unimaginable possibilities point out that passing is much more than just de/re-stabilising of identity categories: it is about the ultimate border – the limit of humanness.

29 My view of the humanising recognition of the other speaks first and foremost to the 'raciology of dehumanisation' (Gilroy 2004) that characterises much of orientalist thinking, including that of many Israelis and Russian-speaking immigrants, where the oriental other – in this case the Palestinian – is racialised through denying him or her the status of the human. I return to a more detailed discussion of Gilroy's work and of my own vision of humanness and dehumanisation in the conclusion.

PART III

Flaming Figures

I conclude my discussion of violence and belonging by taking a journey into the world of on-line fights, known in cyberculture as 'flame wars'. If the first part focused on the homophobic attacks within the immigrant community as a way of excluding queerness from the nation, as well as from class respectability and humanness; and the second part explored how queer attachments to the nation worked through violence towards outsiders – 'intruders', 'trespassers' and 'enemies'; the last two chapters zoom in on the interpersonal violence *within* the queer immigrant cyberspace. My task here is not so much to separate between the different groups subjected to injury – as my discussion will demonstrate, on-line fights among the participants were intertwined with multiple vectors of ethnic, class, racial and gendered violence. Rather, my aim is to explore the cyberviolence of flame wars as a form of *being together though injury and irresolvable ambivalence.*

The social studies of queer spaces (bars, community centres, gay neighbourhoods, and, recently, also newsgroups, chatrooms and websites) frequently examine gays and lesbians as objects of violence. These studies describe GLBT spaces as constituted around the feeling of safety versus the potential threat of homophobia-related hostility and attacks (Corteen et al. 2002; Moran et al. 2001; Moran and Skeggs 2004). They also examine the symbolic violence of heteronormativity, by looking at social landscapes as 'liberatory or oppressive sites for the performance of [...] sexed selves' (Bell and Valentine 1995: 98; see also Kitchin 2002; Knopp 1995). Similarly, researchers of cybercommunities note the potential for establishing on-line queer spaces of belonging (Alexander 2002; Campbell 2004; Munt et al. 2002; Wakeford 1997). And yet there is very little research that addresses the role of violence *within* queer communities; attacks and aggression are typically attributed to outsiders. With the exception of some research on domestic abuse in same-sex partnerships (Cruz 2000; Mason 2002), there are not many accounts of how relations between queers can be based on violence – physical, verbal or symbolic. One very significant exception can be found in literature by queers of colour who emphasise the racial violence of white queer spaces (see, for example, Cruz-Malave and Manalansan 2002; Haritaworn et al. 2008; Held and Leach 2008; Petzen 2004). But even there one finds little conceptualisation of how violence from within, as a complex cultural and psychic phenomenon, can work to produce belonging.

It is this violence from within that interests me here. The following two chapters examine flame wars about *At Shunya's* – the only 'Russian' queer club in Tel-Aviv – that took place on the Forum at the time of my fieldwork. The club was closely linked to the website. Its programme was advertised on the homepage: a flashing permanent banner was located at the top of the page, and drag shows and other special events were announced with large and colourful temporary banners. Many participants of on-line discussions on the Forum met face to face for the first time when they came to *At Shunya's*; many of them even used their Forum nicknames rather than real names to address each other at the club. The Forum served as a place to plan events at the club, for example, when someone proposed a Karaoke night, or to arrange a lift for those coming from another town. It was also the space in which to discuss the club itself. It was these discussions that often developed into flame wars, turning the Forum into a battlefield. Among the 70 discussion threads about *At Shunya's* that I collected from the archives, about one third were passionate and long-lasting fights in which people called each other names, behaved aggressively, insulted, cursed, and mocked the club and each other.

'Why is it that every time *At Shunya's* is mentioned, there are always fights, floods of insults and curses?' – wrote Alex, a Russian-speaking gay man and a frequent visitor to the Forum, in one of the discussions. The following two chapters are based on close reading of some of these fights, their themes, genres and structure. Following Alex's question, I want to ask: what was it about the club that caused constant fights? In Chapter 5, with this question in mind, I will turn to the discussions which positioned *At Shunya's* as the queer immigrants' 'place of their own'. I will show that in these on-line discussions, *At Shunya's* was transformed from a concrete place into a tropic figure of the Club, a 'condensed map of contestable worlds' in Haraway's words (1997: 11). The Club, I will argue, emerged in the flame wars as a material-semiotic-psychic figure that linked together many seemingly disparate elements: smells, tastes and sounds of the night scene; memories of a Soviet past, visions of the immigrant present and future, and a melancholic mourning of impossible belonging. And while each flame war may at first appear to be simply about *At Shunya's* as a place, I will show that it is the Club's tropic quality as a figure that produced the emotional intensity and violence of the fights.

While Chapter 5 focuses on the Club which was at the centre of the endless fights, Chapter 6 takes a closer look at the figure of the Flamer – the one that generated the flame wars, disappeared in them and re-emerged time and again, like a phoenix coming out of the flames. In cyberculture the term 'flamer' usually refers to the person who initiates flame wars, provokes, disturbs and causes fights. But the Flamer, as this chapter will demonstrate, was never just a particular person. Rather, it 'collect[ed] up people' (Haraway 1997: 23) into a material-semiotic figure that conjured and exposed experiences, fantasies, desires, disidentification and loss and mapped the contested world of queer migranthood itself.

My focus on the intra-communal violence in cyberspace may at first appear odd and somewhat out of place in relation to homophobia and nationalism discussed in the first two parts of the book, because the on-line exchanges of insults seemingly exist on a different level and operate on a different register. However, as the two following chapters will show, the flaming debates about the Club and the contradictory figure of the Flamer conjure up precisely the complexities of sexual, ethnic and national belonging of queer immigrants in cyberspace and beyond. What's more, by focusing on the movements and the effects of flame wars, I aim to grasp the complexity of cyberviolence itself, its ambivalence, its slippery trans-formations and constant refigurations, and its reverberating effects across material, semiotic and psychic terrains.

CHAPTER 5

The Club

At Shunya's

In 2001 Shunya (Tanya Shunevich),[1] an immigrant woman in her early 50s who had been a long term lesbian activist in Russia before emigrating,[2] began organising 'Russian evenings' for women at Tel-Aviv's Lesbian Feminist Community Centre.[3] After several months of success Shunya and her partner decided to open a small club – *At Shunya's* – in a rented apartment in South Tel-Aviv.[4] After another year *At Shunya's* moved to a bigger venue, still in South Tel-Aviv. The club remained there for several years, until Shunya's sudden death in 2006[5] – an event that shocked and saddened the many queer immigrants who frequented the place. At the time of my

1 Tanya Shunevich died of heart illness in 2006. This chapter is dedicated to her memory.

2 She took an active part in the emerging lesbian scene in St Petersburg, Russia, since the 1980s.

3 The evenings were part of a broader initiative by several women, including Anna Talisman who later became the coordinator of the RFAHD, to create a network of and a social space for queer immigrant women.

4 South Tel-Aviv, bordering on the city of Jaffa, is an area of cheap housing and slums, established in place of a Palestinian village, and populated by the *Mizrachi* poor in the first several decades of the establishment of Israel. Later, the cheap rents attracted students and immigrants. Since the 1990s the area has been predominantly populated by migrant workers from Eastern Europe, Asia and Africa, as well as by some Russian-speaking immigrants. Today, the area has two open-air food markets and a mixture of small shops, nightclubs and industrial buildings. One section, Florentin, has been a bohemian haunt since the 1990s, and also has a growing gay neighbourhood.

5 After that the club changed hands and location; the new place, *Norvick,* continued to be advertised on the website.

ethnography in 2003–2004, though, it seemed that the club would be there forever. 'It is already impossible to imagine our life without it', wrote Guy, the website's co-administrator and a journalist, in 2002 in an essay posted on the site, and continued, citing the many references to the club: 'Do you go to *At Shunya's*?', 'Yesterday *At Shunya's* was full!', 'Last night it was great at *Shunya's*' (http://www.aguda.org/lesbi/shunya.php, saved March 2004). An inseparable part of queer immigrants' life, *At Shunya's* was also known to Israeli queers as 'the Russian club', which they occasionally visited in search of novelty or exotic atmosphere. For both Israeli and immigrant queers *At Shunya's* became an iconic marker of the Russian-queer scene, and a synecdoche for Russian-immigrant queerness itself.

I remember how Shunya herself told me that what she really wanted was to make a queer club for immigrants. In winter 2000 we were sitting in Tel-Aviv's Lesbian Feminist Community Centre, a place that was seen by many Israeli lesbians as 'their' space. Shunya's words struck me with their pain and longing, and also with their sense of alienation from – and disidentification with – the Israeli scene. 'I do not want to ask anything from *them*', she said, meaning the Israeli women who run the centre. 'I want a place of our own'.

A desire for a 'place of our own' is a familiar experience for many immigrants (as well as other minoritised subjects). Located in different geo-political contexts, some of them leave a national home behind, others arrive at a 'new home', and yet others move between different locations simultaneously coded as 'homes'. Some have a place (or places) they can call 'home'. Others, not having that luxury, still long for – and actively establish – places of attachment, driven by what Avtar Brah calls 'homing desires'. In her *Cartographies of Diaspora* (1996), Brah emphasises that homing desires are not the same as a desire for a national homeland, and are not necessarily linked to a fixed place of origin. Home, for Brah, is first and foremost a 'mythic place of desire in the diasporic imagination' (Brah 1996: 192).

The notion of homing desires has also become a familiar trope in queer studies. Narratives of queer identities often evoke the trope of home: home as memory, home as 'the lost heterosexual origin' (Eng in Fortier 2001: 408–409), and coming out as coming home (Fortier 2001). Scholars of queer diaspora, working at the intersection of sexuality and migration, have approached this notion critically. They have pointed out that many queer communities do not carry the same promise of belonging for all, alienating, excluding or ignoring many queers of colour (Manalansan 2003; Petzen 2004). At the same time they emphasise that for many diasporic and immigrant queers, a desire for places of attachment and belonging is crucial. For example, in a study of Turkish queers in Berlin, Jennifer Petzen notes that while for those 'living with discrimination and misunderstanding on a daily basis, home might be too much to hope for' (Petzen 2004: 28), they can still create 'homelike spaces'. Critical of the linear narrative of moving into a (white) queer home/subculture, Petzen and others (see, for example, Manalansan 2003) nevertheless emphasise the importance of homely places and homing desires in queer immigrants' lives, shifting the discussion from a register of travel/movement to one of affect/attachment (Fortier 2006).

But these discussions of diasporic homing desires seldom address the violence within such homes: queer migrants are assumed to welcome a 'place of their own' univocally. Insightful in their attention to notions of desire, theories on queer homes and queer diaspora can tell us little about the disagreements and raging fights that galvanised the Forum when *At Shunya's* was discussed. In these fights the club was often envisioned as a site of Russianness and migranthood. But while for some participants this diasporic nature of the club signified warmth, welcome, connectivity and 'diasporic intimacy' (Boym 2001), for others it was a sign of provinciality, backwardness and clinging to one's ethnicity. The participants of the Forum, in other words, did not share the same vision of the queer scene, even when they shared the desire for such a scene; their views clashed violently, causing passionate and long-lasting fights and exposing the ambivalence and anxieties of queer migranthood as they were condensed into the 'place of their own'. So what are the different figurations of a 'place of one's own'? How is the Club figured through homing desires? And how can queer immigrant belonging be constituted simultaneously through longing for such a place, and repeated attacks of it, and of each other?

What interests me here are the relations between violence and homing desires, as they unfolded in the flame wars, where the views of Russianness, Israeliness, and queerness clashed time and again. Throughout the chapter

I will follow the complex psychic processes of condensation, displacement and mourning of an unknown and unattainable ideal, involved in figuring the Club. In other words, I will trace the ways the Club emerged as a figure through endless fights in cyberspace, exceeding the particular club *At Shunya's* and transforming it into a tropic entity. I will argue that the 'structure of feeling' (Williams 1997; see also Eng and Han 2003) that guided these flame wars was that of melancholia, leading to the repetition of the fights and to their, often self-inflicted, violence. Melancholia figured the Club as *both* the site onto which homing desires were projected, and as an object of impossible attachment and possession.[6]

In my use of melancholia I am informed by Freud's *Mourning and Melancholia* (1917/1934) as an analysis of the individual psyche, but also by the *social* reading of melancholia, in particular in the context of race and ethnicity (Eng and Han 2003). I address melancholia not (only) as an individual but as what Mark Steinberg (2009) describes as a *social condition* that characterises times of dramatic change and collective uncertainly, what Bell coins 'melancholia that is discursively given' and what Butler refers to as 'culturally instituted forms of melancholia' (Butler in Bell 1999a: 170). Figuring the Club through melancholia, the flame wars, as this chapter will show, were also about 'the making of worlds' (Castañeda 2002), mapping the very condition of immigration and othering and the forms of ambivalent belonging that emerge there.

6 Here I am also informed by Fortier's conceptualisation of migrant community centres as 'cultural objects, as collective property, as a *scene* for referring to and experiencing collective affective belonging' (Fortier 2006: 65, italics in original).

A Russian welcome

Many participants described *At Shunya's* as a place with a soul. Defending the club against one of the critics, one participant posted: 'Do you know the word "soul"??? Show me the soul of *Shirazi*, show me the soul of *Vox*[7] ... But I can show you *Shunya's* soul.' Another one wrote: 'Maybe some need crystal lanterns and other tinsel ... soulless tinsel'. 'But what is there *At Shunya's* is the soul, the soul that is put in you', continued a third one. The soul, here, appeared as an object, both internal to the club, and transferable onto its visitors. For other participants, *At Shunya's* was a place *for* the queer immigrants' souls, a place that welcomed them in a particular way. Explaining his need for a 'Russian' queer club, Boris, for example, wrote:

> <Boris>: We see Israelis in our own way. They see us in their own way. The older generation of immigrants doesn't see GLBT the way Israelis do. We, as Russian-born or as their descendants, naturally have something special in the breadth of our soul and our way of relaxation. Shunya's club warms up this particular part of our soul. That's why it exists.

Boris described *At Shunya's* as a place for his particular needs as a queer immigrant: a place to *be*, rather than *to be seen* (as different). Israelis and immigrants seeing each other in 'their own way' points to – although leaving mainly unsaid – the many experiences of otherness and everyday racism, experienced by queer immigrants. But his posting also hints at the experiences of homophobia, especially vis-à-vis the older generation of immigrants. The raging anti-queer hatred and the erasure of queerness from the Russian-speaking community, described in Chapters 1 and 2, makes Boris's desire particularly clear. He – and many other participants too – wanted to be part of an immigrant space, but as a queer; he wanted to share the space with those who have had similar experiences of both ethnic otherness and homophobia. His poetic narrative of naturalised cultural differences, where the Israelis and the immigrants appear to have

7 *Shirazi* and *Vox* are two well-known queer dance clubs in Tel-Aviv.

different souls, figured the Club of his dream as a place that welcomed, 'warmed up' precisely this immigrant soul. By doing so, it also figured the queer immigrants as having a Russian soul that could only be truly embraced in a 'Russian' space.

The idea of hospitality for the soul has its roots in the Russian tradition of welcoming and turning strangers into guests by opening for them the doors of one's home. Dale Pesmen in her analysis of 'soul' in Russia notes, that 'a common description of hospitality implied that a host or hostess' job was to create a substitute home' for the guest (Pesmen 2000: 161). Being welcomed and being made to feel at home was, too, a common trope in the postings about *At Shunya's*, where it was used to emphasise the club's uniqueness:

> <Alex>: In my opinion, there is something about this place that makes me feel like at home. Is it because I know Shunya, her partner and other frequent visitors very well? But this feeling, I must tell you, is worth a fortune. I have been to many gay places, but have never felt as free [comfortable] anywhere else.
>
> <Smiley>: Alex and the girls are right. *At Shunya's* there is something that you cannot buy for any money in the world. You are like at home there and everyone accepts you like kin, all you need is smile to the people around you.

Alex and Smiley were both describing *At Shunya's* as a home away from home, as a place where their homing desires – framed as a desire for family and acceptance[8] – were met. For Alex the homing desire was first and foremost about *feeling*. The expression he used – to feel free/relaxed/comfortable – is in fact best translated into English as 'feeling at home'. Alex felt at home because he knew Shunya personally. But the idea of feeling 'free', as opposed to feeling constrained, tense and self-aware, is also linked to the Russian language. As several participants noted, one of the things that attracted them to *At Shunya's* was the ability to communicate in their mother tongue, while also being in a queer place.

In these and other references to the soul, belonging was constituted simultaneously as embodied – the sensory comfort of body in place – and as

8 Or rather, family *as* acceptance, which in itself is a very particular figuration of kinship.

non-material, spiritual, juxtaposed to the commercial logic that underpins most of the queer scene, in Tel-Aviv and many Western urban areas. This was a sense of connectedness that could not be bought, as Smiley emphasised. Another person, Snake, similarly noted, in response to someone's critique of the quality of food at the club: 'Not by bread alone … Even the best and tastiest steak cannot compare to [the pleasure of] sitting with friends over a beer (although I personally love good food)'. 'Not by bread alone' refers to the commonly known quote from the Bible: 'Man shall not live by bread alone, but by every word that proceeded out of the mouth of God'.[9] Rooted in Judeo-Christian tradition, widely known and commonly used in Russia, the phrase does not necessarily carry a religious connotation but rather refers to the secular-spiritual emphasis on the non-material, which in turn is seen as a sign of having a soul.

Snake's idea of sitting and drinking with friends evokes very particular cultural associations of connectedness. Her reference to the Judeo-Christian notion of spiritual life in the context of drinking might appear as puzzling, after all, drinking, just like eating, is a bodily act. But Snake's text would better be understood in the context of the role sitting and drinking has traditionally played in Russian and Soviet society, where it was a highly ritualised act, loaded with social meanings. Drinking and sitting together, emphasises Pesmen (2000), is a genre of communication central to Russianness. 'Rituals including alcohol were the epitome of hospitality, condensing economic, socio-cultural, philosophical and psychological *dusha* (soul, Russian). […] Drinking situations […] were also privileged contexts for other *dusha*-related activities, such as playing music, singing, cursing and reciting poetry' (2000: 171). Drinking together, continues Pesmen, can act as a communion, and as a way of establishing the boundaries of terms like 'friends' or 'one of us'. 'The "we", established or assumed while sitting could be exclusive and lasting, or as fleeting as the high from one shot of vodka' (2000: 181).

9 These words appear twice, first in the Old Testament (spoken by Moses to the Israelites in the book of Exodus), and in the New Testament (The Gospel according to St Matthew).

Similarly, in Snake's posting, sitting and drinking was what made *At Shunya's* a place for the soul. The club became a place for the immigrant queers not only because it targeted a particular group in the population, but because of the form of communication that it allowed. It is what Boym calls 'diasporic intimacy': a form of connectedness between immigrants, as 'a precarious cosiness of a foreign home' (Boym 2001: 254). Indeed, the connection between the club's visitors sitting and drinking together is, at the same time, deeply rooted in the Russian heritage, and fragile, because of its status as a marginal, immigrant space on the Israeli queer scene.

In these descriptions of *At Shunya's* Alex, Smiley and Snake figured the Club as an idealised 'substitute home' that, because of its Russianness, privileged the eternal and the spiritual, rather than the material and the trendy. But the Club was not just a place where traditional Russian laws of hospitality and connectedness should operate. Rather, the Club emerged as particularly precious because of the ways its visitors could be figured through it: as those who could – and did – belong, not only and not so much on the national level of entitlement to a home, but on the immediate, tactile level of bodily comfort, familiarity and relaxation. In other words, they were figured as subjects with a soul and as subjects of welcome; as those who were displaced or on the move, but could be embraced unconditionally, as opposed, for example, to the racialised and ethicised logic of immigration, where belonging to the nation is always conditional – on blood, cultural practices or political loyalty.

But not all the participants regarded *At Shunya's* as a place they could or would want to consider their own. Many related to it as a site of failed hospitality, as a disgusting and unwelcoming place. All these notions were also linked to the club's Russianness. Importantly, such views of *At Shunya's* did not move away from immigrants' homing desires; rather, these desires were displaced elsewhere, refiguring the 'Russian' Club as a site of disidentification and loss.

'Bad' / 'old' Russianness

One of the most frequent criticisms of *At Shunya's* was what was described as inadequate service and failure to provide appropriate food and drinks: what was served at the club was of the wrong kind, not properly made, or lacking in variety. Strikingly, the many complaints about the food and drinks depicted them as specifically 'Russian' or Soviet, and therefore, unattractive and even bad. Nice Tree, for example, wrote that the food offered at the club did not look appealing, was not fresh – grilled meat, he noted, was prepared in the morning and not cooked on the spot – and reminded him of a Soviet public dining centre. Soviet dining centres were known for their low-quality food. They could also be seen as an antonym of welcome, both because of the poor cooking and because these were very public spaces, subjected to the state's surveillance and control, and opposed to the intimacy of informal communication (and of home-made food). But it was not only the opposition of the (bad) Soviet to the (good) Israeli/Western/capitalist service. Nice Tree also noted that the window display of *At Shunya's* resembled a 'Russian' shop, meaning a shop established and run by immigrants. 'Russian shops' appeared in Israel during the 1990s, following the big wave of immigration; today they are part of the local scene, mapping sites and routes of nostalgia and transnational connections (Bernstein 2006). But for Nice Tree they are first and foremost signs of a past one wants to move away from; his critique resembled other complaints where clinging to the past or being stuck in Russianness are seen as highly undesirable.

Drinking at the club, too, was depicted in a negative way. Many participants noted that they were repulsed by the drunkenness of *At Shunya's* visitors; some graphically described their encounters with people puking in or outside the club. Their feelings and the vivid materiality they described signalled passionate and tactile rejection and disidentification. Not only did they not want to be associated with these other visitors, but they also repeatedly created distance between themselves and others through expressions of disgust which, as I showed in Chapter 1, is a material-semiotic boundary between subjects and/or communities. But most interestingly, in many postings, sitting with friends and 'spiritual' drinking were refigured as 'Russian' drunkenness. One of the complainers, Tim, wrote that the selection of drinks at the club, and in particular, the service provided by the barwoman, were unacceptable. The barwoman, according to Tim, was not pleasant, but more importantly, she was not as proficient as he would have expected. He ordered 'one Ballantine' ('Ballantine Ale'), and was furious when the barwoman brought him a jug of water. 'She has never heard of Ballantine', he wrote mockingly, 'and therefore misheard my order as a jug of water' (*kankan maim* in Hebrew). Using taste and knowledge of drinks as tools of class distinction (Bourdieu 1984), Tim was stating that the barwoman's lack of professionalism shamed *At Shunya's* vis-à-vis 'any proper bar'.

Tim and Nice Tree's performance of taste illuminates how food and alcohol – their taste, their 'appeal', and the practices of serving and consuming them – act as a form of 'cultural capital' (Bourdieu 1984).[10] In his discussion of class, Bourdieu notes that while taste (for certain food, drinks, clothes, art, etc.) seems to be personal and individual, it is in fact an expression of one's class position. What's more, notions of taste and tastelessness are frequently used to maintain the boundaries – the distinction – between classes. Tim's arrogance towards the barwoman (and by association, also towards other visitors who, unlike Tim, accepted the service gratefully), and similarly Nice Tree's scorning of the food, indeed shows how the expectation of particular cuisine or particular expertise in alcohol put Shunya's club in a negative light. It lacks what is seen as needed cultural capital: this way class is naturalised, and classed judgement becomes a universal category of good/bad. In the same move, Tim and Nice Tree have positioned themselves as people of higher class and taste, or rather, they are performing their aspirations of Western middle-classness.

Another complaint about alcohol demonstrates that drinking is not only a classed, but an ethnicised and historicised figuration: the lack of

10 For an interesting discussion of taste and cultural capital in the case of 'ethnic' food, consumed by the white society *and* by the immigrants, see Hage (1997).

taste in drinking, just as the lack of freshly cooked food, mentioned by Nice Tree, appears to be specifically Soviet.

> <Crazy Ala>: We ordered Whisky-Cola but it turned out that there isn't enough whisky for the second portion (this completely shocked my friend from Moscow) ... We were offered 'Sir Kent' which we decided not to drink for hygienic reasons. At the bar [people were] drinking beer, probably 'Baltic' [...] Due to the lack of whisky at the bar we ordered a Vodka-Red Bull which was more expensive than Whisky-Cola (surprise!), but we survived that. [...] A woman at the bar could not figure out the price for the whisky and called from the back room for a woman named Olga, whose drunken mug confirmed the cult status of this place. [...] We decided not to waste money on dubious alcohol, got a taxi and went to *Carpe Diem* where we had a few high quality cocktails that somewhat improved the bad taste left by *At Shunya's*.

The two visitors (Crazy Ala and a companion) have claimed the position of sophisticated drinkers: they ordered fancy and expensive drinks, and were 'shocked' when these were not stocked; they knew the prices and avoided drinking 'Sir Kent', a vodka that is considered as low-quality and therefore unhealthy. When their demands were not satisfied, they left to raise their spirits with 'high quality cocktails' in the fancy and bohemian Tel-Aviv gay bar *Carpe Diem*. But how did they see those people at the club they left behind, having mocked its 'cult' status? Those at the club were drinking dubious alcohol: cheap vodka and soviet beer ('Baltic' is the name of a Soviet beer, still produced today). In other words, they drank without differentiation, in order to get drunk.

The woman at the bar – a 'drunken mug' – becomes a collective face of all visitors. Her 'ugly' appearance is clearly associated with Russian and Soviet signs of alcoholism, and constitutes the opposition between drinking for pleasure and getting drunk. She synechdochically marks the whole place as a site of unsophisticated and unpleasant alcohol consumption that is inseparable from the club's Sovietness. The latter is emphasised by the presence of 'Soviet' beer. Sovietness here appears both as a sign of class position and as ethnicity frozen in time: Crazy Ala's companion, a guest from Moscow, was well informed about the 'right' drinks. The immigrants – or more specifically, those among them who went to *At Shunya's* – appear to be stuck in their past.

This historicised and classed figuration of lack of sophistication, tastelessness and being stuck in time re-emerges in other postings about *At Shunya's*. For example, one frequently repeated theme in the complaints was that it looked like the Soviet Union of the 1980s. 'It feels like 1989, the place is like a Soviet dining centre', wrote Nice Tree. 'What is the club rated for? Bad taste and provinciality?' asked another participant. 'When I see it I feel that the time stopped in 1990'. And yet another one wrote: 'When I go to a club, I come to dance, surrounded by good-looking people. I don't want to languish in a corner with a plastic cup, watching what looks like a disco in Zhitomir in 1987'.

Zhitomir is the name of a small town in Ukraine, known for its rich Jewish life in the late 19th and 20th century. As one of the places with large Jewish communities, it can be characterised as a *shtettl*, a Jewish village/town, one of many that existed beyond the 'Pale of Settlement'[11] during the tsarist regime, and remained after the revolution. But in pre-Soviet and Soviet-Jewish mapping, *shtettl* is also a marker of provinciality, the opposite of the assimilated Jews who live in big cities.[12] The image of the *shtettl* is a separate topic that lies beyond the scope of this book. What interests me here is how a *shtettl* figures as a sign of Jewish as well as Soviet provinciality. In the encounter between Russian-speaking Jews from different parts of the former Soviet Union that occurred in Israel, provinces, and in particular small towns with a large Jewish population such as Zhiromir, were often constructed as an attribute of the 'other Other': the antithesis of the metropolitan Jewish intelligentsia, coming mainly from Moscow and Leningrad/St Petersburg. In the internal distinctions between the immigrants, in particular those of the 'middle generation' who grew up in the Soviet Union and arrived in Israel in their late teens or twenties, *shtettl* provinciality and Sovietness often merged. Being 'Soviet' was seen as shameful *because* provincial. It seems as if the repeated notion of 'Soviet'

11 Jews in tsarist Russia were only allowed to settle beyond the 'Pale of Settlement', in rural areas and not in big cities.

12 A Russian word for the Yiddish *shtettl* is *mestechko* (little place), that also forms a noun *mestechkovost'*, meaning provinciality, backwardness and narrow-mindedness.

in conjunction with the notion of provinciality signals the desire to shake off the associations with both diasporic Jewish and Soviet pasts.

But Sovietness is also the opposite of modernity, in particular, queer modernity. It is not accidental that the Soviet Union always appears as a moment frozen in time: the late 1980s. One thing that comes to mind is of course the collapse of the communist regime that began with the destruction of the Berlin Wall and was soon followed by the fall of the Soviet Union itself. The late 1980s, for the West, is probably registered as the last days of the Soviet Empire. But for the Russian-speaking immigrants of the last wave, and in particular, for the immigrants in their late twenties and thirties, the late 1980s also carries a deep personal and generational significance. For them the Soviet 1980s is the time (and place) of their adolescence or early adulthood. It was also the last moment of their lives in a country that no longer exists. It became fetishised and frozen in their memories, living through particular images, through moments of longing but also through shame and disidentification. So while some of *At Shunya's* visitors may have embraced the nostalgic pleasures of listening to old pop-music or watching a drag performance that involved songs and personae of their childhood, others wanted to merge with the shiny and up-to-date Israeli scene, as they perceived it. They refused to be associated with an immigrant site, a place that welcomed the *Russian* soul, because it was this Russianness that they wanted to move away from, in order to become queer Israelis. The Israeli scene in itself – in its mixture of multi-cultural consumption, racist and classist exclusions, its fantasies of Westerness and depoliticised sexuality – is a complex and contradictory cultural site. But in the postings that criticised *At Shunya's* and glorified Israeli gay clubs, the Israeli scene appeared as an idealised place, welcoming for everyone and not burdened by a past.

The figuration of the Club as a piece of Sovietness, stuck in time, can also be found in the two articles about 'the Russian club', that appeared in the Hebrew language GLBT magazines in 2003 and were then translated and published on the queer immigrants' website, in the *Community* section. These articles portrayed *At Shunya's* with a mix of patronisation, exoticisation and excitement. One journalist, Oren Ziv, described the club as located at the margins of queer Tel-Aviv: 'outside the pretentious posturing of the (gay/night) scene, alongside the straight clubs of South Tel-Aviv' (http://www.aguda.org/community/shunya.php, saved March 2004). The outsider status of *At Shunya's* was repeated twice: once when it was metaphorically located beyond the Israeli queer scene, and then when it was geographically placed in South Tel-Aviv – the area of slums, migrant labourers and urban poor. 'Do you want to feel as if you're abroad, in another country? Come to the place called *At Shunya's*', wrote the other journalist, Rinat Haimov, informing her readers that 'with the assimilation of "Russians" in Israeli society, it was decided to open the club's doors for those born in the country, who were thirsty for new experiences' (ibid.).

If *At Shunya's* was narrated as being spatially distanced form the Israeli queer scene, the visitors' differences were presented simultaneously on three levels: they came from far away; they were culturally and racially exotic; and they were linked to the past. The queer immigrants were described as having blond curls, blue eyes and athletic bodies; they danced *Kazachok* and other Russian dances to the sounds of Russian pop-music from the 1980s, and projected 'the air of uninhibitedness, which characterizes only those who came here from far away, and now celebrate freedom, having defrosted from the Siberian ice' (Ziv). One of the journalists included some words in (broken) Russian, to contribute to the overall aura of a foreign and exotic place and to make her description look more authentic: she completed her article with '*Fashes darovie*, comrades' (Haimov). This is a distortion of *za vashe zdorovje* – 'to your life', a Russian toast that rarely escapes Western popular narrations of Russia.

Both articles deployed the familiar icons of Russianness and Sovietness, icons that are part of the Western technologies of 'knowing' and representing Soviet Russia in various sites of cultural production from Hollywood films to commercial adverts of vodka. But these icons – and in particular the blond hair and blue eyes – also painfully resonated with the way Russian-speaking immigrants were represented in the Israeli media of the 1990s as 'too white', that is, as carrying 'Slavic blood', as non-Jewish (Golden 2003) or not Jewish enough. Within the framework of their immigration as national homecoming, and within the Israeli economy of Jewishness, blond hair and blue eyes became the synecdoche for the Russian-speaking immigration, marking their desirability as Europeans and at the same time their marginality as racially mixed and 'Russian' rather than Jewish. Russian-speaking immigrants were often seen as 'failing' Jews who have not maintained blood purity and lost their Jewishness to numerous mixed marriages, as well as loosing their cultural and religious identity due to assimilation in the Soviet Union. Not surprisingly, depicting the 'Russian club' as 'another country', forever marked its visitors with difference, despite 'assimilation' – this time in Israel.

When the translation of the two articles was published on the website, some participants laughed them off, but others were clearly upset. 'This is all they see in us, Russians', wrote one person, Will. 'That we drink vodka non-stop and dance *Kazachok*'. But how do they see themselves? What does 'Russianness' mean for Jewish immigrants, whose identification with Russia is complicated and ambivalent? For example, the figure of the Russian drunk has often been seen as the antipode of the Soviet-Jewish intelligentsia, both in terms of class and ethnicity (Lomsky-Feder and Rappoport 2003). Figuring the Club as a place of drunkenness juxtaposed with fashionable drinking is undoubtedly linked to the middle-class Western queerness. But the disidentification with the Russian Club because of its drinking culture is also a form of claiming one's Jewishness, against the 'Russianisation' of immigrants by Israeli society. As many of the Russian-speaking immigrants in Israel repeatedly noted, referring to their racialisation, 'we were Jews in Russia and became Russians in Israel'. They emphasised the irony of finally becoming 'Russians' in the country that welcomed them as Jews, after having been rejected from Russianness in the Soviet Union. This ambivalence of desire, rejection and (dis)identification is what figures the Club as welcoming because of its 'spiritual' drinking, and as repelling because of its unsophisticated drunkenness; as too Jewish (provincial, from a *shtettl*) and simultaneously as too Russian. It is not surprising that the ambivalent longing for a 'place of our own', projected onto the figure of the Club, is so often experienced as impossibility and unattainable loss.

Loss

'I don't care about Shunya's soul, I just want to be served', wrote one of the participants, Richie, in response to the description of *At Shunya's* as a place for the soul, 'Shunya doesn't listen to her clients and loses their trust'. Like Nice Tree, Tim and Crazy Ala, Richie envisions the Club first and foremost as a site of commercial hospitality and exchange. He and many others expressed anger and disgust towards *At Shunya's*, with its drunkenness and bad food; they emphasised that they wanted to leave, go elsewhere and shake off the bad impression left by Shunya's club. Shunya was losing (or would lose) her clients, noted some of them: dissatisfied with the service, they would not come again.

But was it her loss, or theirs? It seems, that in many of the passionate attacks on *At Shunya's* the one who felt the loss was, in fact, the complainant him/herself.

> <Nice Tree>: 'Push off to Shunya's'
> Friday night, the eternal search for entertainment ... Where should we go? For the Russian gay crowd there isn't much choice: all roads lead to 'Shunya's'. I remember the old place[13] where everything was nice, and the music was good, although the place was tiny. [...] My last visit to the place brought only negative impressions. The music at the club is such a mishmash that you don't want to dance at all.
> 'First we need to have vodka', I heard two women saying when entering the club. Indeed, if you want to stay at this place for even 5 minutes you have to be drunk [...] And the window display [that looks like] a Russian shop with all kinds of products. Grilled meat from the morning, reddish, and hell knows what else... looks not too appealing. So what is it? Reminds me of a Soviet [public] dining centre of the late 1980s. And the prices at the bar are so expensive they scare me away .... And the people are no longer the same ... Well, here I won't say a word, you know it yourself. The toilet was inaccessible because some boy covered with make-up was puking into the sink.
> I felt so sad, and afraid. It's 2004 now, but feels like 1989. Shunya's lack of taste and business initiative makes the place go from bad to worse. Of course, the administra-

13 One year after opening, the club moved to another venue.

> tor will erase my terrible thoughts, but I am posting them not to hurt anyone, I just want Shunya to take this into account ... Life is a complicated thing.

Nice Tree seems to be consumed by his own repulsion. His outcry about the drinks, the visitors, the puke, the food, the music and the overall atmosphere went over each of his bodily senses – the sight, the taste, the smell and the sound. This is an embodied, tactile experience of disidentification; it mirrors the bodily feeling of welcome and comfort, described by Alex, Smiley and Snake. Despite the differences in seeing *At Shunya's*, all of them related to it in the same way: through the multi-sensory comfort – or discomfort – of the body. However, if for Alex and others *At Shunya's* was a place where they could find kinship and belonging, for Nice Tree it was a site of both desire and painful disappointment. His complaints (as well as many other postings criticising *At Shunya's*) are written in a genre that Nancy Ries characterises as 'litany' (Ries 1991, 1997). In her work on distinctive Russian speech genres, Ries describes litany as

> passages in conversation in which a speaker would enunciate a series of complaints, grievances, or worries about problems, troubles, afflictions, tribulations, or losses, and then often comment on these enumerations with a poignant rhetorical question ('Why is everything so bad with us?'), a weeping, fatalistic lament about the hopelessness of the situation, or an expressive Russian sigh of disappointment and resignation (Ries 1997: 84).

Indeed many complaints about *At Shunya's* include the fatalistic elements of lament about the fate of gays in general and of Russian gays in Israel, in particular. But it is not only the genre that is at stake here; litanies create an affective regime of longing and loss, through which the Club is figured as the object of melancholic attachment. Nice Tree's posting, for example, presents the gay immigrant as being trapped by his longing for a night scene and his dissatisfaction with its realities. He tried to move away from *At Shunya's* and its visitors, but was always drawn back, hoping – and failing – to find the 'good old club' that was no more. There is something masochistic in Nice Tree's detailed description of his suffering, paired with an urge to go to the club anyway. Just like many other complainers, Nice Tree was simultaneously drawn to and disgusted by the club, and this double urge bursts out violently. The violence is clearly expressed in the title of the posting, 'Push off to Shunya's!' This is the best translation of the original Russian text that literally says 'You all, get to Shunya's!'. Grammatically, it is very close to 'Let's go to Shunya's'. Yet in Russian, this small syntactic change shifts the meaning of the sentence from invitation to an insult. Nice Tree's witty game of words signals this linguistic ambivalence as well as the ambivalence of his own feelings.

Nice Tree's mourning, emphasised by his 'I feel so sad, and afraid', and the sense of being trapped in the wrong place, resonate with many other postings that criticised *At Shunya's*. The dissatisfied, sad and disgusted visitors were looking for a different Russian queerness which they could not find there. Their hopes turned into loss, and their loss, in turn, became an attack. For some, like Nice Tree, it was a loss of the place that they once had and liked. But for many others the Russian queer 'place of our own' was never there in the first place, at least not in the way they wanted it to be, and they mourned its impossibility. For example, one participant, Spring Breeze, wrote a long posting about her desire for a *Russian-speaking* queer scene and for the sort of intimacy she could only find in her mother tongue. She then turned to her negative impression of *At Shunya's*, written in the style of 'poignant rhetorical questions' (Ries 1997: 84):

> <Spring Breeze>: I probably have really strange demands of the owners of *At Shunya's* ... if I order something non-alcoholic, why do I have to wait until the woman serves everyone who came after me? Why can't I drink from a clean glass, why do I get my orange drink in a disposable plastic vessel? And by the way, drink and juice are not the same, so why if I asked for juice, do I get a drink? Why is the change always either sticky or wet?

She concluded her long list of complaints (only partially reproduced here) by exclaiming:

> <Spring Breeze>: This is all so sad, and there is no hope for change. That's why I don't come to *At Shunya's*, and go to meet women in Hebrew-speaking places, where the unexpected sound of the mother tongue comes like life's unintentional gift.

Ries points out that litany, widely used by people in Russia in their everyday conversations as well as in public performances in media and politics, constitutes a recognisable Russian stance, a 'posture that expresses particular perspectives, values, desires or expectations' (Ries 1997: 88). This is often the stance of the victim, the perpetual sufferer, whose suffering gives him/her a position of moral sanctity. At the same time, litanies are an important cultural tool to 'create multiple fields of identification and belonging' (Ries 1997: 113). Taking Ries's argument further, I read the litanies about the club as performative speech acts (Butler 1990, 1993). The repetition of complaints, and the flame wars they generated, constitute the imagined community of Russian-Israeli queers, as a community of irresolvable suffering, and indeed of melancholia – of endless mourning of the loss that cannot be fully comprehended or resolved. The queers' suffering is a double bind: it is embedded in the racial structure of Russian, Soviet and Israeli societies; but is at the same time self-inflicted. While visitors kept rejecting *At Shunya's*, writing extensively about the unpleasant atmosphere and dissatisfying service, they seldom walked away. On the contrary, they returned to the Forum to weep and to attack, time and again. Their flaming words injured *At Shunya's* and those participants who regarded it as a 'place of their own'. But in starting a flame war they also exposed themselves to injury: in every thread that contained a complaint about *At Shunya's* the attack on the complainer followed immediately. The repetition of the inflammable postings and flame wars functioned in ways similar to Nice Tree's masochistic move, combining longing with repulsion. The suffering subject always returned to the lost object, to multiply, rather than to resolve, the suffering: it was both the pain of not having a place to go, and the pain of being attacked by others.

Melancholic belonging

This chapter followed the ways the Club was figured and refigured through flame wars, once as a site of hospitality for the soul, that welcomed queer immigrants unconditionally, and once as a site of disgust and disappointment that was stuck in time, keeping the queers from moving forward, towards deracinated queer modernity. Figuring the Club as a 'place of one's own' made it a ground for various claims: of diasporic welcome, intimacy and of bodily comfort, of capitalist service and of ethicised and classed queerness. The queers were figured through the Club once as part of family, connected to their roots in a home away from home, and once as mobile subjects, free from their past and from the burden of their ethnic otherness. The twists and turns of the flame wars with their grotesque descriptions and passionate attacks turned *At Shunya's* into a figure that 'brought disparate elements together' (Castañeda 2008: n.p.) and at times, it seemed, conjured up almost too much – the lived memories of the Soviet Union and their Western and Israeli stereotypes; the taste of vodka or beer and the connectedness of drinking to the soul; the tactile comfort of being at home, and the unbearable physical proximity of undesirable bodies; the experience of exoticisation and othering and the smell of puke; the sticky change and the longing to hear one's mother tongue. The queer immigrant Club had a tropic character: every complaint and every fight was embedded in a particular figuration (hospitality for the soul, Soviet and Jewish provinciality, queer modernity etc.); every fight, seemingly focussed on praise or critique of *At Shunya's*, was about queer immigrants' homing desires and ambivalent belonging. The figure of the Club, in other words, mapped the condensed and contestable worlds of queer migranthood across material, semiotic and psychic domains.

But what about violence? The flame wars, generated by the debates about *At Shunya's*, were undoubtedly violent; I return to discuss their structure and effects in the next chapter. What I want to emphasise here, however, is the self-inflicted violence of the homing desire itself, or rather, of melancholia as a structure of feeling by which these desires were shaped. As my discussion has shown, the Club was figured not only as a scene for belonging, but also as an object of longing that cannot be fulfilled, and a loss that cannot be grieved. In his discussion of mourning and melancholia, Freud (1917/1934) distinguishes between mourning in which the lost object is grieved until the subject can move on; and melancholia, where the grief is not resolved because the subject refuses to let go of the object and thus cannot redirect the affect/desire to another object. Freud further elaborates that, while in the case of mourning the lost object is fully known, in melancholia it is not always clear what has been lost: the melancholics themselves do not know what they have lost. Melancholia can also occur when a person knows whom s/he had lost but not *what* s/he had lost in that person. For Freud, melancholia, unlike mourning, is mainly an unconscious process that is hard to comprehend and cure. It is this sense of loss of what is not known – and therefore cannot be grieved – that can best describe the endless and always returning complaints about *At Shunya's*. The intense emotions of the flame wars circulated in lamenting the impossible Club, not in constructive proposals for its creation. This was not because of an unwillingness to change the actual place, as some participants had suggested. Rather, it resulted from the ambivalence of Russian-Israeli-queer subjectivity itself which turned the Club into an object of melancholia: a loss without an end for the mythic place that was never there.

Of course, the term melancholia should be used cautiously: I do not aim to pathologise the immigrants' longing for a 'place of their own' and their dissatisfaction that generated endless flame wars. My analysis is also in no way a 'diagnosis' of a disorder, whether individual or collective. My deployment of Freud's work differs from the therapeutic use of the terms mourning and melancholia: I am not addressing them as 'normal' versus 'pathological' processes and do not read melancholia literally, as an illness (as Freud defines it in 1917).[14] Following Eng and Han, I am interested in melancholia as a 'depathologised structure of feeling' (Eng and Han 2003: 344) and as a socio-cultural, rather than only an individual, process (see also Butler 1997b and Steinberg 2009). In their discussion of race and the American myth of immigration as assimilation, Eng and Han note that for Asian-Americans (and other groups of colour) the process of assimilation is suspended and unresolved. Whiteness for them remains 'at an unattainable distance, at once a compelling fantasy and a lost ideal' (Eng and Han 2003: 345).

14 In his early work on the subject (1917/1934) he distinguishes between the 'normal' process of mourning and the 'pathological' melancholia. In his later work he rethinks the relations between the two and suggests that subject formation always includes melancholia (Freud 1923/1964).

Eng and Han's reading of immigration within the melancholic framework is useful for my understanding of Russian-speaking queers' longing for an impossible 'place of their own'. This impossibility, I would like to suggest, is embedded in their ambivalent position as Russian Jews, as Russian-speaking Israelis, and, of course, as Russian-speaking queers. For many of them both Russianness in the Soviet Union and Israeliness in Israel remain at an unattainable distance, although of course there are significant differences between the two modes of inclusion and exclusion in these two societies. The Club as the object of their desire and longing embodies the ambivalence of the immigrants' collective identification with two nations as those who 'were Jews in Russia and are Russians in Israel'. They want a place to speak Russian, but reject manifestations of 'bad' Russianness. The 'Sovietness' is ambivalent, too: it can evoke nostalgia for music and the atmosphere of one's childhood and adolescence. At the same time, however, it signals exclusion from the Israeli queer scene with its 'pretentious' modernity, so the Club figures its visitors' uncomfortable ambivalent position, as homecomers without a home.

'The loss of a love-object', writes Freud, 'constitutes an excellent opportunity for the ambivalence in love-relationships to make itself felt and come to the fore' (Freud 1917/1934: 161). Indeed, as this chapter demonstrated, the ambivalence of Russian-Israeli queerness comes out in the open in the endless fights about *At Shunya's*. Reading the immigrants' affective relations to the Club as melancholic ambivalence one can better understand the violence of the flame wars about it. Freud notes that melancholic grief and the refusal to let go of the lost object can turn the violence inwards, to the self. He describes it as the 'self-torments' of melancholics, which are both painful and pleasurable. 'If the object-love, which cannot be given up, takes refuge in narcissistic identification, while the object itself is abandoned, then hate is expended upon this new substitute-object, railing at it, depreciating it, making it suffer and deriving sadistic gratification from its suffering' (Freud 1917/1934: 161–162).

'Railing at and depreciating' indeed characterises the endless flame wars and the ways many participants figured the Club, themselves and other visitors. In many postings, *At Shunya's* appeared as a poor substitute for the Club queer immigrants lost without ever having. Their violence was directed towards the existing club, but also towards those visitors who did not mourn the loss but found what they longed for, as queers and as immigrants. But the flame wars, I believe, were also a form of displaced bitterness towards the Israeli queer scene, where the much desired sound of Russian could only be 'life's unintentional gift' (Spring Breeze) and where their own club was seen as 'another country' (Rinat Haimov). Queer immigrants simultaneously desire and resent this Israeliness and the de-ethnicised queer scene, where any immigrant presence becomes a foreign country but where they nevertheless want to be at home, as immigrants and as queers. In other words, they long for belonging which is at once a 'compelling fantasy and a lost ideal' (Eng and Han 2003: 345). This is why the flame wars were full of passion and pain; this is why every time *At Shunya's* was mentioned the Forum went up in flames.

CHAPTER 6

The Flamer

Flaming choreography

> One of the things that I don't like about the Forum is the constant fights and attacks on each other.
>
> —Lilith, Forum participant, e-mail interview.

> I really enjoy the fights about *At Shunya's*. I rarely participate in them, but it is so much fun to watch. It's like a theatre, except that it's for real.
>
> —Dana, Forum participant, from fieldwork conversations.

... Every time *At Shunya's* was mentioned the Forum went up in flames. Most flame wars started with a complaint about the place, the service, the food, the drinks or the music, lamenting the miserable fate of the Russian queers who have nowhere else to go or mourning the club's 'good old days'. The complaints were aggressive or sarcastic, sometimes also personally insulting towards Shunya or her staff. Other, more satisfied club-goers, protested. 'It was only a joke', said the author of the original post. Some indeed laughed, while others responded: 'It is not at all funny', and attacked yet again.

The attacks started a ping-pong of poisonous words, name-calling and curses. Then someone would post a flirtatious message, accompanied by smiling (☺) or winking (☺) 'emoticons', playfully breaking the tension of the fight. The Forum would thus be transformed from a battlefield into a queer space, almost a 'virtual bar' (Corell 1995) where visitors would wink, smile and check each other out. At the same time, one participant would reject the flirtation, insult the author of the original message, and return the discussion to *At Shunya's*, while someone else would threaten to expose the 'provocateur's' off-line identity. Yet another would call on the administrator[1] to erase his postings. Then along would come another critique of the club,[2] followed by another passionate defence of the latter, and so on, and so forth.

Although the original message often seemed deliberately provocative, it was also welcomed, and even explicitly enjoyed, by some participants. Some suggested that the complainer – labelled as 'flamer' – in fact worked for Shunya and that the fights had been created deliberately, to draw attention to the club. However, many voiced their distress at the name-calling and the flamer's brutal sarcasm. There would be an invisible audience, too: participants who, like Dana, cited above, enjoyed 'watching' (reading) the fights, yet seldom participated in them; those who, like Lilith, disapproved, but chose to remain silent; or maybe others, like myself, who preferred not to engage in a flame war but to understand why it happened. And there was Shunya herself, who very seldom took part in those discussions, yet seemed to be very aware of and hurt by them.[3]

Each flame war about *At Shunya's* would continue for days and sometimes weeks. The debate could change direction several times, moving away from *At Shunya's* to the experience of migration, the meaning of Russianness, racism and discrimination. Disagreements over these and other issues brought another explosion of insults, but also more laughter and flirtations. Then another participant would appear on the site with a new complaint, and it seemed that the flame war was going to enter a new cycle. 'These are cloned nicknames, generated by the same person', stated

1 At the time of my ethnography the website had three and then two co-administrators, one of whom was responsible for the technical running of the site and was in charge of the Forum. In this chapter I refer only to the latter as 'the administrator'.

2 Due to the structure of the Forum, participants can reply to the opening message of the thread before seeing the rest of the discussion. Each thread is divided into short pages of about 10–15 postings, and one can post a response from any page, before reaching the end of the thread. New arrivals to the thread, therefore, often respond out of synch, and the discussion returns again and again to the original message, in this case the critique of *At Shunya's*.

3 I base this on my observations and personal communication with Shunya on- and off-line.

the administrator. 'I am issuing the last warning to these clowns, before I ban[4] them from the Forum. This discussion is now closed'. And so the flame war that at times looked like it could have lasted forever, finally – and abruptly – ended.

***

At the time of my participation on the Forum I saw a lot of 'flame wars' on a variety of topics; later I saw many more in the archives of older discussions. The themes and the styles of the fights varied. On-line conversations that took place on the website, on whether and how to fight homophobia, issues of national economy and politics, and debates about community spaces, very often turned into vicious fights. The most notable – even if not the most frequent – among them were the fights about *At Shunya's*. They would appear every now and then, striking in their resemblance to each other. Most of them shared the same circular trajectory and the same internal rhythm of repetitions and variations. The fights always moved from the topic of the club, to interpersonal attacks, then to the discussion of the Forum, and then to life in Israel, and then back to the club.

In the previous chapter I discussed how the Club was figured as an object of melancholic attachment through repetitive flame wars; this chapter focuses on the structure and the effects of flaming itself. In my reading of flame wars I follow Steven Vrooman's insight that '[f]laming as a negotiation of the individual and the social, the oral and the literary, can no longer be looked at as monolithic' (2002: 54), and it is this non-monolithic nature that I want to look at. The polyphony of flame wars, as outlined at the opening of this chapter, can be described as an example of Bakhtinian

4 Banning refers to an administrative measure, used in on-line communication. If a certain nickname is banned it can no longer be used. Since participation in discussions requires registration, the banned participant will need to register again. If they chose to do so, they have to use a different email address, since the banned nickname was linked to the banned registration profile; sometimes they also had to change a computer or use special software to prevent identification of their IP number – a unique number each computer receives when connecting to the Internet.

'heteroglossia' – a multiplicity of voices and discourses that coexist simultaneously, at times competing and even contradicting each other (Bakhtin 1981).[5] But what is particularly interesting is not just their multiplicity, but the ways flame wars move. Their movement is choreographic, navigating between topics and genres, often shifting in register from one moment to another and moving virtuously between playfulness and wounding words.[6] The flame wars' waltzing rhythms are like ritual dances, drawing everyone in by virtue of their familiarity and repetition. Their repetitive structure can also be understood as what Freud, in his 'Remembering, Repeating and Working Through', calls the 'compulsion to repeat' (1914/1964: 154) – the endless return to what is not resolved and not even remembered. And of course, the repetitive character of flaming resembles the obsessive 'self-torment' of the melancholics, who, unable to let go of the love object, are compelled to return to their ungrievable loss.

Flame wars are far from being a new phenomenon, and are well known to both researchers and on-line dwellers. Many scholars of cyberculture view flaming and trolling (deliberately provocative messages that aim to distract and incite) as examples of hostile and violent behaviour, and tend to explain them by reference to the anonymity of multi-user domains, forums and chat rooms (Carter and Weaver 2003; Reid 1999; Turkle 1995). Several studies of on-line fights classify the flamer as a negative and disturbing intruder into on-line communities. Herring et al., for example, describe the flamer's acts, such as the deliberate change of discussed topics, provocation or offensive messages, as 'mechanisms of on-line deception and disruptive behaviour' (Herring et al. 2003) that are particularly threatening for what they call a 'vulnerable on-line community' – a feminist discussion forum. Gay, lesbian, bisexual, transgender and queer on-line spaces are often seen as vulnerable, too, subject to homophobic intrusions, 'on-line gay bashing' and hate speech (Campbell 2004; Corell 1995). The flamer, in other

5 For an interesting discussion of heteroglossia in cyberspace see Stivale (1997).

6 My use of the term 'choreography' is also inspired by Charis Cussins's work in science studies and her concept of 'ontological choreography' as 'the coordinated action of many ontologically heterogeneous actors in the service of a long-range self' (Cussins 1996: 600).

words, is usually understood as a hostile outsider who hurts and disrupts the otherwise peaceful and harmonious community. Such understanding of flaming and flamers, however, tells us very little about why so many participants of the Forum seem to enjoy the fights, whether as initiators, participants or viewers. In other words, approaching flaming merely as intrusion cannot conceptualise forms of violence from within.

Other Internet scholars, in turn, have argued that flaming is mistakenly conceptualised as disruption. Instead, they present it as a game or a social ritual that existed long before the Internet which has been transferred into a new medium. Vrooman, for example, positions flaming within a long history of ritual verbal assaults and rhetorical competitions (Vrooman 2002). Similarly, Nancy Baym has linked flaming to 'sporting relations' among men (Baym 1995). Using Baym's approach, John Campbell in his book on gay chatrooms discussed flaming as a particularly queer ritual whose origins predate the Internet but are then transferred into on-line communication (Campbell 2004). '[It] is not inconceivable to compare witty insults and snappy posturing of on-line flaming to the queer practice of camp', he suggests (Campbell 2004: 89–90). Vrooman, Baym and Campbell view the flamer as an inherent part of community, and flaming as an enjoyable collective entertainment. Such an approach is linked to a wider anthropological concept of 'ritual violence', where violence is legitimised (and controlled), and works to create or maintain collective boundaries. But the emphasis on the ritual tends to dismiss the hurtful effects of legitimised violence. It also overlooks the possibility that the ritual can be rejected, turning a 'game' into an injury.

Both approaches offer important insights into flaming as a form of on-line communication and as a frequent event on the Forum. Indeed, flame wars about *At Shunya's* were linked to on-line anonymity and were experienced by at least some participants as a hurtful disruption. At the same time, the flaming choreography undoubtedly had elements of ritual, and some of its tropes, as I will discuss below, were specifically queer, supporting the idea of flaming as camp. But the conceptualisation of flaming as either disruptive and violent or as playful and enjoyable misses the complexity of flaming as a form of melancholic attachment, which in itself is a complex move of desire and repulsion, loss and aggression. Both painful and pleasurable, the violence of melancholia is based on the confusion of self and the other. The melancholic is indirectly attacking the other while ostensibly attacking the self (Freud 1917/1934),[7] as for example, we could see in the case of attacks on the club as a displaced attack on the unwelcoming Israeli scene. What's more, the violence of melancholia and the flame wars it generates brings to the fore the ambivalence of the (lost) love object itself. But most importantly, these either/or approaches fail to grasp the ambivalence of the very figure of the Flamer. Always (mis)recognised, destined to be both embraced and rejected, dismissed and glorified, what kind of 'shared meanings' does this figure embody, and what are the stories, that 'inhabit [its] audiences' (Haraway 1997: 23)? Who are the queers, figured by it? And what is the interplay between the two, seemingly contradictory, figurations: the Flamer as a clone, and the Flamer as a clown?

A clone and a clown

> These are cloned nicknames, generated by the same person. I am issuing the last warning to the clowns, before I ban them from the Forum. This discussion is now closed.
>
> —The administrator.

Mikhail Bakhtin, in his famous work on the chronotope of the novel, conceptualises the clown as a figure of metaphorical significance, one that has no existence of its own but is a 'reflection of some other mode of being' (Bakhtin 1981: 159). Clowns are 'masks of life', whose function is to 'exter-

7 Freud, for example, describes a woman who 'loudly pities her husband for being bound to such a poor creature as herself is really accusing her husband of being a poor creature in some sense or other' (1917/1934: 158).

nalise', in the sense of making hidden things visible and bringing them to the fore. The clown (and the fool)[8] are

> 'not of this world', and therefore possess their own special rights and privileges. These figures are laughed at by others, and *themselves* as well. Their laughter bears the stamp of the public square where the folk gather. They re-establish the public nature of the human figure: the entire being of characters such as these is, after all, utterly on the surface; everything is brought out on to the square, so to speak; their entire function consists in *externalising things* (true enough, it is not their own being they externalise, but a reflected, alien being – however, that is all they have). This creates that distinctive means for externalising a human being, via parodic laughter (Bakhtin 1981: 159–160, emphases in the original).

Bakhtin's conceptualisation of the clown[9] offers several directions which we can take in thinking about the Flamer as a figure. Firstly, Bakhtin emphasises the special privilege of the clown/jester – the right to be 'other' to every common cause and the right to expose the 'falseness of every situation' (1981: 159), thus breaking ideological taboos and speaking out against the ruling and the powerful. Indeed, it is not accidental that the critique of *At Shunya's* was almost always presented in a clownish manner, creating a unique 'chronotope' (Bakhtin 1981) – a space/time of the flame war –where one can criticise both Shunya and the administrator and break the rules of the Forum. These could be the rules of using the site, or, as I will demonstrate in the later section on erasure, the very ownership of cyberwords.

Secondly, 'the stamp of the public square' invites us to think about the Forum as a cybersquare of sorts, not so much in the sense of the Internet as a new public sphere, but in the sense of an imagined collective space where longings, anxieties, fears and desires are externalised through the figure of the Flamer. The idea of the clown's public performance also turns our attention to the relations between the clown and its audience – I will return to these relations in the following section on exposure.

8 Who, in medieval Russian tradition, appear as interchangeable (Partan 2007).

9 Or, in a more exact translation from Russian, the jester.

Thirdly, Bakhtin addresses the historical and cultural roots of the clown: in his discussion of the medieval novel he points out that the mask of the clown goes back to ancient religious rituals. Similarly, when examining the appearance of the Flamer-as-clown, we must be attentive to various cultural tropes conjured up by this figure. For example, the particularly Russian history of the jester as highly placed in the tsarist court (some of them were representatives of the Russian nobility), influential and powerful but also frequently and publicly humiliated. Then there is the rebirth of this tradition in Soviet and post-Soviet times, in the Communist Party and later, under Putin (Partan 2007). There, those made into jesters, were at times the only ones able 'to look at the king'. There are also the subversive figures of jesters in Soviet popular culture and those of drag queens-as-jesters, in Russia and in the West – both carry the ability to mock rigid social hierarchies and break the rules, even if temporarily and within a contained and safe time-space.

The clown, then, has both synchronic and diachronic significance: it bears material-semiotic histories *and* carries transgressive powers in the present. But most importantly, while clowns can be inhabited by a particular person at any particular moment, their presence, Bakhtin emphasises, should not be understood directly, but metaphorically, and their significance 'can be reversed – but one cannot take them literally, because they are not what they seem' (Bakhtin 1981: 159). The idea of the Flamer as a clown who is 'not what he seems' invites us to think through the Flamer's laughter, laughter that at time appears strangely out of place. Marked by multiple smiling, winking or laughing emoticons, the cyberlaughter of the Flamer often accompanies violent exchanges during flame wars. In my discussion I go against the common perception of emoticons, which are widely interpreted as 'neutralising' signs: positioned alongside a harsh or aggressive message, they are supposed to mark the message as 'just a joke'. But instead of approaching emoticons in the simplistic sense, as an expression of the speaker's intention, I want to think about them as masks[10] in the Bakhtinian sense, masks that have no existence of their own but whose function

10 I thank Debra Ferreday for suggesting this.

is to externalise other modes of being. Later in the chapter I will propose a more complex reading of flaming, laughter and jokes as deeply ambivalent and even uncanny. My reading will be informed both by Bakhtinian analysis *and* the psychoanalytical approach to jokes (in particular, Freud's work and Kalpana Seshadri-Crooks's (1998) analysis of racial jokes). The Flamer-as-clown, I will show, bears both social *and* psychic significance.

If the clown points to the carnivalesque elements of the flame war, the notion of clones takes us to the world of science fiction. In particular, it leads us to the extensive cinematic tradition of envisioning clones through fascination with sameness and difference, copy and original, singularity and multiplicity. In her work on replicants and clones in popular film, Debbora Battaglia, for example, conceptualises clones as a form of supplement that 'supplies, or makes apparent, insufficiencies'. She then draws distinctions between replicants that have no connection to an original and clones that 'embody the closest relations to the original' (Battaglia 2001: 496). Jackie Stacey takes on Battaglia's idea of clones as a relation rather than a single subject. She explores cinematic fantasies of cloning 'constructed as the monstrous embodiment of relations of sameness' (Stacey 2007: 80) that bring to the fore both the cloned embodiment and questions of passing. Both Battaglia and Stacey note that clones do not just trouble spectatorial identifications, but illuminate various cultural anxieties, such as those about humanness, or sexuality, or race.

Although there are substantial differences between cinematic fantasies of science and the everyday communication on the Forum, Battaglia and Stacey's insights are useful for understanding the figuration of the Flamer as clone. The term 'clone' was frequently used on the Forum (as well as in many other on-line discussion boards) where the rules of conduct prohibit one user from having more than one name. Some participants of the Forum were notorious for having clones – while writing under one main nickname, they used other names to create additional cyberpersonae. The case of Daughter of Palestine and her clone, described in Chapter 4, is one telling example of how the possibilities of multiplicity and copying offered by on-line communication shed light on anxieties about politics, national borders and sexual subjecthood.

Condemning all those who criticised the club as 'cloned nicknames', and whose critique, therefore, was deemed invaluable for it allegedly only multiplied the dissatisfaction of one person, the administrator (cited at the opening of this section) appeared to be authoritative and knowledgeable. Of course, he was the one who had the ability to end the choreography of a flame war by closing the discussion thread. He was also the one who could ban a particular nickname or block a person's access to the site. But there was no ontological certainty behind the administrator's words. The Flamer emerged on the Forum as an indefinable figure that always escaped knowledge and fixity. It enchanted and enraged because of its parodic laughter, but also because of the almost eerie sense of sameness it evoked: whoever initiated a flame war was immediately suspected to be the same person who had flamed before, had been banned and then returned under a new name. And yet, this figure was always about difference, in the sense of a new complaint generating a new fight; but also in a sense of whoever complained about the club was always seen as 'someone else' and not who he claimed to be. The Flamer, in other words, was everyone and no one, but its figuration was that of relationality, since its potential multiplicity (there were many complainers and their complaints looked the same) or singularity (there was only one 'real' person wearing many masks) tied all the participants into the everlasting game of detection.

But the clone's ambivalence also mapped the Russian-speaking queers' anxieties about belonging. Here I am informed by Freud's link between melancholia and ambivalence but also by Bhabha's notion of ambivalent colonial subjectivity and of the other 'as a subject of difference that is almost the same but not quite' (Bhabha 1994: 86). The sameness and difference of the Flamer was not only about (im)possible knowledge of the complainers' identities or intentions. Rather, the Flamer's figure should be understood as a 'condensed map' (Haraway 1997: 11) of queers' desire to belong, as Israelis and as Russian-speaking immigrants, located between different modes of colonisation and mutual colonisation (Gershenson 2005), privilege and marginality, entitlement and exclusion. They are caught between sameness (Jews, Israelis) and difference ('Russians', marginalised immigrants, queers); their homing desires and homing anxieties work through indefinable longing and melancholic loss, causing a flame war every time *At Shunya's* was mentioned.

Simultaneously figured as a clone and a clown, the Flamer mapped the troubled world of the queer immigrants' collective subjectivity and of their contested belonging. But what is important here is that the Flamer was not simply ambivalent, but was constantly transforming. The Flamer's presence was shifty, its figuration changed from one moment to another. This shiftiness was unsettling, as much as it was illuminating. In the remaining part of the chapter I look at the two processes that followed the Flamer's presence on the Forum: exposure and erasure. The two were closely linked to the figuration of the Flamer as a clone and a clown. Exposure, discussed in the next section, was part of the mechanism of laughter and jokes, but was also related to the Flamer's queerness. The Flamer-clown both exposed and was exposed, mapping the relations between the immigrants' Soviet past and Israeli present; their belonging to the queer scene and to Israel as a whole. Exposure, as I will show, is fraught with violence and pain, and at the same time, can be hilariously funny. I will conclude the chapter with a discussion of erasure. Erasure in cyberspace can be understood an act of extreme violence. In a text-based communication a nickname is more than just a few letters, it is an on-line life, manifested in postings. Erasing one's words is equal to a wound, and erasing or banning a nickname can be considered a 'virtual killing'. On the other hand, the ease with which the participants of the Forum call for erasure – and self-erasure – might suggest that it is merely a game that diminishes the weight of words. The easiness of erasure is undoubtedly linked to the figuration of the Flamer as a clone: in that sense, endless erasure simply mirrors the endless cloning. I, however, would like to propose a third option: looking at erasure as *simultaneously* pleasurable and painful, as an act embedded *both* in the world of cyberspace and in the melancholic subjectivity with its self-inflicted torment, and also as a mechanism of belonging *though* violence.

Exposure

> <Crazy Ala>: '*At Shunya's*. (Administrator, you can delete this post)'
> I would like to comment on my first and last visit to the cult club *At Shunya's*. I was expecting a friend from Moscow, and decided to kill two birds with one stone: to go and see the club *At Shunya's* and to surprise my pretentious Moscow guest with the Israeli gay scene. [...] The advertisement said it was going to be a 'boys' night, an evening of poetry, dance and song...My friend, inspired by all this, also desired to see this fashionable and glamorous place.

This is how Crazy Ala, a participant, briefly introduced in the previous chapter, began a new discussion thread which quickly turned into a flame war. Starting with the sarcastic description of the club as pretentious, fashionable and glamorous, the rest of the text employed various stylistic and rhetorical methods in depicting the club as the opposite. Scorning the place, the music, the lack of sophisticated cocktails, the service and the people, Crazy Ala ended the message with the following words: 'If anyone wants to talk to us, you can call the Intercontinental Hotel, room number 106. We would be happy to talk to you'.

The message caused an immediate and outraged response. 'We love our club, and your floods of dirt won't change that', stated one woman. Another participant wrote: 'Crazy Ala, get fucking lost.' Another two cursed her. And yet another one posted:

> <Butterfly>: I called the hotel and found a freaking out Israeli guy. He didn't know any pretentious homosexuals from Moscow ☺ [...] I am asking everyone here (who goes to the club) to support Shunya. And administrator, I am asking you to erase these kind of messages. It's fucking enough!

Butterfly opposed Crazy Ala's critique by exposing her story as fake. She followed the details provided by Crazy Ala and rang the hotel where her friend supposedly stayed. Butterfly also took on the position of community leader, calling others to speak out for the club and the administrator – to police the critique. Crazy Ala's response followed immediately:

<Crazy Ala>: I am reading this and laughing to myself. I can't believe someone took it seriously, so seriously that they called the hotel, probably to curse me there, no less. 'I am asking to support.. I am asking to erase ...' – well, I myself asked to read this piece and then throw it away, since it was *habalstvo.* [...] I would like people to read it with humour, to have a laugh and to draw their conclusions.

Habalstvo is the name for Russian gay slang. Like other gay slangs, such as Polari[11] or Swardspeak,[12] *habalstvo* is both a language – a use of certain words – and a form of speech. *Habalstvo* is characterised by the use of feminine gender by male speakers, a mannered tone, and theatricalised aggression and rudeness. Defining someone as *habalka* or labelling a conversation as *habalstvo* is often used by speakers to describe themselves as gay ('we sat at a café and *haballed*', Zapadaev 2001: 4). Crazy Ala's response to Butterfly signalled that the author was not a woman but a queerspeaking gay man.[13]

After Crazy Ala's self-exposure, the thread continued like other flame wars about the club. The reference to *habalstvo* – that is, as a queer joke – was not supported by other participants, until much later, when another gay man, Kikis, referred to those fighting in an exaggeratedly rude manner: 'YOU NEED SOME DISCIPLINE!!! Here I come, my dear, my sweet pussies. You need some beating up, and here I come, my lovely faggots, my little cunts!' Crazy Ala immediately responded to Kikis, and the two exchanged several messages that looked more and more like a stage dialogue between two clowns or two drag queens. In this exchange, Crazy Ala's performance of a scandalous *habalka* became much clearer. The nickname 'Crazy Ala' was explained, too, when after a long exchange of postings with Kikis and others Crazy Ala wrote: 'Ala Borisovna is now leaving the scene, covered with confetti and flowers'. Ala Borisovna is the full name of a Russian popsinger, mainly known as Ala Pugacheva. Pugacheva became famous in the late 1970s and is one of the most memorable pop stars of the 1980s. She is still performing today; her stage image has always been, and still remains,

11 A slang used by British gay men (Cox and Fay 1994).

12 A slang used by Filipino gay men (Manalansan 2003).

13 Crazy Ala's reference to 'boys' night' can also be seen as a giveaway of his identity, despite the fact that his postings were written in a female gender.

that of a female jester (Partan 2007). She also serves as a favourite icon for drag queen shows. In particular, Russian-Israeli drag queens have impersonated her several times, including in performances at *At Shunya's*.

The dialogue with Kikis – the final, if short, acceptance of Crazy Ala's attack on the club as a joke – turned the Forum into a queer audience at a drag show. Many participants began sending Crazy Ala 'virtual applause' or kisses. But Butterfly rejected such interpretation. She confronted Crazy Ala again and wrote that calling the complaint *habalstvo* was just an excuse Crazy Ala was making up once caught lying about the hotel. Many other participants, too, refused to acknowledge Crazy Ala's status as a (harmless) *habalka* or to agree to his (humorous) attack on the club. Was it simply a case of 'not getting the joke'?

Jokes, of course, are never simply funny, nor do they have a single and unequivocal meaning. Freud reminds us that jokes are based on complex unconscious processes, produce pleasure from displacement and exposure, and can express anxieties and desires (Freud 1905/1960). Tendentious jokes, in particular, are a way to release aggression in a socially acceptable form, often allowing the expression of things otherwise forbidden. Crazy Ala's *habalstvo* can indeed be read as displaced aggression. Critiques of the club, frequently contested by others and/or censored by the administrator, return to the Forum in a form of a joke. What's more, this joke, figured as *habalstvo*, is specifically queer. It is also specifically cyber, for it uses the possibilities of cyberspace for linguistic gender cross-dressing. Tendentious jokes and the pleasures they generate also work to create a sense of collectivity by sharing laughter. In the cases of displaced hostility, notes Freud, jokes work as if building an army: those laughing join forces against the one who is the 'victim' of the joke (Freud 1905/1960). In that respect *habalstvo* can be read as a performative speech act that constitutes the queer collective. This is also a particular, post-Soviet queerness, based on both language and recognisable cultural icons. And yet, there was something else, slippery and indistinct, that made Crazy Ala's joking about the club painful and insulting.

Seshadri-Crooks notes that racial jokes do not necessarily inhibit aggression as Freud suggests; rather they are 'symptomatic of the re-channelling of hostility' (Seshadri-Crooks 1998: 363). Indeed, as I showed in

Part II of the book, smileys that accompany hate speech and fantasies of torture accentuate, rather that neutralise, the violent effect of wounding words. Can we say the same about Crazy Ala? In order to better understand the complex effects of Crazy Ala's *haballing* and the (mis)recognition of his/her 'jokes' we need to take a closer look at the ways Crazy Ala was figured by the Flamer-as-clown. What kind of mask was it, and what other forms of being and unconscious processes did the Flamer externalise here, to paraphrase Bakhtin?

The figure of the Flamer as a queer clown – a *habalka* – is based on the condensation and displacement[14] of several gendered, classed and ethnicised images. 'Crazy Ala', the character, was an Israeli (and presumably an immigrant) woman, visited by a friend from Moscow. She stayed with this friend at the Intercontinental Hotel. This hotel, located on Tel-Aviv's beach, is among the most expensive in the country. Its main clients are wealthy tourists but also upper class Israelis on business or holiday. 'Russian' women – immigrant-citizens and migrant labourers – frequent this hotel, too: as cleaners or escort girls. The figure of a prostitute, the prevailing Israeli stereotype of a Russian-speaking woman in the 1990s (Lemish 2000), was what many immigrants were confronted with in the media and on the streets in the first years after arrival; the figuration of 'Russian woman as prostitute' is less prevalent today, but is still painful when it emerges. It is not accidental that later in the thread the theme of Russian women as prostitutes came up. 'This is how they [the Israelis] see us', noted one of the participants bitterly, when the discussion turned to ethnic stereotypes.

A man impersonating a woman and a Russian/immigrant woman in a fancy Israeli hotel, the character of 'Crazy Ala' felt acutely – and hilariously – out of place. Giving her room number – suggesting that she was staying at the hotel – made her into a pretender who could be exposed at any minute (and was indeed exposed by Butterfly). The 'fakeness' of Crazy Ala was displaced onto her critique of the club which, too, turned out to

14 Freud describes condensation and displacement as the main mechanisms of joke-work (Freud 1905/1960).

be a fake: Crazy Ala's friend from Moscow was expecting a fashionable club with boys and poetry, but instead he discovered a small and smelly place, with few visitors, a drunken barwoman and bad alcohol.[15] And what about the *habalka* herself? Crazy Ala refer referred to – but was *not* – the famous singer.[16] And her class aspirations – to stay in a fancy hotel, to go to a pretentious club and to drink sophisticated cocktails – contrast drastically with the original meaning of the word *habalka* which means 'rude, loud and vulgar woman' (Ushakov 1935–1940/2000). According to *The Explanatory Dictionary of the Russian Language* (ibid.), the word was historically used for low-class provincial women working as vendors at food markets.

The figuration of the Flamer as *habalka* is based on a double exposure: of the club and of Crazy Ala herself; and this exposure in turn has a double-bind: Crazy Ala exposed and was exposed. Notably, one of the *queer* definitions of *habalka* is a loud and scandalous homosexual, who compromises his partners by demonstrating his homosexuality and therefore exposing theirs. An ultimately gay figure in today's Russia and Russian-speaking queer diaspora, *habalka* is a queer clown of sorts, but it is also a figure fraught with the anxiety of sexual (and classed) exposure, not necessarily of the person inhabiting the role of *habalka*, but that of his partners and surroundings. In other words, *habalka* as a queer figure is ambiguous: adored by some as a powerful parody of heterosexuality, it is seen by others as an epitome of low-classness and lack of respectability, and as such, is often embarrassingly rejected by those, longing for normativity and acceptance. Similarly, Crazy Ala's joke was embarrassing and hurtful because of the anxieties of those in his/her audience; the Flamer's condensed figure spoke to the (exposure of) ambivalence of the queer immigrants' homing desires embedded in *At Shunya's*. The homely space of the club turned out to be a 'small and smelly garage'; Israel, their national home, too, is not exactly welcoming:

15 See previous chapter for details.

16 The choice of the name is interesting in itself, it raises once again the theme of the Soviet 1980s, discussed in the previous chapter.

Jewish 'homecomers', the Russian-speaking immigrants have to erase their Russianness and Sovietness in order to become Israelis.

Building on the parallels Freud draws between joke-work and dream-work, Seshadri-Crooks suggests that racial/colonial jokes are uncanny, in a sense that their meaning 'develops in the direction of ambivalence, until it finally coincides with its opposite' (Freud, cited in Seshadri-Crooks 1998: 359). The uncanny and jokes, she notes, share the process of exposure: the uncanny exposes the familiar that was repressed and returns as strange; the jokes expose repressed desires and anxieties. According to Seshadri-Crooks, colonial jokes expose the 'inherent performativity of the identity of the coloniser' and thus signal possible moments of performative failure, fraught with racial anxiety, when 'the mask of the colonial authority begins to slip' (Seshadri-Crooks 1998: 366). Seshadri-Crooks's analysis of racial jokes informs my interpretation of the Flamer as a queer clown. *Habalstvo* is structured around exposures, and is indeed uncanny as *habalka* is strangely familiar yet refuses fixity, and always fluctuates between one reading and its opposite (in that respect, it is reminiscent of the ambiguous figure of Daughter of Palestine, discussed in Chapter 2). But what I find particularly interesting in Seshadri-Crooks's reading is the relationship between performativity and performative failure. So too flaming, as I describe it here and in earlier chapters, can be thought of as a form of performative violence that constitutes the queer immigrants' belonging through repetition. But it is also always fraught with impossibility and performative failure, where the borders of identity and belonging refuse fixity, and where the mask of authority slips away, giving way to uncertainty and angst of non-belonging.

Erasure

If the Flamer-as-clown brings to the fore the ambivalence of laughter, the Flamer-as-clone draws the boundaries of cyberspeech itself, by making erasure and deletion as part of its figuration. 'I am asking [the administrator] to erase these kind of messages', wrote Butterfly in response to Crazy Ala's 'joking' critique of *At Shunya's*. She was not the only one: many participants called for this 'protective' censorship and suggested banning the flamers and deleting their complaints about the club; the administrator had indeed done so more than once.

Censorship is common practice in many on-line communities encountering flaming and trolling. For example, in a Usenet group studied by Paul Baker participants contacted the net-administrator demanding to take e-mail rights from a person who had been provoking them (Baker 2001). Herring and others, in their description of flaming in a feminist forum, note the call for administrative banning issued by some participants, and the technical and ideological obstacles they encountered (Herring et al. 2003). Censorship is not an univocally accepted practice. Viewed as unquestionable in some on-line communities and forums, it is constantly debated as politically problematic in others. Similarly, the Forum participants were divided in their view of the administrator's erasure and banning. Experienced and appreciated as a necessary protection by some, these were seen as acts of extreme violence by others. The latter sometimes tried to confront or question the administrator, only to face the danger of being banned themselves.

Much can be learned by looking at the topics that evoke censorship in a particular on-line space: topics that are seen as disturbing or provocative (such as politics), can point to the internal divisions and tensions, as well as to the violent silencing of some participants within supposedly welcoming spaces, as indeed I showed in earlier chapters (see also Gajjala 2004). However, it is not so much the mapping of censorship that interests me here; rather, I am interested in the failures of censorship and the recurring threats of erasure that are part of the Flamer's figuration. Erasing some participants' on-line presence in the name of protecting the others and the Forum itself, the administrator was constituted as the authority. His act might have been seen as performative in Butler's sense of censorship as 'a productive form of power' (Butler 1997a: 133). Censorship, according to Butler, produces the subject through regulating speech in the public domain and law. We can extend Butler's reading of law to censorship in on-line communities. The administrator, as well as the 'administrated' participants, were constituted through acts of erasing the Flamer. But then how are we to understand the insistent re-appearance of the Flamer? The figure of the Flamer, it seems, resists erasure because figured as clown, the Flamer is already 'not of this world' (Bakhtin 1981: 159); but also because as clone, the Flamer undermines the very possibility of erasure. The Flamer clone signals moments of the performative failure of censorship and of the administrator's authority, but also, that of the collective identity, produced by the Forum.

Failure to erase the Flamer can generate a further circuit of interpersonal violence, for example, in the form of threats to discover and disclose the 'real' identity of each complainer, and in the atmosphere of a general 'witch-hunt' of all those who disagreed with or criticised either Shunya or the administrator or their friends. There was always someone – the administrator or one of the other participants – who would suggest they knew the complainer as well as the reason behind the attack on *At Shunya's*: a personal grudge against Shunya, or against the administrator. 'You must be X', someone would say to the person, criticising the club, 'I can recognise your style of writing'. 'I know it is you, I saw you at the club yesterday, can't believe you dare to come to the Forum and open your filthy mouth', would add another one. 'You are definitely Y', would write the third. 'I have proof; I can see your IP number, it is the same one used by Y'. Such postings were angry, and were often intertwined with insults, swear words and threats of on-line and off-line violence. But while these threats may look like a violent purge in an attempt to 'clear' the Forum from flamers,[17] they also

17 Some might even say that the threats recall purges in the Communist Party in the Soviet Union, and the constant – and constantly failing – effort to keep the purity of rank by suspecting everyone to be an enemy.

created a striking sense of interconnectedness of all those involved, be it an intimate knowledge of one's whereabouts in and out of cyberspace, or what seemed to be a never ending game of 'cops and robbers', the detective and the not(detected). Or indeed, a deep connection between the king and the jester, whose existence is that of mutual dependency and who mirror each other and can transform into each other.[18]

Thinking about such interconnectedness takes us away from the idea of performative censorship. Instead, I suggest, we should approach erasure, whether enacted or desired, as a way of connection, as a form of being together *through* violence. Understanding erasure as connection becomes even clearer when we look at the proposition of self-erasure by some of the complainers. Some of the messages that criticised *At Shunya's* and caused flame wars, included the possibility of their deletion from the start, and sometimes even explicitly requested it. 'Of course, the administrator will erase my terrible thoughts', wrote one complainer, Nice Tree. 'Administrator, you can delete this post' was the title of Crazy Ala's *haballing* message. 'I wanted people to have a laugh and to draw conclusions', Crazy Ala wrote later, following Butterfly's call for the administrator's censorship, and added: 'I will erase my posting in the evening'. These references to erasure can each be read within the framework of their genres. Provoking the administrator from the first line of the thread fits well into the queer ritual of *haballing* teasing: here I am to annoy you, see who loses it first. Completing one's long lament with 'of course this will be deleted' contributes to the 'Russian' stance of eternal hopelessness used in litanies, as discussed in the previous chapter.

But the repetitive mentioning of deletion is not just a matter of rhetoric. Erasure – or the fear of it – was an inherent part of social life on the Forum at the time of my fieldwork. The administrator was periodically erasing, or threatening to erase, 'spamming' and advertising by third parties; but also some of the flaming messages by the participants; and some of the threads of a political nature, in particular those relating to left-wing activities. In addition to such targeted deletions, the archives of the Forum

18 This transformation is discussed by Bakhtin, and also figures widely in the literature.

discussions were periodically cleared, old discussions disappearing irreversibly and without notice.[19] And lastly, all the registered participants could edit or delete their own postings, whether immediately after they'd been created, or months later, by going through the archives of all the discussions. Each of these erasures had its own internal justification; each appeared to be an individual act with a clear purpose. But their effects were always more profound. Whenever individual messages or whole threads were deleted from the archives, they affected the fabric of what Gajjala calls 'shifting yet fetishised frozen homes (shifting as more and more people get on-line and participate, frozen as their narratives remain on websites and list archives through time in a timeless floating fashion)' (Gajjala 2002: 178).

Thinking about the archives of a bulletin board as a precious record of everyday life in cyberspace and as a fetishised home, one might mourn the mutilation of the archives' wholeness. Indeed, this was the reaction of some participants, when one person decided to commit 'virtual suicide' by deleting all of the messages he had ever posted on the Forum. 'The old discussions don't make sense now', someone lamented, 'because parts of the arguments are missing ... How could he do that?'[20] Similarly, some of the veteran participants and former co-authors of the website I spoke to during my field visits to Israel, were angered and sad about the current administrator's 'careless' and disrespectful treatment of the archives that did not preserve every single publication and interaction, something they said they would have done. 'The early days of the Forum are a unique record of the queer immigrants emerging presence', they suggested, 'it is our history, our lives'. Looking at the purge of parts of the archives at the time of my

19 Such clearance was explained as a need for space to develop additional applications on the site. It is interesting, however, that not all old discussions were equally subjected to deletion. As I discovered one day, it was the archives of the women's section of the Forum that were cleared more often, whereas those of the general (but male-dominated) discussion space were left intact for longer. The women's section was often referred to as 'just chatter' by many male participants; the deletion of its archives undoubtedly echoes the social hierarchies that see men's words as more valuable than women's.

20 Following this 'suicide' the website's administrator decided that from now on participants could only edit their last posting but could not make any retrospective changes to the archives.

ethnography I, too, felt a piercing sense of loss and of the precariousness of cyberhomes: now you see them, and now you don't.

The constant present of erasures, however, reminds us that the archives of the Forum were never whole; erasure was embedded in them from the very beginning. The 'shifting yet fetishised frozen home', therefore, is more of an 'archive of feelings' (Cvetkovich 2003), rather than a full documentation of publications and on-line conversations. It is made of affective 'wrything' (Gajjala 2002) and affective reading and re-reading of cyber-words; of memories of the Forum's events and of one's own place in it; of desires for a homely space in cyberspace (and beyond) and of mourning of its impossibility. Such mourning can best be understood as melancholia: a loss of that which never existed; a mourning of wholeness which is in fact impossible. For the website-as-home was always incomplete and troubled, haunted by the words and webpages that never made it into the archives; or words that were written but then deleted; and of course, by what was never said in the first place. Such reading of cyberhomes takes me back to the feminist critique of 'home', mentioned in the introduction: 'an illusion of coherence and safety based on the exclusion of specific histories of oppression and resistance, the repression of difference even within oneself' (Martin and Mohanty 1986: 1996).

The notion of the 'repression of difference within oneself', which was addressed in the previous chapter, sheds light on the role of erasure in constituting belonging, and on the tormented melancholia of the flame wars. The figuration of the Flamer as clone-and-clown further demonstrates how erasure becomes a form of relation, a connection both feared and desired.[21] Flame wars about *At Shunya's* constituted the Forum as a collective space, not through the exclusion of hostile outsiders and their violent speech, but by figuring the insiders as those whose speech was/is/might be erased or, in other words, as those who are being potentially subjected to violence from within. An essential part of the Flamer's figuration, erasure maps the uncertainties of the queer immigrants, their desire for welcome

21 For an interesting discussion of on-line communities as created through erasure and self-erasure, see Ferreday (2003).

and their fear of exclusion, but most of all, erasure maps their ambivalent, melancholic belonging, in cyberspace and beyond.

Ambivalent figurations

The choreography of the repetitive flame wars was almost magical and had its own charm. As this chapter demonstrated, the fights did not simply merge the painful and the pleasurable, but drew in and enchanted all the participants, regardless of their stand towards *At Shunya's*. One may be surprised to see how those, who cherished and defended the club, also welcomed the fights about it. Some described the fights as a wonderful relief from boredom, others said: 'A negative advertisement is still an advertisement'. One may find it puzzling that several participants suggested that the person who initiated flame wars about the club was, in fact, Shunya's own employee, sent on purpose, to attract attention. But I think it is not surprising at all. Regardless of who the actual complainer might have been in each and every flame war, the ambivalent figure of the Flamer seemed to be a creation of the Forum itself. The flaming came from within the queer immigrants' collective space, and not from without. Indeed, as Alex's rhetorical question stated, every time the club is mentioned, there is a fight. 'Why do *we* always fight?' 'Why is this always happening to *us*?' other participants repeatedly echoed him.

The repetitive re-appearance of the Flamer as something that 'always happens with us' takes us back to the question of melancholia as subjectivity linked to the condition of immigration, and the self-inflicted violence such a condition may contain. The lost and unattainable object, becoming part of the self, turns the violence inwards; the impossible and ungrievable 'place of our own' becomes an endless flame war about such a place. But the violence of melancholia – and the violence of flame wars – is not necessarily destructive. In their move to depathologise melancholia as a form of collective subjectivity, Eng and Han (2003) propose to view it not as damage, but as conflict that structures everyday life and produces particular relations and subjectivities. Exploring the work of racial melancholia they suggest that it can become an intersubjective bond between people, united through their ungrievable loss, negotiating together their ambivalent relations to the lost object – whiteness in the case of the Asian Americans discussed by Eng and Han; Russian-Israeli queerness and idealised belonging at the club and in cyberspace, in the case of the Forum.

The figure of the Flamer indeed maps the intersubjective bonds of melancholia, simultaneously emphasising the connectivity and the ruptures of the queer immigrants' collective cyberspace. Figuring the Flamer as both victim and perpetrator of cyberviolence, and, importantly, as an inherent part of 'us', flame wars illuminate yet another way belonging can work through violence. However, this does not mean that the injuries of flaming disappear, on the contrary. The choreographic circuits of the flame wars, fluctuating between pain and laughter, joke and attack, flirtation and mockery, maps queer immigrants' ambivalent belonging in and out of cyberspace, belonging that is intertwined both with the production and the reception of violence.

In that respect the Flamer is a figure who conjures up many aspects of the queer immigrants' life as contested homecomers, simultaneously victims and beneficiaries of racial and national formations. The Flamer's ambivalence between sameness and difference reflects the immigrants' location in and between Russianness, Israeliness and queerness. The constant (mis) recognition of the Flamer speaks to the immigrants' experience of 'Jewish in Russia and Russian in Israel' and to the racialisation of their lives in both countries. The figuration of the Flamer as a clone and a clown – in the fights about *At Shunya's* as well as in other instances of flaming on the site – is about the immigrants' ambivalent position as simultaneously colonised and colonisers. As immigrants they have to erase their Russianness in order to be recognised as Israelis; but their Russianness and Sovietness haunts their collective places nevertheless. As Israeli-colonisers in an occupied land, their home and belonging is about the erasure of the Palestinians, dehumanised, invisible, but haunting. Cloning here refers to the simultaneous erasure and ghostly presence of that which cannot be erased.

The everyday violence of racism or erasure, reverberating in on-line flame wars, is no joking matter. And yet, the violence of flaming – whether interpersonal or abstract, intercommunal or racist – seems always to generate laughter. This laughter is about the performative failure of the coloniser (and the colonised!), the failure of ontological certainties and of military securities, and the failure of definite home-making within and without the queer scene. As Seshadri-Crooks (1998) reminds us, such laughter does not necessarily inhibit violence, but can re-channel it and, as I emphasise below, can even further intensify it, precisely because laughter dismisses violence as 'innocent'. In other words, the figure of the Flamer maps not just the queer immigrants' ambivalent locations and their contested attachments to their past and present. A ghost in the machine, an uncanny clone of an uncanny clown, the Flamer signals the very ambivalence of cyber-violence and its effects. For example, the Flamer as clown/jester suggests transgression and daring: in the Western, and even more so, in the Russian and Soviet context, this figure is about speaking the truth, against rules and rulers. Similarly, one can read the endless 'cloning' of the Flamer as a form of parody that subverts the injurious effects of his words. But is the figure of the Flamer transgressive? His presence on the Forum may indeed appear as a form of teasing and breaking the rules, yet it can reaffirm and even strengthen hostility and violence. One illuminating example of such ambivalence is the figure of Daughter of Palestine, discussed in Chapter 4, who was also a flamer of sorts. Her constant shape-shifting and her multiple smiling and laughing emoticons may have challenged some foundations of Israeli nationalism, while simultaneously reaffirming national and racial formations, and intensifying anti-Palestinian hatred.

One of the reasons for such ambivalent effects of the Flamer is its constant refigurations. The Flamer seems to be always in motion, changing masks and shapes from one instant to another. As a clone, he always assumes the contours of somebody else; as a clown, he always becomes an opposite, simultaneously transforming the very opposition into something else. As Bakhtin poignantly notes, '[t]he clown and the fool represent a metamorphosis of tsar and god – but the transformed figures are located in the nether world, in death' (1981: 161). These constant transformations of the Flamer are an inherent part of on-line communication with its fantasies of anonymity and tactics of disguise, possibilities of passing and returning, and with the ambiguity of on-line words and actions. But the Flamer's refigurations are also about the incredibly complex work of sexual, racial and colonial violence in Israel/Palestine, where hate is refigured as love or protection, devotion to one's nation is manifested through torture, and the most disturbing, wounding words are presented as art,[22] or as 'just a joke'.[23] The trope of jester as a romantic bearer of truth is what allows refiguring racism or homophobia as an act of care or bravery (remember, for example, how Kamyanov described himself as 'the first one who threw the stone into the swamp of Israeli pederasty' and who felt obliged to speak out again, out of concern for the nation's future). And the endless repetition of cloning is what multiplies, intensifies and deepens the injury of wounding words.

22 For example Kamyanov's poem, discussed in Chapter 1.

23 See the interpersonal attacks discussed in this chapter, or racist speech, discussed in Part II of the book.

CONCLUSION

Belonging through Violence

I began this book by asking questions about the relationship between violence and belonging with regards to queerness, migranthood and nationalism, in cyberspace and beyond. These questions, while focusing on queer immigrants, have broader relevance – and particular urgency – in the context of Israel/Palestine, where the affective regimes of love and hate, the practices of warfare and welcome, and the processes of home-making and the destruction of homes are intertwined so intimately, and in so many complex ways. The concerns, raised in this book also have a broader significance for queer politics in various contexts, for example, in the context of cybercultures, where cyberspace is often envisioned as an unproblematic site of unlimited possibilities – of passing and border crossing, of freedom of speech and of identity games, of erotic encounters and of community formations. They are also significant to the context of post-Soviet Russia and post-communist Europe and their global émigré diasporas, where formations of queerness are caught between different, and at times conflicting, discourses of sexuality, between East and West and between haunting pasts and uncertain futures. And lastly, the issues discussed here have, I believe, a broader resonance in the context of the globalised 'war on terror', where anti-Muslim hatred skilfully mutates to fit various national needs, while remaining a form of global connection, political as well as affective; where dangerous alliances are often formed between right-wing patriotism and gay rights (Haritaworn et al. 2008), and between normative gayness and the 'global dominant ascendancy of whiteness' that produces both 'terrorist *and* citizen bodies' (Puar 2007: 2, emphasis mine).

In this concluding chapter I expand on some of these broader issues. However, my discussion will also keep returning to the specific and the particular: the Russian-Israeli queer immigrants, the beginning of the twenty-first century when the queer immigrant scene emerged, the daily encounters in cyberspace. The participants of the queer immigrant website, described here, were far from a homogenous collective, in their experiences, actions and opinions. I do not claim to have represented them as a group; nor, as I have noted in the opening of the book, did I aim to speak on their behalf. Rather, this book was born out of my own ambivalent position in relation to queer immigrants' politics and organising, as they evolved on the website at the time of my ethnography. My position was a mixture of commitment and fundamental disagreements, participation, appreciation and critique. The book emerged out of my search for a different Russianness and a different queerness and was motivated by the desire to 'speak to': to those, whom I met on the Forum, to other Russian-speaking queer immigrants, to Israelis, and to other queers. But it also came out of the overall sense of responsibility, political and theoretical, to address the complicity of queerness within racial and national formations *while simultaneously trying to conceptualise the complexity* of queer lives that emerged at the intersection of privilege and marginality, production and reception of violence. This complexity, as I tried to demonstrate throughout the book, should not be reduced to simplistic distinctions of material and virtual, of positive and negative, of victims and perpetrators, and should not slide into either 'caricature[s] of absolute evil' (Back 2007: 84) or apologies for racism and hatred.

Throughout the book I showed that in the many forms of violence – physical and verbal, social and psychic, material and semiotic – queer immigrants were both victims and perpetrators. Yet it is not enough to distinguish between different vectors of violence: directed from the outside towards them, from them towards the outside and between themselves (although such distinction initially informed my analysis). More importantly, this book suggests that belonging is always constituted *through* violence, and that the different vectors and forms of violence are always linked. Such understanding leads to a more complex analysis of violence, for violence of a particular type never stands alone. Homophobia and nationalism, militant patriotism and gendered violence, uncanny jokes and ghostly hauntings – all these are always related, as I shall elaborate below. Their relationship takes us away from questions of inclusion and exclusion

– questions that often guide discussions of violence and belonging – as well as from the clear-cut distinction between victims and perpetrators. Instead, my focus on figures and figurations maps the complex domains of the material, the semiotic, and the psychic, where belonging is troubled, ambivalent, and intertwined with violence in many, at times contradictory and unexpected, ways.

Figurations of violence and belonging

So how do figures map condensed and contestable relations between violence and belonging? Throughout the book I have addressed three types of figures: haunting, border and flaming. The three, I would like to suggest, can be examined as particular 'practices of figuration' (Haraway 1997: 9): the processes by which figures come into being, or what Castañeda describes as 'domains of practice and significance' through which 'a concept or an entity is given a particular form' (Castañeda 2002: 3).

The first part of the book followed two haunting figures: the Shadow by the Latrine and the Jewish Victim. In Chapter 1, I showed how belonging to the Israeli nation was claimed and performed by heterosexual, Russian-speaking immigrants through expelling the homosexual abject. This chapter began my engagement with wounding words and their injurious and performative powers. I showed that the attempt to expel the queers – performed in speech acts of disgust – worked through the haunting memory of the Gulag. The figure of the Shadow by the Latrine – the ghost of the Gulag homosexual – constituted national belonging through ethnic (Russian-speaking, post-Soviet) as well as classed (the educated intelligentsia) terms; and marked boundaries of respectability and nationhood by evoking acts of Gulag violence and abuse of the monstrous other. At the same time, the Shadow by the Latrine signalled the impossibility of escaping the past: after all, it was the intelligentsia's own shadow that lived in their literary memory, their language and their subjectivity.

In Chapter 2, I turned to another figure, the one evoked by queer immigrants in *their* claims of national belonging vis-à-vis the homophobic attacks. Comparing the damages and the dangers of homophobia to those of anti-Semitism and Nazism, the queers nationalised their injury and positioned themselves within the Jewish collective, haunted by the Holocaust. The figure of the Jewish Victim that came to stand for the victim of the Gulag had the double effect of ultimate welcome and of uncanny horror. On the one hand, claiming that their injury from homophobia was similar to the injury of anti-Semitism and anti-Jewish persecution, queer immigrants turned themselves into the ultimate victims who should be welcomed by the nation. On the other hand, the haunting presence of anti-Jewish violence and the relations of substitution between victims of homophobia and anti-Semitism, undermined the very foundations of the homecoming trope, for even in their 'home' Russian-Israeli queers were still experiencing violence similar to that of Jews in Russia and Europe.

Haunting as a practice of figuration is about the structure of feeling (Gordon 1997; Williams 1977), but also about modes of understanding and orientation in the world. Gordon and Gunew, in their discussions of ghosts, indicate that being haunted is a form of necessary vulnerability, as well as a form of knowledge and subjectivity. It is also a form of belonging *through* vulnerability (and in particular, through linguistic vulnerability), when one's sense of and longing for a 'home' is mediated by a ghost, such as the abused homosexual in the Soviet labour camp or the persecuted Jew in Nazi Germany. Both the Shadow by the Latrine and the Jewish Victim demonstrate that the ghost can never be fully expelled nor can it ever be fully included or embraced: the figure of the Gulag homosexual haunts the post-Soviet (Jewish) intelligentsia, and becomes its uncanny shadow that was with them all along. The shadow of the Jewish Victim of anti-Semitism and the Holocaust, so frequent and common in Israeli rhetoric, points to the impossible (and yet very powerful!) claim for a national home, based on past victimhood – the claim that is inseparable from the way (some) victims of Israel's colonial project are silenced and erased.

The two ghostly figures discussed here, emphasise the importance of focusing on the unseen, because, as Gordon reminds us, it makes 'everything we do see just as it is, charged with the occluded and forgotten past'

(1997: 195). In that respect, I see my writing about haunting as a form of political commitment to the uncommemorated and unacknowledged 'lost subjects of history' (ibid.), such as the queer victims of the Soviet Gulag.[1] But my commitment to the unseen is also about the occluded and banished *present*, a present which in a sense is being forgotten *as it is happening*.[2] In this present the queer immigrants are not only victims or bearers of cultural memories of victimhood, as Jews and as queers. They are also complicit, sometimes unwittingly, and sometimes knowingly and proudly, in the violence of Israeli colonialism and the ongoing destruction of what Butler calls 'ungrievable lives' (2004: 35) – lives that are not only devalued by the ongoing machine of war, but whose public grievability is prohibited.[3]

It was not a coincidence that while many of the homophobic texts, published in the immigrant media, were also ragingly right-wing and nationalist, the queers' organising against homophobia rarely challenged this nationalism. Warning against the dangers of homophobia – dangers that were communicated through the comparison of anti-Semitism and Nazism – queer immigrant politics mostly kept silent about the dangers and the victims of Israeli warring nationalism. Of course, this silence, cou-

1 Following the ghosts of Kamyanov's attack led me to an in-depth investigation of the narratives about same sex relations in the Gulag memoirs (Kuntsman, forthcoming), a hitherto unexplored, and often ignored, topic in Gulag historiography.

2 One powerful and insightful analysis of such forgetting of the present can be found in Weizman's (2007) discussion of Israel's 'architecture of occupation'. One of the potent tactics of Israel's land-grabbing is so called 'establishing facts on the ground': a hill is first occupied as a temporary site by a few people, then a barrack is built, then an antenna for mobile connection, then an army outpost to 'guard' the antenna and the few people camping there. And then this becomes a settlement, a 'fact on the ground', a sacred Jewish home that should not be touched, its history immediately forgotten. Another telling example is the growth and expansion of checkpoints, documented and discussed by Kirstein Keshet (2006): from a military jeep, to a roadblock, to a multi-lane electronic gate, acting as a border.

3 Butler refers to the co-existence and interrelatedness of war and killings with social and psychic mechanisms of dehumanisation, where the very notion of suffering and death, voiced by Palestinians or Iraqis, is seen as both a lie and a politically threatening utterance that must be policed or denied.

pled with the mobilisation of Jewish victimhood as a political strategy, was not unique to the queer immigrants. Rather, it was embedded in what Cvetkovich poignantly describes as 'the amnesiac powers of national culture, which is adept at using one trauma story to suppress another' (2003: 16). But the nationalism itself – and its violence – was not only normalised, but sometimes specifically glorified as queer, as the second part of this book demonstrated. In this part, I continued the discussion of queer immigrants' relationship with the nation, by moving on to another practice of figuration, 'bordering'. I looked into how some figures are constituted around the notion of the border, how they move across different borders, and how the borders are figured through them. I discussed the ways borders can materialise through violence, and the ways this violence – or the fantasy thereof – can become a promise of belonging for those, whose location in the nation is ambivalent and contested (Nevels 2007).

The figure of the Soldier, discussed in Chapter 3, condensed the feelings of immigrants' love for the nation, merging homoerotic feelings and patriotism. The Soldier's body marked the national borders as the borders of love and of protection. This figure reveals the importance of masculinities in analysing nationalism and colonialism. The role of masculinities is also constitutive of the figure of the Terrorist, a distorted reflection of the Soldier. The Terrorist, too, marked national borders, but he is the one whose body had to be eradicated and violated in order to protect the nation/the soldier/their admirers. Border figures of the Soldier and the Terrorist demonstrated that the border is performed through crossing (or the prevention of such crossing). In that respect, 'bordering' as a practice of figuration is first and foremost about space. But it is undoubtly also about time and history. The Soldier, for example, collapsed the geographical and sentimental borders of the Soviet Union and the time of WWII into the geo-political present of Israel/Palestine, and the Terrorist became the transhistorical embodiment of 'the enemy'.

Chapter 4 continued the discussion of border figurations, this time looking at the female character of Daughter of Palestine. Discussing the idea of passing in cyberspace, I showed how the boundaries of passing and play on-line evoke and perform national borders, and how national borders become borders of identity, legitimacy, subjecthood and humanness.

Daughter of Palestine was figured as an unimaginable subject, as a failing figuration, that did not simply threaten borders of geographical space, culture and language by crossing them, but collapsed these borders into one unimaginable and impossible figure. And just as in the case of the relationship between the soldier and the terrorist/the torturer and the tortured, Daughter of Palestine's passing was always intertwined with the Forum participants' readings.

Figuring Daughter of Palestine as someone to be detected, fixed, contained and eradicated, constituted the participants' belonging in cyberspace and beyond as ambivalent and fraught with anxiety. For example, in order to mark the Forum's participants as real, knowledgeable and truthful, Daughter of Palestine had to be violated first through orientalist fantasies about Arab sexuality, and then through cloning her and speaking instead of her or through her. Taking her voice, if only temporarily and if only virtually, resembled the absence of the Palestinian voice in Israel's vision of the world and its replacement with orientalist 'knowledge' about the 'Arabs'. But it also resembles the voicelessness of the tortured 'enemy'. Elaine Scarry in her discussion of torture and pain notes the voicelessness of the victim because the confession becomes the voice of the torturer:

> The question and answer also objectify the fact that while the prisoner has almost no voice – his confession is a halfway point in the disintegration of language, an audible objectification of the proximity of silence – the torturer and the regime have doubled their voice since the prisoner is now speaking their words (Scarry 1985: 36).

So too the participants constitute their presence – on the Forum and in Israel/Palestine – through preventing the presence of Daughter of Palestine or by substituting her presence with their visions. Similarly, the figure of the Soldier as a sexy warrior comes into being through the killing of terrorists, but at the same time, through sexing the Terrorist as an object of queer erotic fantasy. These figurations uncover the complex relations between war, gender, queerness and violence. Immigrants' belonging to the nation as Israelis and as queers is intertwined with the 'necessity' of violence, constituting the border though erasure, torture, pain and violation of those whose bodies might be momentarily sexed, but whose lives never count, or, in Butler's words, they are ungrievable (2004). To paraphrase Scarry's words, the queer immigrants double their presence – in and beyond cyberspace – by simultaneously erasing the (queer) Palestinians *and* by speaking their sexuality.

These complex relations of interdependency have material, semiotic and psychic effects: they are about knowledge, meanings, feelings and fantasies, but also about daily lives and deaths within and across the borders of Israel/Palestine. Dehumanised and always already figured as terrorists, regardless of sex, age or occupation,[4] the Palestinians *are* those whose lives are marked as ungrievable by Israeli nationhood. What's more, in today's 'war on terror', which is simultaneously nationalised as a local Israeli struggle, and globalised as the 'fight of the West against the evils of Muslim terrorism', they come to constitute a population destined for death. The Israeli soldiers die, too – and so, of course, do the Israeli civilians, caught in the machine of war – but their deaths are radically different from those of 'the terrorists', because the soldiers' lives appear as highly grievable, and their deaths are seen as the protection of the lives of others.[5]

4 I do not suggest that there are no Palestinian militants (including suicide bombers), nor do I want to underestimate the devastating effect of terrorist attacks on the civilian victims, caught in the ongoing bloody warfare in Israel/Palestine. This is also not a discussion of strategies of resistance – violent or non-violent – to Israeli colonialism; such a topic is very important but lies beyond the scope of this book. What I do want to emphasise is the mapping of Israeli political horizons, where Palestinians are always already constituted as fearful and dangerous; and that this construction precedes their actual acts, and not the other way round.

5 For an interesting discussion on dead or missing soldiers and Israeli national solidarity see Kaplan (2008). There are also important and striking differences in the ways that deaths of the Israeli and Palestinian civilians are figured in Israeli national imagination. The former appear as victims of terrorism, a victimhood often linked to that of the Holocaust. Their names are repeatedly announced nationally; their tragically interrupted lives are extensively and publicly mourned, and often used in political rhetoric to justify military brutality against the Palestinians. The latter, on the other hand, are often presented as inevitable casualties of war; they remain nameless and the very number of their deaths is always framed within a discourse of suspicion, signalling possible exaggeration in 'the other side's' reports about casualties. The Israeli responsibility for those deaths is very rarely claimed, often marking the Palestinians as responsible (for example, Palestinian mothers are repeatedly blamed in the Israeli media for not caring enough about their children,

The notion of life and death and their relations to queerness are particularly important here, for they take us to what Puar calls 'queer necropolitics' (2007). Puar brings together Foucault's (2003) idea of biopolitics with Achille Mbembe's notion of necropolitics – a concept he develops when analysing subalternity, race and war and terror (Mbembe 2003). Puar here positions discussion of race and sexuality 'in the reproduction of the relations of living and dying' by 'keep[ing] taut the tension between biopolitics and necropolitics' (2007: 35). Whereas the former is about the regulation of populations through managing lives, the latter is about populations, destined for – and regulated through – death. When looking at the simultaneous expansion of liberal gay politics and its complicity within the US 'war on terror', Puar calls our attention to the 'differences between queer subjects who are being folded (back) into life and the racialised queernesses that emerge through the naming of populations' (ibid.), often those marked for death.[6] The border figures of the Soldier, the Terrorist and Daughter of Palestine similarly map such relations between some forms of queerness, as 'folded into life', home and safety, while others are destined for death. At the same time, they are also figured through the particular contexts of Russia, the Soviet Union, Israel/Palestine and cyberspace. The simultaneous embeddedness of these figures in specific localities, histories and cultural practices, *and* in the globalised 'war on terror', is what gives them their power.

Scarry's notion of torture as doubling one's voice and Puar's insistence on the tensions between necropolitics and biopolitics offer some illuminating answers to the almost rhetorical question, raised in Butler's *Precarious Life* (2004): why is it that some lives, such as those of the Palestinians

---

and sending them to provoke Israeli soldiers, or for not protecting them enough, or for encouraging young people to become terrorists). Similarly, in the recent Israeli-Lebanese war in 2006, the many civilian casualties were blamed on the militants who used the civilian population as their 'live shield', *not* on the Israeli army who bombed civilian areas.

6 Puar notes an important political shift from those queers who are left to die (through HIV/AIDS or denial of reproduction and parenting), to queers that reproduce life, and asks: 'Which queers are folded into life? How do they give life? To what do they give life? How is life weighted, disciplined into subjecthood, narrated into population, and fostered for living?' (2007: 36).

lost at the hands of the Israeli army, or the Iraqis, killed by the American troops, are constituted as ungrievable? Both Scarry and Puar teach us about relations of interdependency – whether between the torturer and the tortured, or between those 'folded into life' and those killed in their name. And while there are clear differences between physical torture and cyberfantasies about it, or between the American and Israeli contexts of the 'war on terror', border figurations discussed in this book bring important insights to the co-constitutive relations of dehumanisation of 'the enemy' on one hand, and humanisation and sexing of colonial or military violence, on the other.

But what about the grievability itself? Can we think about the relationship between an ungrievable past – that of the Soviet Gulag, for example – and the ungrievable present? Or between the ambivalent, melancholic attachment to the queer scene and the currency of Jewish victimhood in claiming the national home?[7]

Flaming figurations, discussed in the third part of the book, tackled some of these issues. In both Chapters 5 and 6, I approached flaming as a form of melancholia – an ambivalent attachment which is about both longing and rejection, a form of tormented collective subjectivity based on a loss that is not fully known and that cannot be grieved. Chapter 5 focused on the queer immigrants' club, showing how in endless on-line fights the club turned from a place to a material-semiotic figure that condensed taste, smell and sound with memories, dreams and aspirations. In this chapter, I questioned the idealised theorising of homing desires, that does not address violence from within, and explored how longing to belong in the context of post-Soviet immigration, and marginalisation in the Israeli queer scene, worked through the violence of flame wars. Shifting from injurious speech acts that aimed to expel the filth, the ghost or the enemy, I followed the circulation of wounding words *within* a collective (cyber)space. Chapter 6 continued the examination of the role of flaming, this time turning to the figure of the Flamer as clone-and-clown who was constantly shifting yet always remained the same. Following the complex structure of the flame

7 I am grateful to Les Back for encouraging me to explore these connections.

wars, I complicated the simplistic theorising of flaming as either outside intrusion, or a playful ritual of the insiders. I showed that the Flamer was constituted as an ambivalent figure that was always *both* embraced and rejected and suggested that this double move mappped the anxieties of queer immigrants and their troubled and contested belonging within and outside of the queer scene, as both welcomed Jewish homecomers and as othered and marginalised 'Russians'.

Flaming as a practice of figuration was both about the object of melancholia, the Club, and the subject of melancholic, self-inflicted and other-directed violence, the Flamer. I proposed that the violence of melancholia can be a form of connectivity and not only a form of rupture, and that flaming can be understood as a way of *being together through violence.* In that sense, the connection, created by flaming, reminds one of the attempt to connect through shared cultural memory of anti-Semitic violence and loss, as it was performed in the anti-homophobic writings of the queer immigrants. Very different in their aims, forms and contexts, the two moves have some striking similarities. Both are uncanny (see the flamer/clown's uncanny laughter, or the uncanny doubleness of the queer/Jew and the unexpected violence that was there all along); both are about ambivalence and impossible longing – for a 'place of our own', or for the safety of a national home; both have elements of performativity *and* of performative failure.

What's more, the two moves both signal displacement of histories and memories; they are about remembering *as well as* forgetting. I am, of course, referring not to intentional forgetting but rather to complex social and psychic mechanisms through which some histories, lives and deaths are made to count, while others are repeatedly erased and sent to oblivion. For example, the turn to the Jewish victimhood certainly has its currency, both in the immigrant community and in the Israeli nation as a whole. However, embracing this victimhood is inevitably complicit with the past and ongoing erasure of other histories and ungrievable lives, inflicted by the Israeli state, often by explicitly evoking the Holocaust as the ultimate justification. And the melancholic longing for the 'place of our own' is constituted not only in the context of a multi-ethnic society where a group of queer immigrants struggles to create its own social space, but also in the context of ongoing war, figured in the Israeli colonial imagination as a struggle to defend 'our own' country, while, in fact, it is also, predominantly, about the continuous destruction of Palestine. Thinking about the history, the land and the lives of Palestinians that Israeli nationhood renders invisible,[8] I cannot help but recall the promo of the club *At Shunya's*, published on the website after the death of Arafat and discussed in the introduction to this book. In the promo, the mourning of the Palestinians – described as mad beasts – is a cause for queer Jewish celebration.

I do not wish to underestimate the emotional intensity of suffering from homophobia, or that of the longing to belong to a 'place of one's own'. Nor do I want to reduce the complex and contradictory lives of queer immigrants to their complicity within Israeli nationalism and the violence done in their name. But what I do want to do is to think about the politics of mourning and the possible traps of collective melancholia in the context of the simultaneous marginality and privilege of queer immigrants within their colonial nation. Paul Gilroy in his *After Empire: Melancholia or Convivial Culture* (2004) puts forward the notion of 'post-colonial melancholia' as the inability to deal with the colonial past, the inability to mourn and to accept responsibility, which results in melancholia. Post-colonial melancholia, for Gilroy, is about the British society being 'stuck' with guilt and self-loathing and hatred, instead of moving on to a society based on conviviality – a move only possible when the evils and damages of colonialism are appreciated and acknowledged.

Gilroy's discussion, extended from the British context to other imperial nations, is highly relevant to the case of Israel/Palestine, despite the many differences between Britain and Israel and despite the fact that Israeli nationalism is still 'colonial', rather than 'post-colonial' (or rather, it is in the middle of dealing with an anti-colonial struggle). For example, Gilroy notes how a post-colonial nationhood does not accommodate its past atrocities, and instead narrates its history where the imperial nation figures 'as the primary victim rather than the principal beneficiary of its vanished colonial dominance' (2004: 115). Indeed, the inversions of victim/perpetrator

8 It is precisely this invisibility of Palestinians in Israeli 'making of worlds' (Castañeda 2002) that makes Palestinian lives ungrievable.

and victim/beneficiary are much in operation in Israeli nationalism. But what is also important is how these inversions structure all aspects of the nation's life and 'precede and underpin the poetics of racial, national and ethnic difference that makes them comprehensible' (ibid.). In that sense, the currency of Jewish victimhood – powerful as it is to speak about the unspeakable and ungrievable ghosts of the Gulag – is a political trap, not only because it may be complicit with the nationalist use of the Holocaust. It is a trap because it reaffirms the very social conditions that render the queer immigrants' longing for the 'place of their own' as melancholic and impossible. For them, who were Jews in Russia and became Russians in Israel, having a 'place of their own' is forever ambivalent: it is both a luring promise and an unattainable ideal, just like whiteness for Asian-Americans, discussed by Eng and Han (2003) in their analysis of racial melancholia. What forms and fuels the social condition of this melancholia is precisely the multifaceted economy of Jewishness, Europeanness and Westernness, which are also part and parcel of the Israeli national project, and which are closely intertwined with the currency of Holocaust commemoration.

The Russian-speaking queer immigrants are simultaneously welcomed and racialised, embraced and injured by Israeli nationalism (and the complexity of welcome and othering of the local queer scene is just one example of many). Their location within the colonial melancholia is therefore far more complex than that of the white British; alternative collective identity and politics for them might be much more difficult, if not impossible. Writing about Britain, Gilroy notes that accepting the loss of empire and acknowledging 'the brutalities of colonial rule enacted in their name and to their benefit' would involve a multi-layered trauma, but that working through it would bring a 'new phase of psychological and ethnical maturity' (2004: 108). But what kind of trauma would such acknowledgement involve for the queers, who, subjected to the homophobic hate speech and demonisation, turn to the nation in search of safety and recognition (however ambivalent this turn might be)? And what kind of trauma would it involve for the Russian-speaking immigrants, queer and straight alike, whose country of birth – the Soviet Union – has just recently fallen apart, destroying all the foundations of history and sociality?

Post-Soviet immigrants, who today are in their thirties or older (and this is the age of many, although far from all, participants on the Forum), spent a significant if not major part of their lives under communism, and then watched everything they knew and believed in breaking down or turning out to be a lie. With various degrees of resentment towards the Soviet state, most of them still experienced the fall of communism and the massive 're-discovery' of its past horrors as deeply traumatic.[9] Their 'new' country, Israel, seemed to differ from the old one dramatically. It presented itself not only as just and democratic, in contrast to the evil and totalitarian Soviet Union, but also as *theirs*, as a country that does not simply open its doors to all Jews but the one – and the only one – where they would really be at home.[10] It also narrated itself as a caring nation – indeed, Israel (sometimes) cares deeply about its citizens, if they are Jews (and preferably *Ashkenazi*).[11] Coming from a country where the relations of the state towards the individual citizen are based on either brutality or abandonment, knowing that one is 'at home' and is cared for is a deeply comforting change

9 I do not assume that all Soviet citizens believed in communism (although many did); there was even a small movement of active dissidents among the Russian Jews, most of whom immigrated to Israel, during the 70s. What I am referring to here is not simply the belief in government or ideology, but rather, the foundational assumptions about Soviet history and past, which has come under scrutiny since the late 1980s. For example, following Mikhail Gorbachev's policy of *glasnost* ('openness'), many archives and documents were made public, revealing the scale of the Stalinist and post-Stalinist political terror, shocking even for those who had been well aware of mass repression, murder and imprisonment.

10 I am referring here to the official Israeli narrative, which was dominant in all the institutions that dealt with the newcomers (such as the 'Ministry of Absorption' – note the name! – that took care of legal and financial aspects of the newcomers' settlement; or *Sokhnut* – 'The Jewish Agency' which dealt with social and cultural aspects of immigrants' lives before and after immigration; or the compulsory language schools where all newcomers learnt Hebrew in the first months after arrival). The political reality was, and still is, far more complex.

11 If we turn to the state's treatment of the *Mizrachi* Jews, we will discover decades of systematic economic and cultural destruction. Paradoxically, but typically for colonial logic, much of this racialised institutional violence is constructed as 'care'. There are many similarities between the treatment of the 'externally colonised' Palestinians and the 'internally colonised' *Mizrachi* Jews, but also many substantial differences.

for many Russian Israelis.[12] It may be particularly precious for the queers, whose relations with the Soviet past are haunted by the criminalisation of homosexuality and the dehumanisation of same-sex relations in the cultural memory of political terror. The comfort of this colonial embrace, of course, has strings attached to it: the immigrants' belonging is conditioned on their patriotism, loyalty and normative Jewishness. But this is what also makes Israeli nationalism so seductive: it carries a promise of ultimate inclusion, including that of the queers and despite the heterosexual imaginings of both the nation and the immigrant community.

The emotional price – individual and collective – of questioning the foundation of this welcome is high, because it might feel like losing the (newly acquired) home all over again. In the country, insistently clinging to its colonial melancholia,[13] victimhood of the past and heroism of the present,[14] it is easier to claim one's participation in the history of suffering or one's contribution to militancy.[15] The move towards political, psychological and ethical 'maturity' (Gilroy 2004: 108) and the responsibility for

12 As long as they don't find themselves on the other side of this care, as, for example, do those who reject Zionism; or those who marry or are engaged sexually with the Arabs – Palestinian Israelis or those form the Occupied territories; or simply the many non-Jewish newcomers who immigrated as family members of Jews, but who are of only 'partial' Jewish heritage.

13 This colonial melancholia characterises not only the mainstream and right wing politics. As Kirstein Keshet's illuminating analysis of the Israeli radical left demonstrates, the political vision of many Zionist, *Ashkenazi* and upper-middle-class Leftists is based on melancholic mourning of the nations' 'golden days', to which they hope to return. Such vision is based on unwillingness to questions the colonial, racial and classed foundations of the Zionist project (Kirstein Keshet 2007).

14 In the Zionist mythology, the establishment of Israel is figured as transition from victimhood (the Holocaust) to heroism (the new Jew, defending himself and his nation).

15 For an interesting ethnographic study of old Russian-speaking immigrants, veterans of WWII and former Soviet soldiers, see the work of Sveta Roberman (2005). Roberman demonstrates that the old immigrants mobilise memory to claim national belonging in the present. They challenge the Zionist narrative of Jewish victimhood during WWII, by positioning themselves as *Jewish* soldiers who were not passive victims and whose heroism contributed the establishment of the Israeli state. With regards to the queers, many scholars have demonstrated how Israeli militarism is embraced precisely through queering (see, for example, Kadish 2001; Michaeli 2004; Yosef 2004, 2005).

the national violence of past and present, will therefore only be possible if it includes the queers and the non-queers, and both the immigrants and the Israeli society as a whole.

Metonymies, reverberations, genealogies

So far, I have pointed out the ways different practices of figuration are related to each other, or at least, can be thought through together. But what about the relationship between the figures themselves? What I want to suggest now is that the figures presented in this book are linked, and that violence and belonging should be examined not only through each figure and its circulation, but also through *the connections between them*. These connections, as I will show, work in two registers: spatial (including the spatiality of texts) and temporal, linking the figures metonymically and through genealogies, and connecting material, semiotic and psychic domains through what I call reverberations.

First of all, the figures are connected because they were part of the same 'archive of feelings' (Cvetkovich 2003) and had circulated in the same ethnographic and textual space: the website of Russian-speaking, queer immigrants living almost exclusively in Israel/Palestine. And while these figures had different histories and genealogies – the aspect I return to below – at the time of my ethnography they were located close to each other. This closeness created metonymic connections, where the figures could be linked to, transformed into, substituted – or even mistaken – for each other. I address metonymy here following Roman Jakobson's analysis of literary texts: according to Jakobson, metonymy is the substitution of objects that are located in textual proximity (Jakobson 1935/1987; see also Ahmed 2004). Jakobson primarily addressed the aesthetics of transformation and substitution (for example, of spatial and temporal categories) in poetic texts; Ahmed focuses more specifically on the politics of connection and 'contact' between texts and figures. Ahmed emphasises that the very making of one's archive – the suggestion that some texts '"belong" together' – is a form of 'contact zone': not a 'conversion of self into a textual gathering' but 'an effect of multiple forms of contact', both institutional and personal, where 'the individual and the social [...] shape each other' (Ahmed 2004: 14). For Ahmed, figures of speech stick together metonymically, precisely in such contact zones, through repetition, resemblance and other forms of textual closeness.

The metonymic connections between figures that I am proposing here are, too, a result of contact zones that involve both the appearance of the texts in cyberspace, and my selection of them for discussion. But the contact zones are also formed because the constitution and the circulation of the figures, discussed here, took place through similar affective and literary technologies of wounding words and performative feelings, similar practices of cybercommunication, or even similar forms of wit. For example, hatred and disgust towards gays and lesbians were expressed through name-calling, distorted words[16] and naming of feelings and actions. Similar practices were also used by attempting to shame the homophobes as fascists, or name-calling of the flamer or the club-goers or leftists, or naming of hatred or threats of torture of 'the enemy', or expressions of disgust towards the club. Many of these also used sarcasm, or smileys, or laughter, to constitute wounding words as a 'joke'. Attempts at erasure were exercised towards the queers in homophobic hate texts; the same erasure was evoked in relation to disturbing cyberpersonae. The latter were connected, too: for example, the Flamer who questioned the notion of Russian-Israeli collective spaces as welcoming and hospitable, and Daughter of Palestine who questioned Israeli nationhood, colonial knowledge and everyday racism, were simultaneously attacked as intruders and dismissed as 'made up characters'. And last but not least, some figures were also linked through particular words: for example, the 'place by the latrine' in the Gulag, designated for the humiliated and abused *pidor* (and, although this was never explicitly mentioned, for the political prisoner from the intelligentsia), reappeared in praise of Israeli soldiers who kill terrorists by the latrines.

16 Such as 'pederation', see Chapter 2.

These metonymic connections create a movement of violence *between* figures, violence that expands each particular figure and gathers them into a cumulative effect.[17] In that sense, the relations between figures point to what Ahmed describes as 'affective economy' (2004: 45–49). Combining insights from Freudian psychoanalysis and Marx's discussion of capital and commodity (1976), Ahmed notes that 'emotions work as a form of capital: affect does not reside positively in the sign or commodity, but is produced as an effect of its circulation' (Ahmed 2004: 45). Importantly for Ahmed, the movement of emotions is not contained within the contours of a subject – the subject is only one 'nodal point' in the economy – but rather it is about the 'relationality of subjects, objects, signs and others' (2004: 46), and, as such, it emphasises that affective economies are social, material and psychic.

The notion of the cumulative and economic effect of the links between figures sheds light on the ways violence can intensify through the figures' circulation, expanding beyond the effects of each one of them. But Ahmed's notion of affective economies also invites us to think about violence beyond cyberspace, or rather, it opens up a way of conceptualising the effects of violence that does not recreate the separation between on-line and off-line worlds. When presenting different parts of this project in conferences and seminars, I was sometimes asked, whether the on-line racism in particular, and, more generally, the wounding words in cyberspace , reflected the 'real' social life off-line, in other words, how representative were on-line discussions of what was 'really' happening. I was also asked what impact the cyberviolence I observed had on real daily interactions. Both types of questions encouraged me to think carefully about the specificity of cyberspace in analysing violence. And yet I never had, and still do not have, a satisfying answer to either question, because I think the questions themselves are the wrong ones. Leaving aside the assumption that off-line interactions are somehow more 'real' – assumptions that I do not share,

17 I owe my attention to the cumulative effect of figurations to Castañeda's work on the figure of the child, where she notes that 'the child's value for adult discourses is constituted through its accumulated particularity across multiple figurations' (Castañeda 2002: 45).

and that are already extensively problematised and questioned by many scholars of cybercultures – I suggest that what is also problematic here are the visions of origins and impact.

The first question positions off-line social life as the authentic 'origin', which can be reflected or represented on-line; the movement of meaning here comes from off-line to on-line. The second question, on the other hand, presumes that it is the cyberspace that creates violence which then affects social relations off-line. What I suggest instead is that neither is the sole origin, and that our attention should be shifted from origins and impact to movement and figuration. The movement of violence in and out of cyberspace creates complex and messy relations, relations that cannot be grasped through concepts of reflection, representation or influence – models often used in the analysis of media texts.[18] In my discussions, I insisted that these relations are about the inseparability of the material and the semiotic: words can wound, and, as Daughter of Palestine's clone reminds us, words in cyberspace are sometimes written in blood, even if it is only an html code that creates the effect of red ink. These relations are about the breadth of the potential impact as well as about depth, for example, the deep emotional resonance of cyberwords (the very notion of linguistic injury suggests embodied and psychic effects of words). But just as in the case of Ahmed's affective economies, resonance is never only

18 To some extent, these relations could be conceptualised through terms, such as Paul Virilio's 'logistics of perception' (1989). In his *War and Cinema: The Logistics of Perception*, Virilio addresses the interrelatedness of military and cinematic technologies – such as elimination of distance, simulation and substitution of places – to the point where the boundary between cinema and warfare becomes indistinguishable, and where the violence of war is always also a spectacle. In the age of the Internet and accelerated speed of both communication and warfare, his analysis seems particularly relevant, although Virilio himself suggests that cyberspace brings a new form of perception, which is no longer visual, but tactile (Virilio 1995). For another illuminating analysis of the relations between warfare, technology and perception see Weizman's (2007) notion of the 'politics of verticality' in Israel/Palestine, and Puar's (2007) discussion of terrorist assemblages, and in particular her elaboration on Weizman's work in her reading of the 'data bodies' and the 'technological sublime' (2007: 151–154).

about the subject. Rather, emotions *reverberate*, in and through bodies, psyches and the spaces between them.

My deployment of the term 'reverberation' throughout the book was inspired by acoustics and musicology, although my use of the term is metaphorical, rather than literal. In acoustics, reverberation describes the physical process by which the sound bounces off hard surfaces, reaching the ear with possible delays – if the surface is in the distance, the sound 'returns' with an echo.[19] In discussions of 'acoustic space' or 'soundscape', particularly in relation to music in urban sites, reverberation is about the movement of sound and the ways it can become distorted, intensified or muffled as it moves between physical objects, encountering barriers and mixing with other sounds (see, for example, Tagg 2006). I chose the concept of reverberation as a potent metaphor because it invites us to think not only about the movement of violence in and out of cyberspace, but also about the multiplicity of effects such movement might entail. Reverberation is a concept that makes us attentive to speed and stillness, distortions and resonance, intensification and dissolution; as such, it also allows the tracing and opening up processes of refiguration. Reverberation also takes us away from the questions of ontological origins: even though its definition in acoustics assumes one single origin of each sound, the description of the urban musical soundscape, which predominantly inspires me here, is about *multiple* movements of *multiple* sounds, coming from *multiple* origins and bouncing off *multiple* surfaces, often simultaneously and in contradiction to each other. In that sense, reverberation is multi-nodal and has its own agency; its effects are unpredictable, and as such, can never be fully known.

Metonymies and reverberations both address the movement of violence between figures through immediate, synchronic proximity. However reverberations, in particular when we think about delay and echo, also point to the importance of connections through time, as, for example, I demonstrated in my discussion of haunting. I want to conclude my

19 Importantly, reverberation is always about the interdependency of the sound and the surface: without the encounter between the two, the sound would not exist.

argument about the figures' connection by looking at the ways they are linked diachronically, through what Ahmed calls 'histories of association that often "work" through concealment' (Ahmed 2004: 13). These histories of association only rarely come to the surface, and even then they are only marked through moments of uncanny resonance, such as happened in the case of the latrines. In order to understand them we must turn to the figures' genealogies.

My use of genealogies is informed by Puar and Amir Rai's analysis of the 'war on terror' (Puar and Rai 2002). In their 'Monster, Terrorist, Fag: the War on Terrorism and the Production of Docile Patriots', they suggest that today's figure of the terrorist has multiple genealogies that produce 'both hypervisible icons and the ghosts that haunt the machine of war' (Puar and Rai 2002: 117). Exploring these genealogies, they trace the figure of the terrorist within the history of monstrosity in Western discourse of normality:

> [M]onstrosity [is] a regulatory construct of modernity that imbricates not only sexuality but also questions of culture and race. [...] First, the monster is not merely an other; it is one category through which a multiform power operates. As such, discourses that would mobilise monstrosity as a screen for otherness are always also involved in circuits of normalising power as well: the monster and the person to be corrected are close cousins. Second, the monster is part of the West's family of abnormals, questions of race and sexuality will have always haunted its figuration (Puar and Rai 2002: 119).

Focusing on the genealogy of the terrorist, Puar and Rai point to the deep link between the terrorist and the queer: both are constituted through similar mechanisms of knowledge, quarantine and correction. This link clarifies why the terrorist in particular, and racialised others more generally, are often figured as queer, signalling failing heteronormativity and often also failing masculinity.

The genealogies drawn by Puar and Rai help us understand the uncanny resonance between some of the figures, for example, the shadow of the Gulag homosexual as it circulates in the immigrant attacks on Pride Parades, and the (queer) Arab terrorist as he is imagined on the queer immigrants' website. The two share the genealogies of failed masculinity, state control, silencing and delegitimation. More broadly, the emphasis on genealogies allows us to explore the similarities in the figurations of various monsters, such as Daughter of Palestine and the Flamer: both are figured through suspicion and rejection of authenticity, both dance on the shaky borderline between a joke and an attack.

These and other monsters are simultaneously mobile and frozen in time (or in the virtual fossils of on-line archives); they live with and through their past reincarnations (whether recent, such as earlier fights on the Forum, or more distant); and carry not only the past but also unpredictable, uncharted and haunting futures, futures that are 'already here [...] yet unknown but for a split second' (Puar 2007: xx). All of them have a degree of ambivalence in that they are destined for expulsion and/or erasure and at the same time are impossible to erase or expel. But most importantly, the emphasis on genealogies points to the intimate and very complex connection between victims and perpetrators; or rather, it problematises that very distinction. When I started my fieldwork, I was particularly troubled and confused by the fact that forms of discursive and affective violence used in homophobic attacks were reproduced by queers themselves, towards those defined as their enemies – homophobes, or Palestinians – and among each other. Looking at the genealogies of the figures offers some answers to this confusion: different figures that operate in different domains of belonging (such as belonging to the nation, to the immigrant community, to the queer scene, to cyberspace etc.) share the same genealogies of violence. Those genealogies are not only manifested in circuits of power and in forms of knowledge. Rather, they have a psychic life that moves across geo-political spaces as well as across time and generations. Here violence becomes a form of connectivity – even if painful, and even if unknown and unconscious. Genealogies of violence, then, have their own constitutive power that lies beyond individual speech acts or forms of collective imagination.

Refigurations: Concluding remarks

> To imagine beyond the limits of what is already understandable is our best hope for retaining what ideology critique traditionally offers while transforming its limitations into what, in an older Marxist language, was called utopian possibility.
>
> —Avery Gordon, *Ghostly Matters*, 1997: 195.

Having discussed the complex and contradictory ways in which belonging can be constituted against, with, or through violence, I want to conclude by looking at three issues: the possibilities of dialogue and intervention into violent speech in cyberspace and beyond; the ways of approaching and reconciling with a haunting past; and lastly, the need to reconsider the borders of humanness. I would like to point out some directions for research and politics where violences of haunting, borders and flaming can be rethought and reimagined. I will do so by suggesting the necessity of refiguration – a process of change in world viewing and world-making (Haraway 1997; Castañeda 2002). Refiguration, as has been discussed throughout the book, can be a technology of violence, where relations between victims and perpetrators are skilfully reversed (as demonstrated in Part I); or where hate emerges as love and atrocities become heroism (as shown in Part II); and where injury generates laughter by being claimed as a joke (as described in Part III). Refiguration can be also a form of resistance and 'talking back', as for example, happened when the queers refigured the queer victim as a Jewish one. But refiguration also, I believe, can be a form of hope, a way of moving towards justice by 'imagin[ing] beyond the limits of what is already understandable', to use Gordon's words.

The first issue – possibilities of intervention into violent speech – arises from my thoughts on the many instances of silence on the Forum, for example, the violent silencing of my friend Rita when she attempted to post information about anti-Occupation and anti-war events, or my own silence about politics during my fieldwork. In scholarly and activist discussions of minoritatian politics – feminist, GLBT, ethnic and post-colonial – speech is often figured as a privileged site of empowerment and resistance. The way to work against silences is usually understood to be either by speaking out within the particular space where violence takes place, or by creating an alternative one where it would be possible to 'disrupt hegemonic narratives' (Gajjala 2004: 5), such as those of homophobia or nationalism. In other words, having a voice, being able to speak and being heard often become synonymous with political subjecthood. In cybercultures the privileging of speech – or rather, of 'wrything' (Gajjala 2002) – is particularly evident, since in text-based on-line spaces 'wrything' equals 'being'.[20]

I do not suggest that interventions in the form of 'speaking out' should not be made; no doubt, such interventions are important.[21] However, I also want to put forward a different way of thinking about the relations between speech and silence, in and beyond cyberspace. Firstly, we have to be attentive to the ways speech itself can be complicit with the very formations it aims to disrupt and how it can contribute to and even intensify, rather than stop or inhibit, the circuits of violence. For example, in the context of constant flame wars, as was the case on the Forum, it might be the refusal to take part in the inflammable ping-pong of injurious words – the refusal to speak, rather than the speech itself – that can inhibit the violence.[22] But I also suggest that we should refigure the very privilege

20 The growing presence of non-textual and interactive materials on the Internet is another good opportunity to rethink the privileging of text and speech.

21 For example, the anti-homophobic organising was meaningful and empowering for at least some queer immigrants; and so were Rita's debates on politics. Similarly, I think it is crucial to continue creating alternative sites where homophobia, nationalism and racism can be challenged. One such site is the first 'Russian' feminist group, organised by Rita. Another is the new website for Russian-Israeli LGBTs, *Raduga* (rainbow, Rus.), www.raduga.co.il. The organisers of the site invited me to contribute by sharing my research with the wider audience of queer immigrants. I have already written a piece on homophobia and the Gulag, based on the chapters in Part I, which was met with much appreciation; currently I am working on a piece on nationalism, violence and queerness, based on Part II of the book. Whether or not the latter would be dismissed, opposed or would open up a debate about queer complicities, is a question for the future.

22 For an insightful discussion of refusal to speak, or to be read or represented, as a form of cyber-resistance, see Gajjala (2004). For an interesting ethnographic account of refusal to participate as opposition to violence see, for example, Spencer (2000).

of speech versus silence. Esperanza Miyake in her 'The Voice of Silence: Interrogating the Sound of Queerness/Raciality', writes beautifully about listening to silences:

> [S]ilence is a double-edged sword that can cut either way: silence can mean certain voices, certain narratives are cut off, leaving them omitted from history and representation; but I also want to suggest that silence can be a means to hear a pin drop, a tool to make us listen to the sounds that are made *in* silence (Miyake 2008: 124, emphasis in the original).

Following Miyake, I propose that one way to refigure violent racist or homophobic speech might be by listening to silences.[23] I do not mean the literal lack of voice, but rather, silence as an epistemological category that allows imagining the unimaginable, and listening to those who cannot speak and cannot be spoken for, but whose absence can be a form of 'seething presence' (Gordon 1997: 8). 'To move outside the domain of speakability is to risk one's status as a subject', notes Butler (1997: 133). Yet the unspeakable does not mean not existing. On the contrary, Butler emphasises that the unspeakable is that which brings the subject into being and then haunts its speech, becoming what Linda Randolph, the artist that inspired Haraway's work on figurations, calls a 'metaphysical space in between', a 'place where change occurs' (Randolph 1993 in Haraway 1997: 273).

The notion of haunted speech brings me to the second issue: the relations with haunting figures, and more specifically, the ghosts of the Soviet labour camps. Russian and Western historiography of Stalinist and post-Stalinist Gulag insistently ignores the topic of same-sex relations among political prisoners and accepts the memoirs of survivors as unquestionably truthful testimonies of life in the camps, both those of the fellow political prisoners and of their ultimate other – the criminals. Research on the Gulag, and in particular on the memoir literature of the Stalinist period, overlooks the fact that it is almost always the educated political prisoners

23 In thinking about listening, rather than speaking, I am also inspired by Back's *The Art of Listening*, where he notes that sociology is about 'recognising that what we touch is always moving, unpredictable, irreducible and mysteriously opaque' (2007: 3).

who bear the epistemological authority to narrate and explain the lives and actions of the low-class 'criminal' inmates and to figure them as 'beyond the borders of human' (Ginzburg 1979: 42).

One important challenge to the field of Gulag studies lies in raising the topic of sexual relations as a legitimate object of research beyond penology – the pathologising context in which same-sex relations in Soviet prisons and camps are often described by Russian scholars.[24] But it will not be enough to acquire academic acknowledgement or legitimation of the topic, nor is it enough to simply gather archival information about same-sex relations among 'criminal' as well as 'political' prisoners – a suggestion made repeatedly to me by historians of the period. What is needed is a refiguring of the very relations between sexuality, class and humanness and between all these and memory and historical subjecthood.

Such refiguring is crucial not only for the field of Gulag historiography, Russian- and English-language alike, but also for the public debates on sexuality in various post-Soviet domains, including émigré communities. Simply shaming, and referring to the homophobic violence as unacceptable (which it undoubtedly is), or comparing it with other atrocities will not do the work – it will only displace the horror elsewhere. Neither will the attempt to reclaim same-sex relations as respectable and 'cultural'. Naming famous poets and writers who experienced and glorified same-sex love, or insisting that the political prisoners, too, must have had queer experiences, is a tempting way to resist the intellectualising homophobic attacks, such as those that took place in *Vesti* in 2002 and are still frequent among the Russian-Israeli intelligentsia. It may indeed be empowering for individual queers who see themselves as part of the intelligentsia and for whom the exclusion from this imagined community is extremely painful. But the appeal to this cultural capital only reproduces the 'borders of human' (Ginzburg 1979: 42), the very borders that leave those beyond

24 In Russian-language (Soviet and post-Soviet) research, there is a clear division of labour between studies in criminology and studies in literature. The former pathologises all aspects of prison and camp behaviour, including same-sex relations; the latter looks at the memoirs of political prisoners in the Soviet penal system, who are clearly distinguished from the 'real' criminals and are addressed as writers, dissidents, and survivors.

them as voiceless shadows and as monsters who do not deserve memory, history and recognition.

Denial of history, recognition and remembrance is what connects the two seemingly unrelated topics, the absent presence of same-sex relations in the cultural memory of the Gulag and the troubled colonial realities of Israel/Palestine. This connection brings me to the third issue: the need to refigure humanness, not only in relation to the Gulag shadows, but in immigrant and queer politics and particularly in Israel/Palestine. In a chapter of his *After Empire*, entitled 'Race and the Right to be Human', Gilroy puts forward the concept of raciology, shifting the discussion from 'race' as an ontological category to racisms and their technologies in producing knowledge, hierarchies, histories and geo-political boundaries. One of such technologies is the recognition or denial of human status. 'To be recognised as human was to be accorded an authentic kind of historic being. On the other hand, to be dismissed on raciological grounds as bestial or infrahuman was to be cast outside of both culture and historicality' (Gilroy 2004: 34). Throughout his discussion, Gilroy traces raciologies of dehumanisation across colonial histories, Nazi genocide, apartheid regimes, and other, constantly evolving, forms of legitimised brutality, all united by 'murderous enthusiasm for the proper racial ordering of the world' (2004: 57). His concept of the 'infrahuman', which he also links to Georgio Agamben's 'bare life' (1998), points to profound, even if not always recognised, connections between the Gulag, the Holocaust, and the deadly realities of Israel/Palestine.[25] All of them operate through creating individuals and populations whose social annihilation and physical killings are marked with impunity, and who are also denied historical subjecthood or the right to political sovereignty.

25 By connections I do not mean similarities. I do not claim that the German concentration camps and the Soviet Gulag were similar, or that the systematic destruction of the social and psychic fabric of life in Palestine is 'exactly the same' as the Nazi's annihilation of the Jews (it is not!). Such comparisons, which seem to be a tempting rhetorical device in some political debates, are dangerous both because they constitute one atrocity as a 'valid measure' of another, and because they become deaf to the particular histories of each and, as such, diminish the human suffering by turning it into a generalised model.

As my final point, then, I would like to suggest that the hope for a just future lies first and foremost in refiguring the borders of humanness, or rather, in eliminating such borders altogether. The refiguration I hope for is neither about the rational human of the Enlightenment, nor about the depoliticised notion of liberal human rights. It is also not about narcissistic compassion,[26] where the humanness of the other can be recognised only through sameness, by being figured as someone 'just like us' (Tyler 2006).[27] Rather, it is first and foremost about moving away from raciological distinctions between humans and infrahumans. It is about the recognition of suffering in the present – recognition that, as Tyler suggests, should work 'at the limits of the available lexicon, including rights discourses, while simultaneously contesting the "regimes within which the terms of recognisability take place"' (Butler, 2002: 12 in Tyler 2006: 199). In the context of Israel/Palestine, it is also about acknowledgement of responsibility for past and present erasures and atrocities. Such acknowledgement must replace the insistent one-sided emphasis on and commemoration of Jewish victimhood, and by doing so, refigure the colonial cosmology of Israeliness as Jewishness in the land with no other humans and no other histories.

In July 2008, as I was finishing work on this book, the Israeli parliament – the *Knesset* – held a discussion about whether to grant Atlit detention centre, in the north of Israel, the status of concentration camp. This was where the British held the 'illegal' Jewish immigrants who had fled from Nazi Europe to Palestine between the late 1930s and early 1940s. The suggestion, proposed by a group of Russian-speaking immigrants, caused rage from some Israelis,[28] because they felt that the term 'concentration

26 Forms of compassionate politics and the politics of compassion are a complex issue that has to be addressed separately. For a detailed critical discussion of compassion, see Berlant (2004).

27 In her discussion of humanitarian politics, Tyler shows how the refugee becomes a generalised and disembodied object of narcissistic projection, recognised only through similarity (they are just like us) and subsuming (we are all refuges). This move, Tyler emphasises, 'abstract[s] and disembody[ies] "the figure of the other" from any embodied referent (actual refugees)' (Tyler 2006: 197).

28 I was not univocally accepted by the immigrants, either, as I discovered by observing the Russian-Israeli blogosphere.

camp' should be reserved primarily for the Nazi camps. The leader of the immigrant group, however, argued that his father had been in a Soviet concentration camp and that the detention centre in Atlit looked exactly the same (Galili 2008: n.p.).

The newspaper article by Lilly Galili[29] that described this debate was entitled 'We will teach you how to remember' (*Haaretz*, 25 July 2008). It opened, unsurprisingly, by mentioning the mourning of the most recent Israeli victims of a terrorist attack. The article then moved on to the Russian immigrants' negotiation of Israeli practices of commemoration. The recent initiative by a group of immigrants, among them members of the *Knesset*, included a proposal to increase the commemoration sites of Jewish persecution, so as to cover not only Germany and Poland but also the territories of the former Soviet Union. In addition, the immigrants proposed to expand the current 'memory tours'[30] to include not just sites of victimhood and death but also sites of combat and heroism, such as the sites of victorious battles in the Great Patriotic War led by the Soviet Union against the Germans (1941–1945).

This 'teaching how to remember' appeared to the journalist herself and the many people she interviewed – the MPs, the immigrants, and the two Israeli sociologists of collective memory – as a significant moment for both Israeli-born Jews and the Russian-speaking immigrants. For the latter it signalled inclusion in the national pantheon of victimhood and heroism, and also linked their personal and family history to the history of other Jews in Europe and British Palestine. For the former it was about the threat to their ethnic hegemony and control over national narratives. But nowhere in Galili's article do we see a reference to death and destruction brought by Israel to Gaza or Lebanon, nor to the detention centres currently operated by Israel for Palestinian political prisoners – all of which

29 Galili has a regular column dedicated to Russian-speaking immigrants. Her own representations of the immigrants are far from unproblematic; her article is used here not as a true account of immigrant politics, but as a telling vignette that illuminates many issues of nationhood, memory and belonging.

30 Many Israeli teenagers take part in 'memory tours' organised by the Ministry of Education, to the sites of the mass murder of Jews in the Nazi camps, usually to Auschwitz.

I see as highly symptomatic of the state of mind of both the Hebrew and Russain-speaking Israelis today. Nor do we see the call to include in the national memory the traces of Palestinian life before the establishment of the Israeli state, traces scattered all across the country, vanishing under the new, Jewish, names of streets, neighbourhoods and towns.

The absence is not accidental, and is not simply about the separation of 'immigration issues' from 'political issues', although such separation guides much of Israeli journalistic and academic writing on immigration and ethnicity, and in itself must be rethought.[31] Rather, it is about their invisible pairing. Having discussed the possible reasons for the immigrants' initiative as offered by two sociologists, Galili concludes with her own explanation. She suggests that the immigrants' appeal to the history of combat and heroism might be the result of 'the sense of weakness and defeat' left by the second Israeli-Lebanese war that took place in 2006. The violent inversion of the recent warfare in Lebanon into Israel's 'weakness and defeat' is part and parcel of the raciology of dehumanisation. The exclusiveness of Jewish suffering and commemoration is its other part.

And what about the queers? They were not mentioned in Galili's article, and most probably were not part of the *Knesset* discussion. But as I have demonstrated throughout this book, queer immigrants' politics are intimately tied to both the Russian Israelis' claims for home and belonging *and* to Israeli colonial nationhood. In both, acknowledgement and commemoration of suffering – of queers versus the heterosexual prisoners in the Gulag, for example, or of Jews versus the Palestinians – so often appears as mutually exclusive, as if accepting one is dependent on denial of the other. I believe that it is vital that we move instead to what Gilroy describes as 'planetary humanism' – the capability of 'comprehending the universality of our elemental vulnerability to the wrongs we visit upon each other' (2004: 4). Only then can we hope for different queer politics, not based on national militancy and on raciology of dehumanisation. Only

31 One important intervention into this separation is made by the *Mizrachi* scholarship that links internal colonisation of non-European Jews with questions of Israel/Palestine (see, for example, Lavie n.d.). Another is Majid Al-Haj's (2004) analysis of the Russian-speaking immigration of the 1990s in the context of Israel's treatment of its Arab citizens.

then, when the borders of humanness are refigured – at the limits of available language, in the metaphysical space of silence – would it be possible to move to other modes of belonging and to the unimagined possibilities of existence that can 'transform a shadow of a life into an undiminished life whose shadows touch softly in the spirit of peaceful reconciliation' (Gordon 1997: 208).

Bibliography

Agamben, G. (1999) *Remnants of Auschwitz: The Witness and the Archive*, New York: Zone Books.

Ahmed, S. (1999) 'Passing Through Hybridity', *Theory, Culture and Society* 16 (2), 87–106.

——. (2004) *The Cultural Politics of Emotion*, Edinburgh: Edinburgh University Press.

——. (2006) *Queer Phenomenology: Orientations, Objects, Others*, Durham: Duke University Press.

Al-Haj, M. (2004) *Immigration and Ethnic Formation in a Deeply Divided Society: The Case of the 1990s Immigrants from the Former Soviet Union in Israel*, Boston: Brill.

Alarcón, N. (1996) 'Anzaldúa's *Frontera* : Inscribing Gynetics', in Lavie, S. and Swedenburg, T. (eds) *Displacement, Diaspora and Geographies of Identity*, Durham and London: Duke University Press.

Alexander, J. (2002) 'Queer Webs: Representation of LGBT People and Communities on the World Wide Web', *International Journal of Sexuality and Gender Studies*, 7 (2/3), 77–84.

Alexander, J. M. (1994) 'Not Just (Any) Body Can Be a Citizen: The Politics of Law, Sexuality and Postcoloniality in Trinidad and Tobago and the Bahamas', *Feminist Review*, 48, 5–23.

——. (1997) 'Erotic Autonomy as a Politics of Decolonization: An Anatomy of State Practice in the Bahamas Tourist Economy', in Alexander, J. M. and Mohanty, C. T., (eds) *Feminist Genealogies, Colonial Legacies, Democratic Futures*, New York: Routledge.

Amir, D. and Benjamin, O. (1997) 'Defining Encounters: Who are Women Entitled to Join the Israeli Collective?', *Women's Studies International Forum*, 20 (5/6), 639–650.

——, Remennick, L. and Elimelech, Y. (1997) 'Educating Lena: Women Immigrants and "Integration" Policies in Israel: The Politics of Reproduction and Family Planning', in Lewin-Epstein, N., Ro'I, Y. and Ritterband, P. (eds), *Russian Jews on Three Continents: Migration and Resettlement*, London: Frank Cass.

Anderson, B. (1991) *Imagined Communities*. London: Verso.

Anthias, F. and Yuval-Davis, N. (1989) 'Introduction', in Yuval-Davis, N. and Anthias, F. (eds), *Woman–Nation–State*, London: Macmillan.

Anzaldúa, G. (1987) *Borderlands/La Frontera: The New Mestiza*, San Francisco: Aunt Lute.

Ashrawi, H. (2001) 'Areej – The Scent of Youth and Death', *Media Monitors Network*, http://www.mediamonitors.net/hanan9.html [Accessed February 2006].

Back, L. (2007) *The Art of Listening*, Oxford: Berg.

Baker, P. (2001) 'Moral Panic and Alternative Identity Construction in Usenet', *Journal of Computer Mediated Communication*, 7 (1). http://jcmc.indiana.edu/vol7/issue1/baker.html [Accessed May 2006].

Bakhtin, M. (1968) *Rabelais and His World*, Cambridge, MA: MIT Press.

——. (1981) *The Dialogic Imagination*, Austin: University of Texas Press.

Bal, M. (1999) 'Introduction', in Bal, M., Crewe, J. and Spitzer, L. (eds), *Acts of Memory: Cultural Recall in the Present*, Hanover and London: University Press of New England.

Bardenstein, C. (1999) 'Trees, Forests and the Shaping of Palestinian and Israeli Collective Memory', in Bal, M., Crewe, J. and Spitzer, L. (eds), *Acts of Memory: Cultural Recall in the Present*, Hanover and London: University Press of New England.

——. (2005) 'Cross-Cast: Passing in Israeli and Palestinian Cinema,' in Stein, R. L. and Swedenburg, T. (eds), *Palestine, Israel, and The Politics Of Popular Culture*, Durham and London: Duke University Press.

Bar-On, B. (1997) 'Sexuality, the Family and Nationalism', in Lindemann, N. H. (ed.), *Feminism and Families*, New York: Routledge.

Battaglia, D. (2001) 'Multiplicities: An Anthropologist's Thoughts on Replicants and Clones in Popular Film', *Critical Inquiry*, 27 (3), 493–515.

Baym, N. (1995) 'The Emergence of Community in Computer Mediated Communication', in Jones, S. G. (ed.), *Cybersociety: Computer mediated communication and community*, Thousand Oaks, CA: Sage.

Belanovsky, S. and Marzeeva, S. (1991) *Hazing in the Army: Sociological Papers*, Moscow: Akademia Nauk SSSR (in Russian).

Bell, D. and Binnie, J. (2002) 'Sexual Citizenship: Marriage, the Market and the Military', in Richardson, D. and Seidman, S. (eds), *Handbook of Lesbian and Gay Studies*, London: Sage.

——. and Valentine, G. (1995) 'Sexualised Spaces: Global/Local', in Bell, D. and Valentine, G. (eds), *Mapping Desire: Geographies of Sexuality*, London and New York: Routledge.

Bell, V. (1999a) 'On Speech, Race and Melancholia: An Interview with Judith Butler', *Theory, Culture and Society*, 16 (2), 163–174.

——. (1999b) 'Performativity and Belonging', *Theory, Culture and Society*, 16 (2), 1–10.

Berkovitch, N. (1997) 'Motherhood as a National Mission: the Construction of Womanhood in the Legal Discourse in Israel', *Women Studies International Forum*, 20(5), 605–619.

Berlant, L. (1997) *The Queen of America Goes to Washington City: Essays on Sex and Citizenship*, Durham and London: Duke University Press.

——. (2001) 'Trauma and Ineloquence', *Cultural Values*, 5(1), 41–58.

——. (2004) 'Introduction: Compassion (and Withholding)', in Berlant, L. (ed.), *Compassion: The Culture and Politics of an Emotion*, London and New York: Routledge.

Bernstein, J. (2006) '"Sometimes I feel that this is the Russia we had always dreamed of…". Transnationalism and capitalism: Migrants from the former Soviet Union and their experiences in Germany', *Research Group Transnationalism* Working Paper Number 7, Institute of Cultural Anthropology and European Ethnology, Johann Wolfgang Goethe University Frankfurt am Main.

Bhabha, H. K. (1994) *The Location of Culture*, London, New York: Routledge.

Bhattacharyya, G. (2008) *Dangerous Brown Men: Exploiting Sex, Violence and Feminism in the War on the Terror*, London: Zed Books.

Biemann, U. (2001) *Performing the Border: On Gender, Transnational Bodies, and Technology*. http://www.geobodies.org/video/performing/performtxte.html [Accessed May 2006].

Binnie, J. (1995) 'Trading Places: Consumption, Sexuality and the Production of the Queer Space', in Bell, D. and Valentine, G. (eds), *Mapping Desire: Geographies of Sexualities*, London and New York: Routledge.

Boellstorff, T. (2007) *A Coincidence of Desires: Anthropology, Queer Studies, Indonesia*, Durham and London: Duke University Press.

Borenstein, E. (2008) 'Band of Brothers: Homoeroticism and the Russian Action hero', *Kultura*, 4 (2). www.kultura-rus.de [Accessed May 2008].

Bourdieu, P. (1984) *Distinction: A Social Critique of the Judgment of Taste*, Cambridge: Massachusetts.

Bourgois, P. (2004) 'The Continuum of Violence in War and Peace: Post-Cold War lessons from El Salvador', in Sheper-Hughes, N. and Bourgois, P. (eds), *Violence in War and Peace. An Anthology*, Malden, Oxford, Carlton: Blackwell Publishing.

Boyarin, D. (1997) *Unheroic Conduct: The Rise of Heterosexuality and the Invention of the Jewish Man*, Berkeley: University of California Press.

Boym, S. (1993) 'Loving in Bad Taste: Eroticism and Excess in Marina Tsvetaeva's "The Tale of Sonechka"', in Costlow, J. T., Sandler, S. and Vowles, J. (eds), *Sexuality and the Body in Russian Culture*, California: Stanford University Press.

——. (1995) 'From the Russian Soul to Post-Communist Nostalgia', *Representations* Special Issue: *Identifying Histories: Eastern Europe Before and After 1989*, 133–166.

——. (2001) *The Future of Nostalgia*, New York: Basic Books.

Brah, A. (1996) *Cartographies of Diaspora: Contesting Identities*, London, New York: Routledge.

Bram, C. (2005) 'White Russians?!', paper presented at the *'Russians' in Israel and Beyond: The Meanings of Culture in Discourse and Practice*, Jerusalem, 8–9 June 2005.

Butler, J. (1990) *Gender Trouble: Feminism and the Subversion of Identity*, London: Routledge.

——. (1993) *Bodies That Matter: On the Discursive Limits of Sex*, London, New York: Routledge.

——. (1997a) *Excitable Speech: A Politics of the Performative*, London: Routledge.

——. (1997b) *The Psychic Life of Power: Theories of Subjection*, Stanford: Stanford University Press.

——. (2004) *Precarious Life: Essays on Mourning and Violence*, London and New York: Verso.

Campbell, J. E. (2004) *Getting It On Online: Cyberspace, Gay Male Sexuality, and Embodied Identity*, Binghamton, NY: Haworth Press.

Campt, T. (2005) *Other Germans: Black Germans and the Politics of Race, Gender, and Memory in the Third Reich*, Ann Arbor: The University of Michigan Press.

Carter, C. and Weaver, C. K. (2003) *Violence and the Media*, Open University Press: Buckingham, Philadelphia.

Castañeda, C. (2002) *Figurations: Child, Bodies, Worlds*, Durham: Duke University Press.

——. (2008) Personal correspondence.

Central Bureau of Statistics of Israel (2002) *Statistical Abstract*, Jerusalem: Central Bureau of Statistics of Israel.

Cooper, D. (1995) *Power in Struggle: Feminism, Sexuality and the State*, New York: Buckingham, and New York University Press.

——. (2002) 'Imagining the Place of the State: Where Governance and Social Power Meet', in Richardson, D. and Seidman, S. (eds), *Handbook of Lesbian and Gay Studies*, London: Sage.

Correll, S. (1995) 'The Ethnography of an Electronic Bar: the Lesbian Café', *Journal of Contemporary Ethnography* 24(3), 270–298.

Corteen K., Moran L., Skeggs B. and Tyrer P. (2002) 'Violence, Sexuality and Space: Challenging Homophobic Violence', in Stanko, E. (ed.), *The Meaning of Violence*, London: Routledge.

Cox, L. J. and Fay, R. J. (1994) 'Gayspeak, the Linguistic Fringe: Bona Polari, Camp, Queerspeak and Beyond', in Whittle, S. (ed.), *The Margins of the City: Gay Men's Urban Lives*, Aldershot: Ashgate.

Cruz, M. J. (2000) 'Gay Male Domestic Violence and the Pursuit of Masculinity', in Nardi, P. (ed.), *Gay Masculinities*, Thousand Oaks, CA: Sage.

Cruz-Malave, A. and Manalansan, M. F. IV. (2002) 'Introduction: Dissident Sexualities/Alternative Globalisms', in Cruz-Malave, A. and Manalansan, M. F. IV. (eds), *Queer Globalization: Citizenship and the Afterlife of Colonialism*, New York and London: New York University Press.

Cussins C. (1996) 'Ontological Choreography: Agency for Women Patients in an Infertility Clinic', *Social Studies of Science*, 26, 575–610.

Cvetkovich, A. (2003) *An Archive of Feelings: Trauma, Sexuality, and Lesbian Public Cultures*, Durham and London: Duke University Press.

Daiya, K. (2008) *Violent Belongings: Partition, Gender, and National Culture in Postcolonial India*, Philadelphia: Temple University Press.

Danet, B. (1998) 'Text as Mask: Gender, Play, and Performance on the Internet', in S. G. Jones (ed.), *Cybersociety 2.0: Revisiting Computer-Mediated Communication and Community*, Thousand Oaks, CA: Sage.

Daniel E. V. (1996) *Charred Lullabies: Chapters in an Anthropography of Violence*, Princeton, New Jersey: Princeton University Press.

Das, V. and Kleinman, A. (2000) 'Introduction', in Das, V. , Kleinman, A., Ramphele, M. and Reynolds, P. (eds), *Violence and Subjectivity*, Berkeley, Los Angeles and London: University of California Press.

——. (ed.) (1990) *Mirrors of Violence: Community, Riots and Survivors in South Asia*, Delhi: Oxford University Press.

——, Kleinman, A., Ramphele, M. and Reynolds, P. (eds). (2000) *Violence and Subjectivity*, Berkeley, Los Angeles and London: University of California Press.

Delgado, R. (1993) 'Words That Wound: A Tort Action for Racial Insults, Epithets, and Name Calling', in Matsuda, M. J., Lawrence III, C. L., Delgado, R. and Crenshaw, K. W. (eds), *Words That Wound*, Boulder, San Francisco and Oxford: Westview Press.

Derné, S. (2000) 'Men's Sexuality and Women's Subordination in Indian Nationalisms', in Mayer, T. (ed.), *Gender Ironies of Nationalism: Sexing the Nation*, London and New York: Routledge.

Dhawan, N. and Castro Varela, M. (2006) 'Catachresis: Sexuality, Colonialism and the Production of Cultural Difference', paper presented at *Hegemony and Sexual*

Politics: On Queer and Post-colonial Critique of Economies of Desire in Europe, 14–15 July, Basel, Switzerland.

Elias, N. (1982) *The Civilizing Process: State Formation and Civilization*. Oxford: Blackwell.

Eng, D. L. (1997) 'Out Here and Over There: Queerness and Diaspora in Asian Studies', *Social Text*, 15 (3), 31–52.

——., Halberstam, J, and Muñoz J. E. (2005) 'Introduction', *What's Queer about Queer Studies Now?* Special Issue of *Social Text*, 23 (3/4), 1–17.

——. and Han, S. (2003) 'A Dialogue on Racial Melancholia', in Eng, D. L. and Kazanjian, D. (eds), *Loss: The Politics of Mourning*, Berkeley: University of California Press.

Everard, J. (2000) *Virtual States: the Internet and the Boundaries of the Nation-State*, London and New York: Routledge.

Fanon, F. (1963) *The Wretched of the Earth*, New York: Grove Press.

——. (1986) *Black Skin, White Masks*, London: Pluto Press.

Fernback, J. (1999) 'There is a There There: Notes Toward a Definition of Cybercommunity', in Jones, S. (ed.), *Doing Internet Research: Critical Issues and Methods for Examining the Net*, London, New Delhi: Sage.

Ferreday, D. (2003) 'Unspeakable Bodies: Erasure, Embodiment and the Pro-Ana Community', *International Journal of Cultural Studies*, 6 (3), 277–295.

Fortier, A-M. (2000) *Migrant Belongings: Memory, Space and Identity*, Oxford: Berg.

——. (2001) '"Coming Home": Queer Migrations and Multiple Evocations of Home', *European Journal of Cultural Studies*, 4 (4), 405–424.

——. (2006) 'Community, Belonging and Intimate Ethnicity', *Modern Italy*, 1 (1), 63–77.

——. (2008) *Multicultural Horizons: Diversity and the Limits of the Civil Nation*, London and New York: Routledge.

Foucault, M. (2003) *'Society Must Be Defended': Lectures at the College de France, 1975–1976*, New York: Picador.

Freud, S. (1905/1960) *Jokes and Their Relations to the Unconscious*, London: Routledge and Kegan Paul.

——. (1914/1964) 'Remembering, Repeating and Working Through', *The Standard Edition of the Complete Psychological Works of Sigmund Freud, Vol XII*, London: The Hogarth Press, 147–156.

——. (1917/1934) 'Mourning and Melancholia', in *Collected Papers, Vol. IV*, London: The Hogarth Press.

——. (1919/1934) 'The "Uncanny"', in *Collected Papers, Vol. IV*, London: Hogarth Press.

——. (1923/1964) 'The Ego and the Id', *The Standard Edition of the Complete Psychological Works of Sigmund Freud, Vol XIX*, London: The Hogarth Press.

——. (1926/1964) 'Inhibitions, Symptoms and Anxiety', *The Standard Edition of the Complete Psychological Works of Sigmund Freud, Vol XX*, London: The Hogarth Press.

Fusco, C. (1989) 'The Border Art Workshop/ Taller de Arte Fronterizo: Interview with Guillermo Gomez-Peña and Emily Hicks', *Third Text*, 7, 53–76.

Gajjala, R. (1996) 'Cyborg Diaspora and Virtual Imagined Community: Studying SAWNET'. www.cyberdiva.org/erniestuff/sanov.html [Accessed October 2003].

——. (2000) 'Cyberethnography: Reading Each "Other" Online', http://personal.bgsu.edu/~radhik/Cyberethnography.pdf [Accessed March 2006].

——. (2001) 'Studying Feminist E-spaces: Introducing Transnational/ Post-colonial Concerns', in Munt, S. (ed.), *Technospaces: Inside the New Media*, Continuum: London and New York.

——. (2002) 'An Interrupted Postcolonial/Feminist Cyberethnography: Complicity and Resistance in the "Cyberfield"', *Feminist Media Studies*, 2 (2), 177–193.

——. (2004) *Cyberselves: Feminist Ethnographies of South-Asian Women*, Oxford: Alta Mira Press.

Galili, L. (2008) 'We will Teach you How to Remember', *Haaretz*, 25 July 2008 (in Hebrew).

Garber, M. (1992) *Vested Interests: Cross-Dressing and Cultural Anxiety*, New York: Routledge.

Gershenson, O. (2005) 'Postcolonial Discourse Analysis and Intercultural Communication: Building the New Model', *The Intercultural and International Communication Annual*, 28, 124–145.

Gilroy, P. (2004) *After Empire: Melancholia or Convivial Culture?* London and New York: Routledge.

Ginzburg, E. (1979) *Treacherous Journey, Vol. II*, Milano: Arnoldo Mondadori Editore (in Russian).

Glusman, M. (1997) 'The Longing for Heterosexuality: Zionism and Sexuality in "Altnoyland"', *Theory and Criticism*, 11, 145–162 (in Hebrew).

Goffman, E. (1956) *The Presentation of Self in Everyday Life*, Doubleday: New York.

Golden, D. (2002) 'Storytelling the Future: Israelis, Immigrants and the Imagining of Community', *Anthropological Quarterly*, 75 (1), 7–35.

——. (2003), 'A National Cautionary Tale: Russian Women to Israel portrayed'. *Nations and Nationalism*, 9 (1), 34–51.

Gopinath, G. (1996) 'Funny Boys and Girls: Notes on a Queer South Asian Planet', in Leong, R. (ed.), *Asian American sexualities: Dimensions of the Gay and Lesbian Experience*, London and New York: Routledge.

——. (2003) 'Nostalgia, Desire, Diaspora: South Asian Sexualities in Motion', in Braziel, J. and Mannur, A. (eds), *Theorizing Diaspora*, Oxford: Blackwell Publishing.

——. (2005) *Impossible Desires: Queer Diasporas and South Asian Public Cultures*, Durham: Duke University Press.

Gordon, A. (1997) *Ghostly Matters: Haunting and the Sociological Imagination*, Minneapolis and London: University of Minneapolis Press.

——. (2006) 'Abu Ghraib: Imprisonment and the War on Terror', *Race & Class*, 48 (1), 42–59.

Gregory, D. (2004a) 'Palestine and the "War on Terror"', *Comparative Studies of South Asia, Africa and the Middle East*, 24 (1), 183–195.

——. (2004b) *The Colonial Present*, Oxford: Blackwell.

Gross, A. (2000) 'Sexuality, Masculinity, Military, and Citizenship: Gay Military Service in I.D.F. in Comparative View', *Pelilim*, 95–183 (in Hebrew).

Guberman, I. (2003) *Walks around the Barracks*, EKSMO (in Russian).

Gunew, S. (2003) 'The Home of Language: a Pedagogy of the Stammer', in Ahmed, S., Castañeda, C., Fortier, A.-M. and Sheller, M. (eds), *Uprootings/ Regroundings: Questions of Home and Migration*, Oxford: Berg.

——. (2004) *Haunted Nations: The Colonial Dimensions of Multiculturalisms*, London and New York: Routledge.

Hage, G. (1997) *Home/World: Space, Community and Marginality in Sydney's West*, Sydney: Pluto Press.

——. (2000) *White Nation: Fantasies of White Supremacy in a Multicultural Society*, London and New York: Routledge.

——. (2003) *Against Paranoid Nationalism: Searching for Hope in a Shrinking Society*, Sydney: Pluto Press.

Har'el, A. (2000) 'The Rise and Fall of the Israeli Gay Legal Revolution', *Columbia Human Rights Law Review*, 31, 443–451.

Haraway, D. (1991) *Simians, Cyborgs, and Women: The Reinvention of Nature*, New York: Routledge.

——. (1997) *Modest _Witness@Second_Millenium: FemaleMan _ Meets _ OncoMouse™: Feminism and Technoscience*, New York: Routledge.

Haritaworn, J. with Tauqir, T. and Erdem, E. (2008) 'Gay Imperialism: Gender and Sexuality Discourse in the "War on Terror"', in Kuntsman, A. and Miyake, E. (eds), *Out of Place: Interrogating Silences in Queerness/Raciality*, York: Raw Nerve Books.

——. (2008) 'Loyal Repetitions of the Nation: Gay Assimilation and the War on Terror', *DarkMatter*, 3. http://www.darkmatter101.org/site/category/issues/3-post-colonial-sexuality/ [Accessed 7 May 2008].

——. (2009), 'Hybrid border crossers? Towards a radical socialisation of "Mixed Race"', *Journal of Ethnic and Migration Studies* 35(1), 115–132.

Healey, D. (2001) *Homosexual Desire in Revolutionary Russia: The Regulation of Sexual and Gender Dissent*, Chicago and London: University of Chicago Press.

Heidenreich, N. (2006) 'The "War of Subcultures" and its True Victims', paper presented at *Hegemony and sexual politics: On queer and post-colonial critique of economies of desire in Europe*, 14–15 July, Basel, Switzerland.

Held, N. and Leach, T. (2008) '"What Are You Doing Here?" The "Look" and (Non) Belongings of Racialised Bodies in Sexualised Space', in Kuntsman, A. and Miyake, E. (eds), *Out of Place: Interrogating Silences in Queerness/Raciality*, York: Raw Nerve Books.

Herring, S., Job-Sluder, K, Scheckler, R., and Barab, S. (2003) 'Searching for Safety Online: Managing "Trolling" in a Feminist Forum.' *CSI Working paper*, No. WP– 02–03. http://rkcsi.indiana.edu/archive/CSI/WP/WP02–03B.html [Accessed November 2005].

Hine, C. (2000) *Virtual Ethnography*, London, Thousand Oaks and New Delhi: Sage.

Horowitz, T. and Leshem, E. (1998) 'The Immigrants from the FSU in the Israeli Cultural sphere', in Sicron, M. and Leshem, E. (eds), *Profile of an Immigration Wave: The Absorption Process of Immigrants from the Former Soviet Union, 1990–1995*, Jerusalem: Magnes Press (in Hebrew).

Jakobson, R. (1935/1987) 'Notes on the Prose of the Poet Pasternak', in *Studies in Poetics*, Moscow, 21–44 (in Russian).

Kadish, R. (2001) 'My Zionism is Bigger than Your Zionism: Israeli Lesbians, Gay Men, Gay Rights and National Identity', PhD Dissertation Chapter, University of Berkeley, California.

Kamyanov, B. (2002a) '"The March of Love" in Jerusalem', *Vesti*, 20 June 2002 (in Russian).

——. (2002b) 'Shadows Demand Rights', *The Russian Israeli*, 18 September 2002 (in Russian).

Kandiyoti, D. (1994) 'Identity and its Discontents: Women and the Nation', in Williams, P. and Chrisman, L. (eds), *Colonial Discourse and Post-Colonial Theory*, New York, Columbia University Press.

Kaplan, A. (2004) 'Violent Belongings and the Question of Empire Today: Presidential Address to the American Studies Association, 17 October 2003', *American Quarterly*, 56 (1), 1–18.

Kaplan, D. (2008) 'Commemorating a Suspended Death: Missing Soldiers and National Solidarity in Israel', *American Ethnologist*, 35 (3), 413–427.

Karamcheti, I. (1992) 'The Shrinking Himalayas', *Diaspora* , 2(2), 261–276.

Kendall, L. (1999) 'Recontextualizing "Cyberspace": Methodological Considerations for On-line Research', in Jones, S. (ed.), *Doing Internet Research: Critical Issues and Methods for Examining the Net*, Thousand Oaks, London and New Delhi: Sage.

Khalili, L. (2005) 'Virtual Nation: Palestinian Cyberculture in Lebanese Camp', in Strin, R. and Swedenburg, T. (eds), *Palestine, Israel and the Politics of Popular Culture*, Durham and London: Duke University Press.

Kimmerling, B. (1993) 'Patterns of Militarism in Israel', *European Journal of Sociology* 34, 196–223.

King, T. (2003) 'Rhodesians in Hyperspace: The Maintenance of a National and Cultural Identity', in Karim, H. K. (ed.), *The Media of Diaspora*, London and New York: Routledge.

Kirstein Keshet, Y. (2002) 'Rights of Passage: Dramas of Transition at Israeli Military Checkpoints in the Occupied West Bank', *antiTHESIS*, special issue, *In Transit*, 13, 34–52.

——. (2006) *Checkpoint Watch: Testimonies from Occupied Palestine*, London: Zed Books.

——. (2007) 'In Search of (A) Lost Time: Mourning Innocence in Occupied Palestine', paper presented at *Melancholic States* conference, 27–29 September 2007, Lancaster.

Kitchin, R. (2002) 'Sexing the City: The Sexual Production of Non-heterosexual Space in Belfast, Manchester and San-Francisco', *City*, 6:2, 205–218.

Kleinman, A. (2000) 'The Violences of Everyday Life: The Multiple Forms and Dynamics of Social Violence; in Das, V., Kleinman, A., Ramphele, M. and Reynolds, P. (eds), *Violence and Subjectivity*, Berkeley, Los Angeles and London: University of California Press.

Knopp, L. (1995) 'Sexuality and Urban Space: A Framework for Analysis', in Bell, D. and Valentine, G. (eds), *Mapping Desire: Geographies of Sexualities*, London and New York: Routledge.

Kon, I. (1998) *Moonlight at Sunrise: Faces and Masks of Same-Sex Love*, Moscow: Olimp (in Russian).

Kontorer, D. (2002) 'Gay Censorship', *Vesti*, 20 August 2002 (in Russian).

Kriksonov, P. (2001) *Workshop on Russian Immigration*, Hebrew University, Jerusalem.

Kristeva, J. (1982) *Powers of Horror: An Essay on Abjection*, New York: Columbia University Press.

Kuntsman, A. (2003) 'Double Homecoming: Sexuality, Ethnicity and Place in Immigration Stories of Russian Lesbians in Israel', *Women Studies International Forum*, 26 (4), 299–311.

——. (forthcoming) '"With a Shade of Disgust": Affective Politics of Sexuality and Class in Memoirs of the Stalinist Gulags', *Slavic Review*.

Lambevski, S. (1999) 'Suck My Nation – Masculinity, Ethnicity and the Politics of (Homo)sex', *Sexualities* 2(4), 397–419.

Laskov, M. (2002) 'The Russian Lynch, Deliberate and Merciless', *Vesti*, 5 September 2002 (in Russian).

Lavie, S. (1996) 'Blowups in the Borderzones: Third World Israeli Authors' Gropings for Home', in Lavie, S. and Swedenburg, T. (eds), *Displacement, Diaspora and Geographies of Identity*, Durham and London: Duke University Press.

——. (no date) 'Mizrahi Feminism and the Question of Palestine', work in progress.

——. and Swedenburg, T. (1996) 'Between and Among the Boundaries of Culture: Bridging Text and Lived Experience in the Third Timespace', *Cultural Studies* 10(1), 154–179.

Lawrence III, C. R., Matsuda, M. J., Delgado R., and Crenshaw K. W. (1993) 'Introduction', In Mari J. Matsuda, Charles R. Lawrence III, Richard Delgado, and Kimberlè Williams Crenshaw (eds), *Words That Wound*, Boulder, San Francisco and Oxford: Westview Press.

Lee, V. (2002) 'Geny, How did You Turn up a Lesbian?', *Haaretz*, 2 August 2002 (in Hebrew).

Lemish, D. (2000) 'The Whore and the Other: Israeli images of female immigrants from the former USSR', *Gender and Society*, 14 (2), 333–349.

Lentin, R. (2004) 'Introduction: Postmemory, Unsayability and the Return of the Auschwitz Code', in Lentin, R. (ed.), *Re-Presenting the Shoah for the 21st Century*, London: Berghahn Books.

Lerner, J. (in preparation) 'Introduction: the Pragmatic Power of Culture in Migration', in Feldhay, R. and Lerner, J. (eds), *'Russians' in Israel: the Pragmatics of Culture in Migration*, Jerusalem: Van Leer.

Leshem, E. (2008) 'Being an Israeli: Immigrants from the Former Soviet Union in Israel, Fifteen years later', *The Journal of Israeli History*, 27 (1), 29–49.

Levi, P. (1998) *The Drowned and the Saved*, New York: Summit Books.

Levi-Barzilai, V. (2003) 'Gays? Palestinians? Who Cares!', *Haaretz*, 21 March 2003 (in Hebrew).

Lomsky-Feder, E. and Rapoport, T. (2003) 'Juggling Models of Masculinity: Russian-Jewish Immigrants in the Israeli Army', *Sociological Inquiry*, 73 (1), 114–137.

——., ——. and Lerner J. (2005) 'Orientalism and the Challenge of Migration: Russian Students Read Israeli Ethnicity', *Theory and Criticism* 26, 119–147 (in Hebrew).

Luibhéid, E. (2002) *Entry Denied: Controlling Sexuality at the Border*, Minneapolis and London: University of Minnesota Press.

——. (2008) 'Queer/Migration: An Unruly Body of Scholarship', *GLQ: A Journal of Lesbian and Gay Studies*, 14 (2–3), 169–190.

Malkki, L. H. (1995) *Purity and Exile: Violence, Memory, and National Cosmology Among Hutu Refugees in Tanzania*, Chicago: University of Chicago Press.

Manalansan, M. F. IV. (2000) 'Diasporic Deviants/Divas: How Filipino Transmigrants "Play with the World"', in Patton, C. and Sanchez-Eppler, B. (eds), *Queer Diasporas*, Durham and London: Duke University Press.

——. (2002) 'A Queer Itinerary: Deviant Excursions into Modernities'. In Lewin, Ellen and William L. Leap (eds), *Out in Theory: The Emergence of Gay and Lesbian Anthropology*, Urbana and Chicago, University of Illinois Press.

——. (2003) *Global Divas: Filipino Gay Men in the Diaspora*, Duke University Press: Durham and London.

——. (2004) 'Where Are the Piers? Race, Space, and Violence in the Global City', paper presented at *Queer Matters* conference, 28–30 May 2004, King's College, London.

Markham, A. N. (2004) 'Reconsidering Self and Other: The Methods, Politics, and Ethics of Representation in Online Ethnography', in Denzin, N. K. and Lincoln, Y. S. (eds), *Handbook of Qualitative Research*, Thousand Oaks: Sage.

Martin, B. and Mohanty, C. T. (1986) 'Feminist Politics: What's Home Got To Do With It?' in De Lauretis, T. (ed.), *Feminist Studies/Critical Studies*, Bloomington: University of Indiana Press.

Marx, K. (1976) *Capital: A Critique of Political Economy*, vol. I, Harmondsworth: Penguin Books.

Mason, G. (2002) *The Spectacle of Violence: Homophobia, Gender and Knowledge*, London and New York: Routledge.

Mayer, T. (2000a) 'From Zero to Hero: Masculinity in Jewish Nationalism', in Mayer, T. (ed.), *Gender Ironies and Nationalism: Sexing the Nation*, New York: Routledge.

——. (2000b) 'Gender Ironies of Nationalism: Setting the Stage', in Mayer, T. (ed.), *Gender Ironies and Nationalism: Sexing the Nation*, New York: Routledge.

Mbembe, A. (2003) 'Necropolitics', *Public Culture*, 15(1), 11–40.

McClintock, A. (1995) *Imperial Leather: Race, Gender and Sexuality in the Colonial Conquest*, London: Routledge.

Michaeli, S. (2004) 'Homonational Desire: Israeli Gay Masculinity in Eitan Fox's films', paper presented at *An Other Sex 4: The Fourth Annual Lesbian and Gay Studies and Queer Theory Conference*, 9–10 May 204, Tel-Aviv University.

Miller, D. and Slater, D. (2000) *The Internet: An Ethnographic Approach*, Oxford: Berg.

Mitra, A. (1997) 'Virtual Commonality: Looking for India on the Internet', in Jones, S. (ed.), *Virtual Culture*. London, South Oaks and New Delhi: Sage.

Miyake, E. (2008) 'The Voice of Silence: Interrogating the Sound of Queerness/Raciality', in Kuntsman, A. and Miyake, E. (eds), *Out of Place: Interrogating Silences in Queerness/Raciality*, York: Raw Nerve Books.

Mookherjee, N. (2003) 'Gendered Embodiments: Mapping the Body-Politic of the Raped Woman and the Nation in Bangladesh', in Puwar, N. and Raghuram, P. (eds), *South Asian Women in the Diaspora*, Oxford: Berg.

——. (2004) '"My Man (Honour) is Lost but I Still Have my Iman (Principle)": Sexual Violence and Articulations of Masculinity', in Chopra, R., Osella, C. and Osella, F. (eds), *South Asian Masculinities*, New Delhi: Kali for Women.

Moran, L. J. and Skeggs, B. with Tyrer, P. and Corteen, K. (2004) *Sexuality and the Politics of Violence and Safety*, Routledge: London and New York.

——. (2000) 'Homophobic Violence: The Hidden Injuries of Class', in Munt, S. (ed.), *Cultural Studies and the Working Class: Subject to Change*, London: Cassell.

——., Skeggs, B., Tyrer, P. and Corteen, K. (2001) 'Property, Boundary, Exclusion: Making Sense of Hetero-Violence in Safer paces', *Social and Cultural Geography*, 2 (4), 407–420.

Mosse, G. L. (1985) *Nationalism and Sexuality: Respectability and Abnormal Sexuality in Modern Europe*, New York: Howard Fertig.

Mostov, J. (2000) 'Sexing the Nation/Desexing the Body: Politics of National Identity in the Former Yugoslavia', in Mayer, T. (ed.), *Gender Ironies and Nationalism: Sexing the Nation*, New York: Routledge.

Muñoz, J. E. (1997) 'The White to Be Angry: Vaginal Davis's Terrorist Drag', *Social Text*, 52–53.

Munt, S. R., Bassett, E. H. and O'Riordan, K. (2002) 'Virtually Belonging: Risk, Connectivity and Coming Out On-line', *The International Journal of Sexuality and Gender Studies*, 7 (2/3), 125–138.

Nakamura, L. (2002) *Cybertypes: Race, Ethnicity and Identity on the Internet*, New York and London: Routledge.

Nevels, C. S. (2007) *Lynching to Belong: Claiming Whiteness through Racial Violence*, College Station: Texas A&M University Press.

Ochs, J. (2006) 'The Politics of Victimhood and its Internal Exegetes: Terror Victims in Israel', *History and Anthropology*, 17 (4), 355–368.

Olejnik, A. (2001) *Russian Prison Subculture: In Everyday Life And Power Relationships*, Moscow: Infra (in Russian).

——. (2003) *Organized Crime, Prison and Post-Soviet Societies*, Aldershot: Ashgate.

——. (2004) 'Prison subculture in Russia: marginal subculture or mainstream culture?', *NZ: Debates on Politics and Culture*, 36 (4). http://www.nz-online.ru/print.phtml?aid=25011101 [Accessed 4 March 2006] (in Russian).

——. (2005) 'Prison and Society: The Institutional Congruency between Prison Culture and Russian Economy and Society', *Berliner Journal für Soziologie*, 15 (3), 331–350.

Partan, O. (2007) 'Alla: The Jester-Queen of Russian Pop Culture', *The Russian Review*, 66, 483–500.

Patton, C. and Sanchez-Eppler, B. (eds) (2000) *Queer Diasporas*, Durham and London: Duke University Press.

Pesmen, D. (2000) *Russia and Soul: An Exploration*, Ithaca, New York: Cornell University Press.

Petzen, J. (2004) 'Home or Homelike? Turkish Queers Manage Space in Berlin', *Space and Culture*, 7 (1), 20–32.

Plamper, J. (2002) 'Foucault's Gulag', *Kritika: Explorations in Russian and Eurasian History* 3 (2), 255–280.

Plotkin, V. (2002) 'Do no harm!', *Vesti*, 14 September 2002.

Probyn, E. (1996) *Outside Belongings*, New York and London: Routledge.

——. (2000), *Carnal Appetites: FoodSexIdentities*, London and New York: Routledge.

Puar, J. K. and Rai, A. (2002) 'Monster, Terrorist, Fag: the War on Terrorism and the Production of Docile Patriots', *Social Text*, 72 (20), 117–148.

——. (1998) 'Transnational Sexualities: South Asian (Trans)nation(alism)s and Queer Diasporas', in D. Eng and A. Hom (eds), *Q&A: Queer and Asian in America*, Philadelphia: Temple University Press.

——. (2005) 'Queer Times, Queer Assemblages', *What's Queer about Queer Studies Now?* Special Issue of *Social text*, 23 (3–4), 121–139.

——. (2007) *Terrorist Assemblages: Homonationalism in Queer Times*, Durham and London: Duke University Press.

Puri, J. (2004) *Encountering Nationalism*, Malden, MA: Blackwell.

Randolph, L. (1993) 'The Illusas (deluded women): Representations of Women Who Are Out of Bounds', paper delivered at the Bunting Institute, Cambridge, MA, 30 November.

Rapoport, T. and Lomsky-Feder, E. (2005) 'The Producing of Homecoming in Everyday Life', Keynote lecture presented at the *'Russians' in Israel and Beyond:*

The Meanings of Culture in Discourse and Practice, Van Leer, Jerusalem, 8–9 June 2005.
——., ——., Heider, A. (2002) 'Recollection and Relocation in Immigration: Russian-Jewish Immigrants in Israel and Germany Normalize Their Anti-Semitic Experiences', *Symbolic Interaction*, 25(2), 175–198.
Reid, E. (1999) 'Hierarchy and Power: Social Control in Cyberspace', in Smith, M. A. and Kollock, P. (eds), *Communities in Cyberspace*, London: Routledge.
Reznik, S. (1999) 'The "Blood Libel" in Russia', *Vestnik*, 22 (229), 28 October 1999. http://www.vestnik.com/issues/1999/1026/win/resnik.htm [Accessed May 2006] (in Russian).
Rheingold, H. (2000) *The Virtual Community: Homesteading on the Electronic Frontier*, London: MIT Press.
Richardson, D. (1998) 'Sexuality and Citizenship', *Sociology* 32, 83–100.
——. (2000) 'Claiming Citizenship? Sexuality, Citizenship and Lesbian/Feminist Theory', *Sexualities* 3(2), 255–272.
Ries, N. (1991) 'The Power of Negative Thinking: Russian Talk and the Reproduction of Mindset, Worldview, and Society', *The Anthropology of East Europe Review*, 10 (2), 38–53.
——. (1997) *Russian Talk: Culture and Conversation during Perestroika*, Ithaca and London: Cornell University Press.
Ritchie, J. (forthcoming) 'How Do You Say "Come Out of the Closet" in Arabic? Queer Activism and the Politics of Visibility in Israel-Palestine', *GLQ: A Journal of Lesbian and Gay Studies*, 16 (4).
Roberman, S. (2005) *Memory in Migration: Red Army Soldiers in Israel*, Jerusalem: Magnes (in Hebrew).
Rose, J. (1998) *States of Fantasy*, Clarendon Lectures in English: Oxford University Press.
Said, E. (1979) *Orientalism*, Vintage: New York.
——. (1997) 'Zionism from the Standpoint of Its Victims', in McClintock, A., Mufti, A. and Shohat, E. (eds), *Dangerous Liaisons: Gender, Nation, and Postcolonial Perspectives*, Minneapolis: University of Minnesota Press.
Samojlov, L. (1989) 'Journey to an Upside-down World', *Neva*, 4 (in Russian).
Sasson-Levy, O. (2003) 'Military, Masculinity, and Citizenship: Tensions and Contradictions in the Experience of Blue-Collar Soldiers', *Identities: Global Studies in Culture and Power*, 10, 319–345.
Scarry, E. (1985) *The Body in Pain: The Making and Unmaking of the World*, New York: Oxford University Press.

Schlossberg, L. (2001) 'Introduction: Rites of Passing', in Sanchez, M. C. and Schlossberg, L. (eds), *Passing: Identity and Interpretation in Sexuality, Race and Religion*, New York and London: New York University Press.

Seidman, N. (1997) 'A Stormy Divorce The Sexual Politics of the Hebrew-Yiddish "Language War"', in *A Marriage Made in Heaven: The Sexual Politics of Hebrew and Yiddish*, Berkeley: University of California Press.

Seshadri-Crooks, K. (1998) 'The Comedy of Domination: Psychoanalysis and the Conceit of Whiteness', in Lane, C. (ed.), *The Psychoanalysis of Race*, New York: Columbia University press.

——. (2000) *Desiring Whiteness: A Lacanian Analysis of Race*, London: Routledge.

Shalamov, V. (2003) 'Swindler's Blood', in *Overcoming Evil*, Moscow: EKSMO (in Russian).

Shalom-Shitrit, S. (1999) *The Ashkenazi Revolution is Dead*, Tel Aviv: Bimat Kedem Le-Chinuh (in Hebrew).

Shepherd-Hughes, N. and Bourgois, P. (2004) 'Introduction', in Sheper-Hughes, N. and Bourgois, P. (eds), *Violence in War and Peace. An Anthology*, Malden, Oxford, Carlton: Blackwell Publishing.

Shohat, E. (1997) 'Sephardim in Israel: Zionism from the Standpoint of Its Jewish Victims', in McClintock, A., Mufti, A. and Shohat, E. (eds), *Dangerous Liaisons: Gender, Nation, and Postcolonial Perspectives*. Minneapolis: University of Minnesota Press.

——. and Stam, R. (1994) *Unthinking Eurocentrism: Multiculturalism and the Media*, New York and London: Routledge.

Shumsky, D. (2004) 'Post-Zionist Orientalism? Orientalist Discourse and Islamophobia among the Russian-Speaking Intelligentsia in Israel', *Social Identities*, 10 (1), 83–99.

——. (2005) 'The Janus Face of Russian and Russian-Israeli Orientalism', paper presented at *'Russians' in Israel and Beyond: The Meanings of Culture in Discourse and Practice*, Van Leer Institute, Jerusalem, 8–9 June 2005.

Silver, D. (2000) 'Introducing cyberculture', in Gauntlett, D. (ed.), *Web.studies: Rewiring Media Studies for the Digital Age*, New York: Oxford University Press.

Skeggs, B. (2000) 'The Appearance of Class: Challenges in Gay Space', in Munt, S. (ed.) *Cultural Studies and the Working Class: Subject to Change*, London: Continuum International.

Spencer, J. (2000) 'On Not Becoming a Terrorist: Problems of Memory, Agency and Community in the Sri Lankan Conflict', in Das, V., Kleinman, A., Ramphele, M. and Reynolds, P. (eds), *Violence and Subjectivity*, Berkeley, Los Angeles and London: University of California Press.

Spitzer, L. (1999) 'Back through the Future: Nostalgic Memory and Critical Memory in a Refugee from Nazism', in Bal, M., Crewe, J. and Spitzer, L. (eds), *Acts of Memory: Cultural Recall in the Present*, Hanover and London: University Press of New England.

Stacey, J. (2007) 'She is not Herself: the Deviant Relations of *Alien Resurrection*', *Queer Screen: A Screen Reader*, London and New York: Routledge.

Steinberg, M. (2008) 'The Melancholy of Modern Time: Social Emotion Talk in Russia between the Revolutions', paper presented at *Emotions in Russian Literature and History*, Moscow, 2–5 April 2007 (in Russian).

Stivale, C. J. (1997) *'"Spam": Heteroglossia and Harassment in Cyberspace'*, in Porter, D. (ed.), *Internet Culture*, New York: Routledge.

Stone, A. R. S. (2001) 'Will the Real Body Please Stand Up?: Boundary Stories About Virtual Cultures', in Trend, D. (ed.), *Reading Digital Culture*, Oxford and Massachusetts: Blackwell.

Strukova, M. (2002) 'The terrorist', Zavtra, http://www.zavtra.ru/cgi//veil//data/zavtra/02/439/52.html [Accessed March 2006] (in Russian).

Tachtarova, I. (2005) 'Would Dostoyevsky Have Said That? The Ravikovitch Controversy, Then and Now', paper presented at the *'Russians' in Israel and Beyond: The Meanings of Culture in Discourse and Practice*, Jerusalem, 8–9 June 2005.

Tagg, P. (2006) 'Subjectivity and Soundscape, Motorbikes and Music', in Bennett, A., Shank, B. and Toynbee, J. (eds), *The Popular Music Studies Reader*, London and New York: Routledge.

Takagi, D. Y. (1996) 'Maiden Voyage: Excursion into Sexuality and Identity Politics in Asian America', in Seidman, S. (ed.), *Queer Theory/Sociology*, Cambridge and Oxford: Blackwell.

Tal, K. (1996) *The Unbearable Whiteness of Being: African American Critical Theory and Cyberculture*. http://www.freshmonsters.com/kalital/Text/Articles/whiteness.html [Accessed May 2004].

——. and Lyman, G. (2000) 'Room Full of Mirrors: Virtual Tourism and First World Technogaze', *Artbyte*. http://www.kalital.com/Text/Articles/artbyte.html [Accessed May 2004].

Toker, L. (2000) *Return from the Archipelago: Narratives of Gulag Survivors*, Bloomington and Indianapolis: Indiana University Press.

Trifonov, G. (1991) 'Soviet Homosexualis: Yesterday, Today, Tomorrow' (in Russian). http://az.gay.ru/articles/articles/slav1c.html [Accessed January 2007].

Turkle, S. (1995) *Life on the Screen*, New York: Simon and Schuster.

Tyler, I. (2006) '"Welcome to Britain": The Cultural Politics of Asylum', *European Journal of Cultural Studies*, 9, 185–202.

Ushakov, D. N. (ed.)(1935–1940/2000) *The Explanatory Dictionary of Russian Language*, Moscow (in Russian).
Verstraete, G. (2003) 'Technological Frontiers and the Politics of Mobility in the European Union', in Ahmed, S., Castañeda, C., Fortier, A.-M. and Sheller, M. (eds), *Uprootings/Regroundings: Questions of Home and Migration*, Oxford and New York: Berg.
Virilio, P. (1989) *War and Cinema: The Logistics of Perception*, New York: Verso.
——. (1995) 'Speed and Information: Cyberspace Alarm!', *CTheory*, 18 (3). http://www.ctheory.net/articles.aspx?id=72 [Accessed November 2008].
——. (1997) *Open Sky*, New York: Verso.
Visweswaran, K. (1997) *Fictions of Feminist Ethnography*, University of Minnesota Press: Minneapolis, London.
Vrooman, S. (2002) 'The Art of Invective: Performing Identity in Cyberspace', *New Media and Society*, 4 (1), 51–70.
Wakeford, N. (1997) 'Cyberqueer', in Munt, S. (ed.), *Lesbian and Gay Studies*, London: Cassell.
Walzer, L. (2000) *Between Sodom and Eden: A Gay Journey through Today's Changing Israel*, New York: Columbia University Press.
Warner, M. (1993) *Fear of a Queer Planet: Queer Politics and Social Theory*. Minneapolis: University of Minnesota Press.
Weizman, E. (2007) *Hollow Land: Israel's Architecture of Occupation*, London: Verso.
Williams, R. (1977) *Marxism and Literature*, Oxford: Oxford University Press.
Yanai, N. (2002) 'Hatred as Ambivalence', *Theory, Culture and Society*, 19 (3), 71–88.
Yosef, R. (2002) 'Homoland: Interracial Sex and the Israeli-Palestinian Conflict in Israeli Cinema', *GLQ: A Journal of Lesbian and Gay Studies*, 8 (4), 553–580.
——. (2004) *Beyond Flesh: Queer Masculinities and Nationalism in Israeli Cinema*, New Brunswick, NJ: Rutgers University Press.
——. (2005) 'The National Closet: Gay Israel in Yossi and Jagger', *GLQ: A Journal of Lesbian and Gay Studies*, 11 (2), 283–300.
Yuval-Davis, N. (1997) *Gender and Nation*, London: Sage.
——. and Abdo, N. (1995) 'Palestine, Israel and the Zionist Settler Project', in Stasulis, D. and Yuval-Davis, N. (eds), *Unsettling Settler Societies: Articalutions on Gender, Race, Ethnicity and Class*, London, Thousand Oaks, New Delhi: Sage Publications.
Zapadaev, A. M. (2001) *Dictionary of Habballic Words and Expressions*, St Petersburg, Self-published (in Russian).

Žarkov, D. (2001) 'The Body of the Other Man: Sexual Violence and the Construction of Masculinity, Sexuality and Ethnicity in Croatian Media', in Moser, C. and Clark, F. (eds), *Victims, Perpetrators or Actors? Gender, Armed Conflict and Political Violence*, London: Zed Books, 69–82.

Zorin, A. (2008) 'Feeling across Borders: The Europeanization of Russian Nobility through Emotional Patterns', paper presented at *Emotions in Russian Literature and History*, Moscow, 2–5 April 2007 (in Russian).

Zhuk, O. (1998) *The Russian Amazons: History of Lesbian Sub-Culture in Russia, 20th century*, Moscow: Glagol (in Russian).

Index

Illustrations

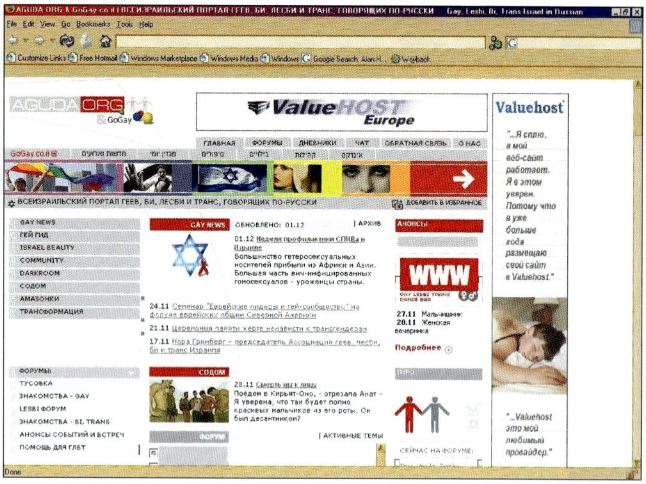

Figure 1: 'The Pan-Israeli Portal of Russian-speaking Gays, Lesbians, Bisexuals and Transsexuals': Homepage (http://www.aguda.org, saved December 2003)

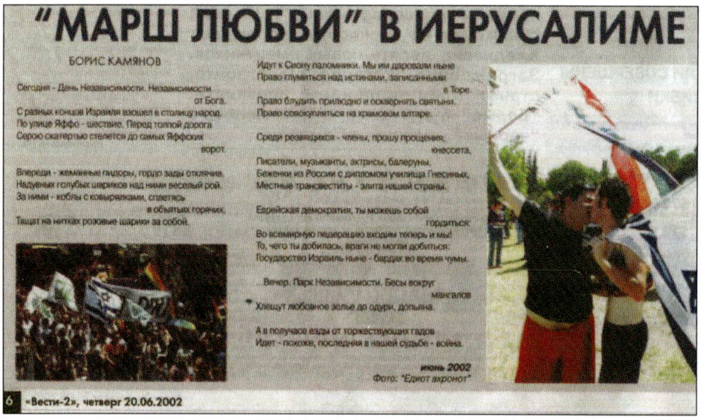

"МАРШ ЛЮБВИ" В ИЕРУСАЛИМЕ

БОРИС КАМЯНОВ

Сегодня - День Независимости. Независимости
от Бога.
С разных концов Израиля вошел в столицу народ.
По улице Яффо - шествие. Перед толпой дорога
Серою скатертью стелется до самых Яффских
ворот.

Впереди - жеманные пидоры, гордо зады отклячив.
Надувных голубых шариков над ними веселый рой.
За ними - коблы с ковырялками, сплетясь
в объятьях горячих,
Тащат на нитках розовые шарики за собой.

Идут к Сиону паломники. Мы им даровали ныне
Право глумиться над истинами, записанными
в Торе,
Право блудить прилюдно и осквернять святыни,
Право совокупляться на храмовом алтаре.

Среди резвящихся - члены, прошу прощения,
кнессета,
Писатели, музыканты, актрисы, балеруны,
Беженки из России с дипломом училища Гнесиных,
Местные трансвеститы - элита нашей страны.

Еврейская демократия, ты можешь собой
гордиться:
Во всемирную педерацию входим теперь и мы!
То, чего ты добилась, враги не могли добиться:
Государство Израиль ныне - бардак во время чумы.

...Вечер. Парк Независимости. Бесы вокруг
мангалов
Хлещут любовное зелье до одури, допьяна.

А в получасе езды от торжествующих гадов
Идет - похоже, последняя в нашей судьбе - война.

июнь 2002
Фото: "Едиот ахронот"

6 «Вести-2», четверг 20.06.2002

Figure 2: Boris Kamyanov, '"The March of Love" in Jerusalem', *Vesti*, 20 June 2002

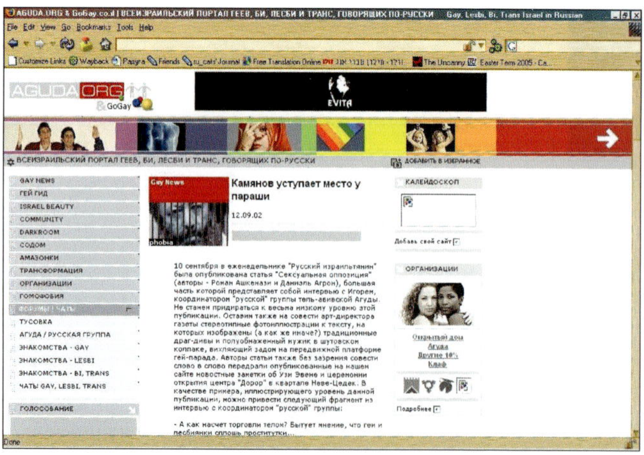

Figure 3: 'Kamyanov leaves a vacancy by the latrine', *Gay News* section of the website, 12 September 2002 (http://www.aguda.org/n.php?mode=lenta&news=133, saved March 2004)

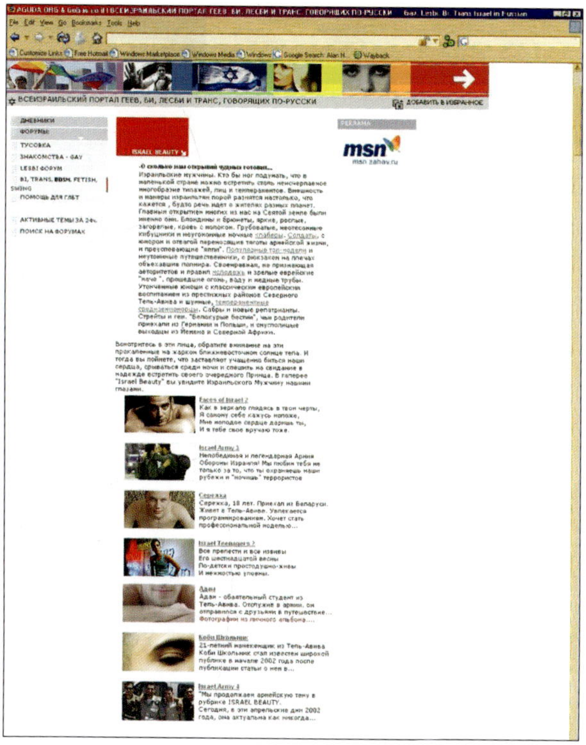

Figure 4: *Israel Beauty* section of the website, the main page (http://www.aguda.org/gallery/, saved March 2004)

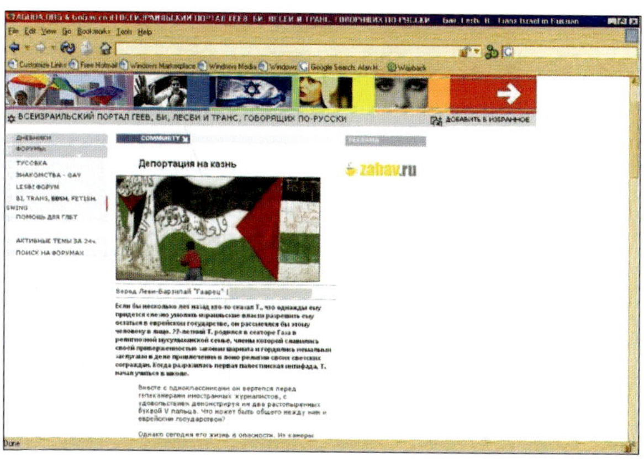

Figure 5: 'Deported to execution', *Community* section of the website (http://aguda.org/community/pales/php, saved March 2004)

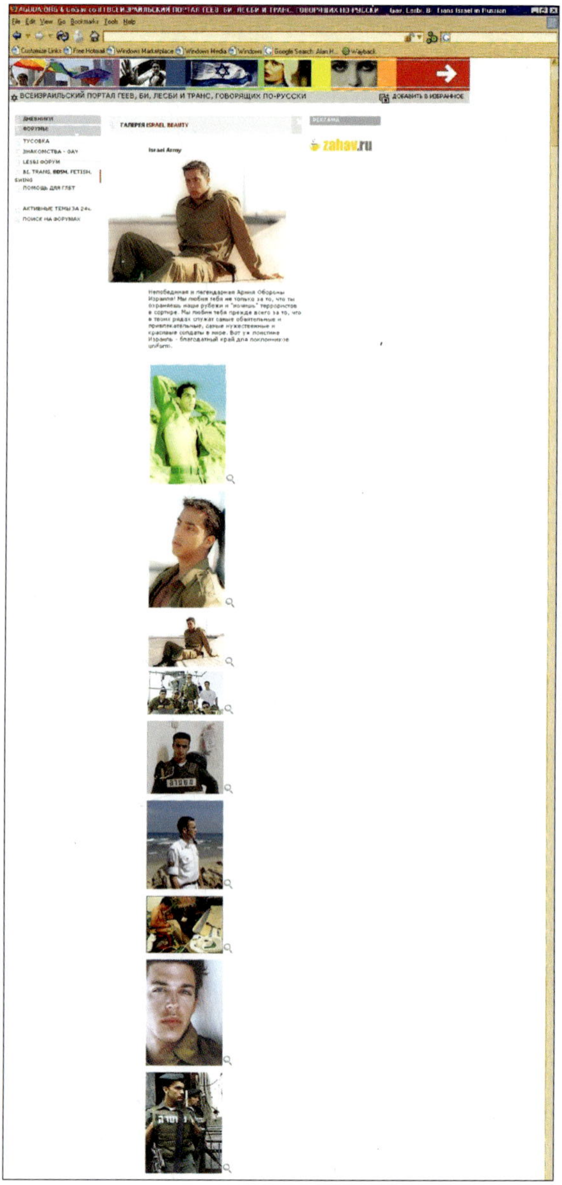

Figure 6: *Israel Beauty* section of the website, gallery 'Israeli Army -1' (http://www.aguda.org/gallery/index.php, saved March 2004)